POLITICAL PHILOSOPHY NOW

Chief Editor of the Series:
Howard Williams, University of Wales, Aberystwyth

Associate Editors:
Wolfgang Kersting, University of Kiel, Germany
Steven B. Smith, Yale University, USA
Peter Nicholson, University of York, England

Political Philosophy Now is a series which deals with authors, topics and periods in political philosophy from the perspective of their relevance to current debates. The series presents a spread of subjects and points of view from various traditions which include European and New World debates in political philosophy.

For other titles in this series, please see the University of Wales Press website: *www. wales.ac.uk/press*

POLITICAL PHILOSOPHY NOW

John Rawls:
Towards a Just World Order

Patrick Hayden

UNIVERSITY OF WALES PRESS • CARDIFF • 2002

© Patrick Hayden, 2002

British Library Cataloguing-in-Publication Data
A catalogue record for this book is available from the British Library.

ISBN 0–7083–1728–6 paperback
     0–7083–1729–4 cased

Typeset at the University of Wales Press, Cardiff.
Printed in Great Britain by Dinefwr Press, Llandybïe.

For Katherine

Contents

1 • Introduction

John Rawls is the philosopher who brought political philosophy back to life in the last three decades of the twentieth century. In 1971 his masterpiece, *A Theory of Justice*, was published to wide critical acclaim.[1] In the years prior to and following the Second World War, political philosophy had suffered a near death brought on by neglect and disinterest.[2] Shunned by thinkers interested more in matters of logic and language than in questions of equality and freedom, political philosophy struggled to retain its relevance in the contemporary world. Since the publication of *A Theory of Justice*, however, there has been a marked revival of interest in political philosophy. In particular there has been a broad resurgence of interest in conceptions of justice, their principles and requirements, and the concomitant elements of just social structures, such as liberty, economic goods and rights.

The present study offers a critical exposition of Rawls's political philosophy, with a special focus on the role that human rights play in regard to his accounts of domestic and international justice. I base this project on the view that human rights discourse is best situated within the broader context of theories of social justice. This is because human rights theory depends in important ways on the terms or principles of social justice, which delineate the conditions of a well-ordered society necessary for the recognition and implementation of claims to human rights. Since conceptions of justice are not all created equally, it is my belief that a theory of justice which fails to locate a robust place for universal human rights is not an adequate account of justice in the contemporary world. With this in mind, then, I examine Rawls's most important writings in order to assess how adequately his theory of justice is able to accommodate claims to universal human rights.

As I have already noted, Rawls's major statement on justice came in his influential *A Theory of Justice*. There Rawls identifies one's right to the most equal extensive liberty compatible with a similar liberty for others as the first of his principles of justice as fairness. Rawls establishes his principles by suggesting a scenario in which individuals representing several generations are to be abstracted from time and space and required to choose principles for an actual society, into which they would be eventually returned, which they could all agree to support as the most just possible. However, in *A Theory of Justice* Rawls restricts his enquiry to single societies only, effectively neglecting the problem of justice internationally or globally.

In light of this omission in his work, it is not surprising that Rawls's theory has received criticism from those concerned with the international aspects of social justice, and in particular with universal human rights. In several of his publications following *A Theory of Justice*, Rawls has attempted to respond to these criticisms and explain how he understands justice as fairness to extend into the global domain and, most recently, its relationship to human rights theory and practice. It is this particular point of debate surrounding Rawls's work that forms the focus of the second half of this book. In looking at what Rawls has to say about human rights I attempt to shed some light on what is still a relatively neglected area of his writings. Yet I also attempt to expose some of the limitations and weaknesses of his work on human rights, while showing that his work can contribute to the construction of a more robust, cosmopolitan approach to issues of international justice.

This book has two parts. Part I sets out the basic framework and principles of Rawls's theory of justice as fairness. In the first chapter I survey the primary ethical and political concerns of the social contract tradition and discuss the influence of this tradition on the development of modern human rights discourse. I also discuss some of the current issues confronting human rights theory, in particular those of social pluralism and globalization. With this as background, in the second chapter I then offer a comprehensive examination of Rawls's theory of justice as fairness. Here I address the role of rights in Rawls's theory and the transformation of this theory in his later writings. The discussion in Part I makes no assumptions of prior acquaintance with Rawls's work and seeks to familiarize the reader with the significance and implications of Rawls's theory. Because *A Theory of Justice* inspired many debates in contemporary political philosophy, attracting a great deal of attention both from critics and sympathetic readers, some account must be taken of the views of important commentators. Nevertheless, given that commentaries on *A Theory of Justice* now comprise a body of work which is enormous, the primary focus will be on setting out Rawls's own arguments.

Part II discusses the international dimensions of justice as fairness. The two chapters making up Part II do not confine themselves to exposition alone, but provide critical commentary and evaluation of Rawls's treatment of international justice and human rights. In Chapter 3 I specify more precisely Rawls's account of international justice. I show that Rawls's account fails to sustain the critical and creative energy of his domestic conception of justice, mainly because he gives priority to the domestic conception and restricts the principles of justice at the international level. In response to these limitations, I argue that Rawls's theory should be reformulated such that the global original position is no longer subordinated to the domestic. The result would be a conception of justice that is more cosmopolitan than the one offered by Rawls. I should make clear at the outset that in this chapter I focus solely on the theoretical shortcomings that are internal to Rawls's account of international justice. Thus I do not fully develop principles of international distributive justice for material resources, nor articulate specific strategies for the distribution of such resources, which would go beyond the scope of the present enquiry.

In the fourth chapter I offer an analysis of Rawls's latest effort to extend justice as fairness globally in his recently published book, *The Law of Peoples*, which grows out of an earlier essay with the same title.[3] I conclude that, although Rawls now attempts to justify the inclusion of universal human rights in his theory, he fails to overcome the same deficiencies that marked his earlier account of international justice. In the end, Rawls sacrifices the normative strength of his theory of justice as fairness in favour of a status quo description of international affairs, thereby weakening his attempt to account for human rights. I argue that an effective system of universal human rights would require a more cosmopolitan system of social justice than is offered in Rawls's own theory of international justice.

In Chapter 4 I also argue that a cosmopolitan system of social justice allows for the articulation of moral and political reasons in support of increased democratization and human rights to global peace and security, issues that are of pressing importance in current political debates. Although Rawls's theory of justice can, I think, be utilized to contribute to a theory of universal human rights, this contribution must depend on a greater commitment to extending the priority and principles of justice to all persons and not only to those already living in established liberal democracies.

I owe a debt of thanks to several people in connection with this project. I owe the largest debt of gratitude to Paul Voice. He provided careful and illuminating comments on an earlier draft of the book, and offered encouragement at just the right moments. For their help in bringing this study to fruition I would also like to thank Darrel Moellendorf, James Sterba, and Howard Williams; I have learnt much from their wise and prudent comments. I am also indebted to Mark Evans for the helpful comments he kindly offered on various aspects of this work, and to an anonymous referee for University of Wales Press, whose constructive suggestions on an earlier draft contributed to revisions which, I hope, helped to improve the final product. Bryan Hilliard, Dennis Kalob, Tom Lansford and James Walsh provided good humour and fine fellowship when most needed. Thanks must also be extended to UWP's Duncan Campbell and Ceinwen Jones, whose advice as the project progressed was consistently good. Finally, I should like to express special gratitude to my wife, Katherine, who was a constant source of support and encouragement throughout the writing of this work. To her, I dedicate this book.

I • The Framework and Principles of Justice as Fairness

1 • Contractarian Theory and the Principles of Justice

> I have suggested that . . . contractarianism is manifesting itself increasingly in our overt consciousness. And this consciousness is spreading more and more widely . . . so that, as more and more people attain self-awareness, they do so in the terms provided by the deep structure of our thought – in the terms, then, of contractarianism. (David Gauthier, 'The Social Contract as Ideology', 163)

In the first section of this chapter, I begin by surveying the basic ethical and political concerns of classical social contract theory. I then develop the primary features of Rawls's contractarian theory of social justice, first by way of a fairly straightforward exposition of Rawls's initial approach to justice and social and political organization as presented in his influential *A Theory of Justice*. The question that drives Rawls's theory is, what are the most important characteristics of a just society? In the third section of this chapter, I discuss the answer Rawls provides in terms of the principles all rational beings would choose as the foundation for a just society. These principles, Rawls suggests, delimit the distributive structure of a just society.

A survey of the contractarian tradition provides a useful introduction to this book for three reasons. First, because this book seeks to examine Rawls's theory of justice as regards the cogency of both the contractarian argument and the theory of universal human rights, the reader will benefit from an understanding of the philosophical principles and reasoning offered in support of the contractarian tradition. Second, many of the basic components of the contractarian tradition are presupposed in the arguments examined more fully in later parts of this book and thus a certain amount of background information is necessary. Third, Rawls's contractarian theory differs in a number of ways from earlier, as well as contemporary, social contract theories, as does his employment of (human) rights.[1] The background material on the contractarian tradition will, I hope, provide the preliminary spadework that helps to define the set of principles Rawls advances for his theory of justice and its concomitant theory of rights, as well as the arguments he gives in favour of those principles.

Contractarian theory

I begin by surveying the basic idea and concerns of social contract theory. The label 'social contract' or 'contractarian' can be applied to a wide variety of theories that address issues of government legitimacy, social justice and political and moral obligation. Despite their differences, however, contract theories typically follow a similar argumentative framework in developing their accounts. The argument usually describes an initial state of nature in which people are situated without a political or legal order, or moral rules. Contractarians then argue that this initial situation is for the most part unfavourable for people to live in, as it exposes them to a host of dangers and problems that undermine the ability to establish a stable social life. Given this situation people come to the conclusion that they would be better off leaving the state of nature, which in turn requires some kind of general agreement in order to establish a political, legal and moral order that will lead to a better life for everyone. Contractarians have used this type of argument to account for the foundation of government, the justification of political obligation and the identification of binding principles of justice and morality.

The central mechanism of the contractarian argument is *agreement*. In its classical forms, contract theory sought to justify the political authority of the state, that is, to account for the legitimate exercise of authority by a sovereign over the members of society. The classical contract theorists argued that the justification of political authority and moral principles rests upon what people have, or would have, agreed upon. Following a contract theory of political obligation, it is possible to develop a theory of social justice that includes an account of the rights, duties and obligations of individuals based upon a form of agreement or contract in which consent has been given by the members of society. Contract theories derive a structure of obligations and duties, what we can call a theory of right, and this structure is erected upon the consent of autonomous individuals.

A theory of right addresses the aims and principles of conduct and choice in terms of what it is right for people to do. Generally, the contractarian theory of right is deontological in nature.

Deontological theories characterize the right independently of the good, that is, they define the concept of right action independently of what might be considered intrinsically good, such as the values of love, beauty and knowledge or the satisfaction of desire.[2] Therefore they base the rightness of acts or rules on criteria other than solely the intrinsic good contained in the consequences of actions. Deontological theories are thus non-consequentialist because they hold that actions or rules are to be judged on the basis of non-consequentialist criteria, such as rights and duties, given the consent or agreement of individuals independent of future consequences. In contrast, teleological theories, such as utilitarianism, characterize the good independently of the right and then characterize the right as a function of the good. For a teleological theory, the right act to perform is that which maximizes the amount of intrinsic good in the consequences. Teleological theories are for this reason sometimes called 'consequentialist' because they require that actions or rules be judged solely by the amount of good contained in the consequences. In teleological theories the right is subordinated to the good and defined in terms of the maximization of the amount of good in consequences.

Deontological theories are often called right-based theories, for the deontic concepts of right and ought are taken to be fundamental and other ethical concepts are defined in terms of them.[3] For instance, when it is claimed that the right is prior to the good this means that principles of right are derived independently of principles of good and serve as 'side constraints' on the pursuit of the good.[4] Side constraints specify kinds of actions one may never perform no matter what goal one aims at. In this way something does not count as good unless it is consistent with the right. Consequently, a contractarian theory places limits or restrictions around what actions may be agreed to in the contract and therefore around what actions can be considered moral. Peter Vallentyne provides a concise definition of contractarianism that captures this last point: 'A contractarian moral theory states that an action (practice, social structure, etc.) is morally permissible if and only if it (or the rules to which it conforms) would be agreed to by the members of society under certain circumstances.'[5]

Contractarian theories differ over the nature of the contract or act which establishes the structure of right. On some accounts, the contract is a historical reality that was actually made and ought to be adhered to. On other accounts, the contract is an ideal construct that either ought to have been made, ought to be made or perhaps ought to serve as a guide or ideal at which to aim. On still other accounts, the contract is one which is only tacitly made, or the contract is a hypothetical entity only and is used to specify what persons would consent to under certain conditions. Each type of contract theory, historical, ideal and hypothetical, has produced its own method of arguing from the contract or expression of consent to a structure of right.

It is also possible to distinguish between versions of the contract which involve a permanent, non-revocable pact and versions which involve a renewable, revocable trust. Further distinctions that can be made concern the actors involved in the contract. For some theories, the contract is between individuals only, while for others it is between agents or representatives of individuals. Moreover, some theories hold that the contract is between all individuals and the state, while for others it is only between the state and those individuals meeting certain qualifications. In this way, some contract theories are inclusive and democratic while others are exclusive and non-democratic.

Social contract theories also employ a normative theory that assigns each individual person moral standing independently of political or institutional considerations. This moral standing is often based upon some feature believed to be possessed by all moral agents, such as rationality or an interest in freedom, and is usually specified in terms of rights and obligations generated by the moral status of each individual. The moral standing specified in a contractarian normative theory is commonly established by employing a description of the pre-political state of nature. Such a description is employed because theorizing about the state of nature allows questions to be asked about the moral status of the person considered under assorted constraints which specify the circumstances of an agreement independently of our real social, psychological and institutional circumstances. This in turn can lead to the development of various normative dimensions of contractarian theory, such as a theory of social justice which includes the notion of 'natural rights'. Natural or moral rights are typically thought to include rights to life, liberty and control over one's own body, and are regarded as the basic rights of individuals which may not be violated.[6] It should be noted that, in their considerations of the nature and status of contractors, classical contract theorists confined their arguments in ways that did not include all of humanity. Women and the poor and propertyless were, for instance, often excluded as possible participants from the consensual process of political association. Contemporary versions of contract theory have rejected these restrictions and adopted more universalistic conceptions of participatory political association.[7]

By employing a description of the state of nature, contractarians offer a representation of what life was like or perhaps would be like without political authority and the institutions of government. Doing so allows for a comparison of the state of nature with an account of society, as well as for the justification of political authority and a system of moral and political rules. This basic approach to moral and political justification, grounded on the agreement or consent of those who coexist in political society, works itself out in a variety of structural models formulated by contractarian theorists. For example, 'express consent' theories appeal to an actual contract in which individuals have expressed their consent to certain institutions or arrangements, while 'tacit consent' theories appeal to the terms of a tacitly made contract in which individuals have implicitly given their consent to certain institutions through their actions. 'Hypothetical consent' theories appeal to an act of consent that would be given if certain specified conditions were obtained. In this case moral and political principles are those to which people could rationally agree if they had the opportunity.

These different versions of the social contract can be illustrated with brief sketches of some classical and modern contractarian theories. Perhaps the very first versions of the social contract theory appear in Plato's *Crito* and *The Republic*. In the *Crito* a historical, pure tacit consent theory is presented through Socrates' discussion with the laws of Athens. If any person chooses to live in a particular city or colony when he could live elsewhere, the laws tell Socrates, then that person has – in virtue of the act of residency – agreed to obey the laws of the state; that person has tacitly given his consent to the existing political authority. A historical, express consent theory is given in *The Republic* when Glaucon suggests that 'when men have both done and suffered injustice and have had experience of both . . . they think that they had better agree among themselves to have neither; hence there arise laws and mutual covenants'.[8]

It is with the work of Thomas Hobbes that classical contract-arianism, and the theory of natural rights, is born. In *Leviathan* (1651) Hobbes begins with an account of human nature and argues that all of our actions are performed for self-interested reasons, primarily to obtain satisfaction and avoid harm, a view that is now referred to as psychological egoism. He also describes an amoral, pre-political stage of human social development, a state of nature, where people live independently under conditions of suspicion, insecurity and conflict. All humans are basically equal in terms of their desires and abilities, Hobbes maintains, yet our natural egoism combined with competition for limited resources leads to a state of perpetual war of all against all, in which life is 'solitary, poor, nasty, brutish, and short'.

Hobbes argues that several motives, including fear of death and the desire to have the material goods needed for a condition of welfare, cause people to form a political society by means of a social contract. The basis of the social contract is natural law, which Hobbes identifies through a lengthy list of specific laws of nature that serve as rational precepts for the maintenance of social order, flowing from self-interested prudence. For Hobbes, the precepts of natural law have their source in the fundamental natural right to life of each person, 'the liberty each man hath, to use his own power, as he will himself, for the preservation of his own nature'.[9] This natural right is the fundamental liberty that each individual possesses in the absence of political authority. Because this liberty is absolute, however, each individual is free to do whatever he or she wants, including violating the rights of others, without fear of penalty or punishment. It is for this reason that Hobbes describes the state of nature as a condition characterized by the 'war of everyone against everyone'. Thus, 'unless the natural right of every man to every thing' is constrained and regulated by enforceable law, nobody is obligated to respect the natural rights of others: 'RIGHT, consisteth in liberty to do, or to forbear; whereas LAW, determineth, and bindith to one of them'.[10] In order to escape the violent state of nature and create a government, however, all persons must agree mutually to transfer their right of absolute liberty (as absence of constraint) to a political sovereign – the state or Leviathan – which is then empowered to enforce security by punishing those who violate the agreement to obey the laws of society. Although Hobbes conceives of the sovereign as the supreme authority, it is important to note that the power of the sovereign is derived not from the divine right of kings but from the natural right of the people through the event of the social contract. In Hobbes's view, the contract originates in an original act of express consent and it is then tacitly renewed by each subsequent generation.

However, the authority established by the contract is restricted when it comes to certain natural rights that Hobbes regards as inalienable:

[T]here be some rights, which no man can be understood by any words, or other signs, to have abandoned, or transferred. As first a man cannot lay down the right of resisting them, that assault him by force, to take away his life . . . The same may be said of wounds, and chains, and imprisonment . . . And lastly the motive, and end for which this renouncing, and transferring of right is introduced, is nothing else but the security of a man's person, in his life, and in the means of so preserving life, as not to be weary of it.[11]

For Hobbes, the foundation that limits the power of the state is provided by the natural rights of individuals which precede the state. Specifically, the existence of the rights to life and to all things which are indispensable to the preservation of life grounds the limits of sovereign authority. The primary weakness of Hobbes's theory of natural rights, however, is his focus on the self-preserving character of those rights. In other words, while Hobbes is concerned to show in his account of the state of nature that humans have natural rights which, at least in part, cannot be fully surrendered to political authority, these rights consist in one's liberty to do or forbear to do whatever is necessary for the preservation of one's *own* life. Hobbes does not adequately account for the possibility of an obligation equally to preserve the rights of *others*.

The classical social contract and natural rights theory born with Hobbes is brought into a more mature age with the work of John Locke. Locke's philosophy often differs sharply from Hobbes's, and plays an important role in the development not only of contractarianism but also of ideas about human rights and the state's duty to respect them.

Locke's description of the state of nature in *The Second Treatise on Civil Government* (1690) is significant in that he asserts that the fundamental law of nature is not simply that of self-preservation, but rather preservation of the life of others as well as oneself.[12] A contract engendering political society is agreed upon for the purpose of securing life and ensuring the equality between and freedom of persons. According to Locke, 'The chief and great end, therefore, of men uniting into a commonwealth, and putting themselves under government, is the preservation of their property'.[13] In this context, however, Locke uses the term 'property' not only in the narrow sense of external possessions; rather, he says it must be understood to mean 'that property which men have in their persons as well as goods', namely, 'life, liberty, and estate'.[14] With this statement Locke establishes the well-known idea that the individual possesses the natural rights to life, liberty and property.

The primary function of the state – the protection of the natural rights of individuals – is thus conferred by the consent of those who enter into the social contract. Yet this function is not conferred absolutely or irrevocably; it is established instead as a trust for the public good. The only way that humans can divest themselves of their natural rights is by mutual consent to a social contract that would ensure not only the comfort and safety of all members, but most importantly the equality and liberty of all:

> [P]olitical power is that power which every man having in the state of Nature has given up into the hands of the society, and therein to the governors whom the society hath set over itself, with this express or tacit trust, that it shall be employed for their good and the preservation of their property.[15]

The contract that Locke derives from the state of nature gives the state far less power than does the contract derived by Hobbes. In Locke's theory, only one contract is made, namely the social contract proper. This contract empowers the majority to erect a government with the state as a trustee and the people as trustor. Such a relationship places all of the rights on the side of the people and all of the duties on the side of the government. In Locke's view, natural rights are inviolable in the state of nature but are enforceable only in a society that recognizes and acts to protect such rights through the mechanism of the social contract.

Locke's contract theory is, then, an example of a historical, mixed theory. After sketching a theory of natural rights which serves to establish a natural moral status possessed by each individual, Locke bases the legitimacy of the state upon two premises. First, all societies originate in contracts expressly made by the original members. Second, this original contract is tacitly renewed by each member of succeeding generations. Each person – by either his residency in society, ownership of property or acceptance of the benefits of society – implies by his actions a tacit acceptance of the contract. However, if a government exceeds the legitimate limits of the authority conferred to it, it can be dismissed for a breach of its trust and replaced by another. A government exceeds its authority when it unjustly encroaches upon or fails to preserve the natural rights and liberties of the people.

Another important member of the social contract tradition is Jean-Jacques Rousseau. In *The Social Contract* (1762) Rousseau develops a tacit consent theory according to which, when a number of individuals voluntarily unite behind a political power, each by his actions tacitly gives his entire self and rights up to the group. A corporate being is thus formed which possesses a general will and which is called the state. The general will aims at the good of all.

For Rousseau, the social contract functions as the fundamental principle underlying the political association whereby the social becomes an embodiment of the personal. The contract is a mechanism for harmonizing the liberty of individuals with the legitimate freedom of others, insofar as natural liberty is exchanged for civil liberty. By the terms of the contract, each person relates to all others as constituent yet equal parts of an 'indivisible whole', under the direction of the general will:

'Find a form of association that defends and protects the person and goods of each associate with all the common force, and by means of which each one, uniting with all, nevertheless obeys only himself and remains as free as before'. This is the fundamental problem which is solved by the social contract . . . The clauses of this contract . . . come down to a single one, namely, the total alienation of each associate, with all his rights, to the whole community.[16]

The social contract gives the political association its characteristic 'existence and life', namely, the intertwining of the individual good with the common good. Rousseau is also concerned to argue that the regulation of the state under the authority of the general will not only allows for the exercise of individual freedom, but also enables people to perfect their natural virtues. By means of the social contract, civil liberty manifests the moral goodness of the entire society. Clearly, Rousseau differs from Locke in relegating the rights of the individual to a collective general will. In other words, the equal natural rights of persons are ultimately grounded in the general will of society, such that these rights are conceived by Rousseau as being properly legitimated in the acts of political association by which society is formed. Rousseau's version of the social contract contrasts with the individualism of Locke's version, in so much as it favours a social conception of rights based on a contract intended to protect not only individual liberty but also social equality and political justice.

Finally, we can mention the contribution of Immanuel Kant. Kant's moral theory, as presented in his *Foundations of the Metaphysics of Morals* (1785), argues that the only thing that is unconditionally good is a good will.[17] According to Kant, a person who acts with a good will acts on the basis of neither the desires that influence the action nor the consequences that result from it, but instead on the recognition that the action is obligatory or necessary. This means the person acts in accord with what Kant calls the categorical imperative. Kant formulated the categorical imperative in several different ways, including 'Act only according to that maxim by which you can at the same time will that it should be a universal law', that is, a rule or law that everyone should obey. He also stated the categorical imperative as 'Act so that you treat humanity, whether in your person or in that of another, always as an end and never as a means only'. As a deontologist, Kant believed that an action willed from the categorical imperative is done with a necessary view to treating all persons, including ourselves, as ends in themselves and not merely as means to other ends. What this implies for Kant is that people have an intrinsic worth or dignity as moral persons and should be respected accordingly. Only in this way is it possible to respect the freedom, equality and autonomy of human beings.

In clarifying the relationship of his moral theory to political practice, Kant discusses how a civil state is justified on the basis of a social contract that expresses the conception of humanity as an end in itself, what Kant referred to as a 'kingdom of ends'.[18] Kant argues that, even if the social contract is a fiction, it is nevertheless 'an *idea* of reason' that provides a regulative principle by which to frame the laws of the state 'in such a way that they could have been produced by the united will of the whole nation'.[19] Kant's point is that a hypothetical social contract provides a practical justificatory tool for determining the legitimacy of the state and its laws. If free individuals could not or would not agree to the state and its laws, then the arrangement is unjust.[20] In a just government the rights of humanity are secured, establishing a reciprocal obligation on the part of each citizen to respect the rights of everyone else. Thus some limitations on freedom do exist, through the rule of law and the state's right to punish, but these limitations are legitimate since they actually increase freedom by prohibiting (and redressing) the types of wrongs characteristic of the lawless state of nature. For Kant, then, the value of legitimate government is that it guarantees our natural right to freedom and provides us with a foundation from which to acquire other rights through mutual consent. Kant powerfully conveys the fundamental role of human rights in identifying the basic human freedoms that are to be respected:

> There is nothing more sacred in the wide world than the rights of others. They are inviolable. Woe unto him who trespasses upon the right of another and tramples it underfoot! His right should be his security; it should be stronger than any shield or fortress. We have a holy ruler and the most sacred of his gifts to us is the rights of man.[21]

Influenced by Kant's work, John Rawls has developed his own theory of justice under the explicit inspiration of the contractarian tradition. In *A Theory of Justice*, he describes the idea of justice as fairness formulated therein as a theory 'that generalizes and carries to a higher level of abstraction the traditional conception of the social contract' (1971: 3). In his major work, Rawls identifies one's right to the most equal extensive liberty compatible with a similar liberty for others as the first of his principles of justice. This first principle, the liberty principle, is to be secured, whenever possible, prior to the implementation of the second principle, which includes both the difference principle and the equality of opportunity principle.

Rawls establishes his principles by proposing that they would be the object of mutual agreement by persons under fair conditions. Starting from the idea of a hypothetical social contract, he specifies a point of view from which a fair agreement between free and equal persons can be reached on those principles that they could all agree to support as the most just possible. This 'original position' would allow these individuals knowledge of general facts about social and political life, but not of the specific place they would be occupying in society, a restriction Rawls calls the 'veil of ignorance'. Particular conceptions of the good are thus disallowed in the original position and the parties to the contract 'do not know what final aims persons have' (1971: 563). Rawls stipulates that this is so because, first, the only relevant aspect of the self in considerations of justice (in the original position) is 'moral personality' and, second, allowing knowledge of substantive standards of the good would compromise the priority of liberty (1971: 327–8). From this presumably impartial situation Rawls sets out a contemporary version of contract theory, since the occupants of the original position would use the principles upon which they have agreed as guides for constructing actual socio-political institutions.

In this manner Rawls offers a unique attempt to conceptualize the problem of social justice and support the priority of the right over the good. What this means is that each person is to choose his or her own conception of the good and devise his or her own pursuit of that good. However, this pursuit must take a path which does not violate the public principles of right. In other words, people should be free to pursue their own ends within a general framework of rules that is neutral toward these ends, yet that nevertheless enforces the right. Even more specifically, the idea here is that the common structure of political action should constrain and limit what elected governments may decide in the name of the state, what citizens may do in pursuit of their own conceptions of the good life and what economic actors may do in pursuit of economic gain. Consequently, Rawls holds that people are moral agents capable of adopting, pursuing and changing their own beliefs about what constitutes a morally good life for them, while the legal and political institutions of the state enforce right actions between individuals. This position reflects the strong contractarian emphasis on the fundamental rights of individuals within the sphere of social justice. These issues will be discussed in more detail in the next chapter.

Rawls's contractarian approach to justice

The contractarian tradition to which Rawls's theory belongs rose to prominence during the Enlightenment and has long served as an important inspiration to many liberal theorists concerned with social justice and human rights. Rawls explains in *A Theory of Justice* that his 'aim is to present a conception of justice which generalizes and carries to a higher level of abstraction the familiar theory of the social contract as found, say, in Locke, Rousseau, and Kant' (1971: 11). In this section I present an account of Rawls's hypothetical consent theory of justice. I do so for two reasons. First, even a basic description of the elements of Rawls's theory is needed if we are to understand his approach to rights and liberties. Second, because our discussion of international justice and human rights in the following chapters seeks to extend Rawls's initial domestic or intrastate account of justice, it will be useful first to work through the initial account itself. Thus, the general analysis offered here will be an essential guide to our later inquiry.

In place of the original compact postulated by the various contract theories, Rawls describes what he calls an initial situation. This is a hypothetical choice situation from which the principles of social justice and the principles assigning basic rights and duties are to be chosen. Of course, a large number of descriptions of such an initial situation might be constructed, each determining a choice of principles of social justice. Rawls calls his preferred interpretation of the initial situation the 'original position', and he provides substantial arguments in support of the claim that the original position is the most appropriate interpretation of the initial situation from which people enter into an agreement on the principles of social justice.

A general definition of the original position is introduced early on in *A Theory of Justice*. The original position is a purely hypothetical state of affairs in which all the members of a particular society are free, rational, equal and concerned to further their own interests. They are to choose once and for all what is to count in their society as just and unjust. Thus, a set of principles must be chosen that will define the fundamental terms of their association, namely, the principles covering the major institutions or 'basic structure' of society.

The parties in the original position are behind what Rawls calls a 'veil of ignorance'. Behind the veil of ignorance no person knows his or her social position or status. No one knows the particular circumstances of his or her own society, such as its economic or political situation, or its level of civilization and culture. Furthermore, no one knows to which generation he or she belongs. No one knows how he or she fares in the distribution of natural assets. That is, no one knows his or her talents, intelligence level, abilities, health, gender, appearance, race or ethnic origin. In addition, nobody knows his or her level of income or wealth, career, religion, conception of the good, psychological orientation toward risk and the personal characteristics of his or her parents. However, the parties know the general facts of economics, political science, anthropology, sociology and human psychology – presumably in the form in which this general information is known in society upon 'entry' into the original position (1971: 136–7).

The veil of ignorance provides part of the sense in which all of the parties in the original position are equal, for the veil of ignorance removes from consideration all personal characteristics which serve to differentiate one person from another and it eliminates knowledge of natural and social factors that set persons at odds. The result is arguably a 'symmetry of everyone's relations to each other', for all are 'similarly situated' (1971: 12). The veil of ignorance also serves to ensure that the choice of principles is impartial or unbiased. Thus, nobody is able to tailor principles to favour the particular circumstances of his or her own case.

Another source of impartiality in the original position is the way in which decisions are made in light of the maximin rule. The term 'maximin' is from *maximum minimorum* (the greatest of the least) and the maximin rule is derived from a theory of rational choice, designed for situations of choice under conditions of uncertainty. The rule directs the decision-maker to rank alternative choices by their worst outcome and to choose the option which results in the best worst outcome possible. Because the persons in the original position are operating under a veil of ignorance they must make choices under conditions of uncertainty. Thus they must make decisions according to maximin, choosing the alternative which yields the worst outcome that is superior to the worst outcomes of the other alternatives. To illustrate, Rawls offers the example set out in the gain-and-loss table

	Circumstances		
Decisions	c_1	c_2	c_3
d_1	−7	8	12
d_2	−8	7	14
d_3	5	6	8

(1971: 153): (d) stands for the individual's decision and (c) stands for the possible circumstances the individual faces. The numbers in the table represent the values of the goods yielded by each of the individual's decision and circumstances. While the best possible outcome is achieved by d_2 under c_3, d_2 might also yield the worst possible outcome under c_1. The maximin rule requires the choice of d_3 because the worst that can happen is a gain of five, which is better than the worst for the other choices. Given the constraints of the veil of ignorance, the parties in the original position are uncertain of the nature of their society and of their place in it. Thus the parties, it is assumed, will not take risks in choosing principles that jeopardize important aspects of their own lives as well as those of future generations: 'They must also take into account the fact that their choice of principles should seem reasonable to others, in particular their descendants, whose rights will be deeply affected by it' (1971: 155). An impartial solution is required that will optimize the lots of the parties in the original position if they should turn out to be among the less favoured. The parties will therefore choose in light of the maximin rule in order to secure a satisfactory minimum whatever the circumstances of their lives turn out to be.[22]

In light of these constraints, we can see how the correct principles of social justice are those that would be chosen in such a situation of equality. Rawls calls this way of regarding the principles of social justice 'justice as fairness', for the reason that the original position exemplifies what is considered to be a fair choice situation (1971: 11–12). Thus, 'justice as fairness' is the name of the view which conceives the correct principles of social justice to be those that would be chosen in a hypothetical choice situation having the features of the original position. In this way, Rawls defines a procedure for the selection of principles of social justice, one which involves discovering the principles that would be consented to by persons in the original position.

Brian Barry defends an approach to justice that is somewhat similar to that proposed by Rawls. Barry's theory of 'justice as impartiality' articulates the notion of a test that can be applied to the moral and legal rules of a society. This test is grounded on the contractarian idea that principles and rules ought to be capable of forming the basis of agreement among individuals seeking agreement on reasonable terms. The aim of justice as impartiality is to establish justice on reasonable agreement between well-informed people with equal power who hold competing conceptions of the good. This agreement emerges from a kind of original position which excludes some information that might bias the process of deliberation about principles of justice, but not as much as Rawls would have it. Barry is critical of Rawls's original position because, as he puts it, people in the original position are 'clones' or 'computers'.[23] In Barry's view, Rawls's veil of ignorance is too stringent in its excising of personal knowledge, particularly of individuals' conceptions of the good. While the original position is intended to be a procedure for collective bargaining, Barry worries that in fact there can be no bargaining since people in the original position 'are faced with identical information and reasoning in an identical fashion'.[24] Given this situation, Barry contends, there is very little if any basis for disagreement and thus for bargaining.

Barry holds that there exists an irreducible pluralism of conceptions of the good and disputes about the good are unresolvable since no single conception of the good will be universally acceptable. It is for this reason that justice as impartiality is neutral between different conceptions of the good, seeking principles of justice that can be endorsed by all members of society whatever their conception of the good. Because it allows ample room for people to pursue their own conceptions of the good, justice as impartiality distinguishes between first-order impartiality, which excludes preferential treatment from the relationships of our everyday lives, and second-order impartiality, which applies to the moral and legal rules of a society.[25] Nevertheless, Barry does recognize that some restrictions on certain conceptions of the good must exist, namely, those that are incompatible with justice as impartiality.

The primary criticism Barry makes of Rawls's account is that it introduces the problem of bargaining power into the original position. Barry characterizes Rawls's account as containing a version of justice as reciprocity, grounded in the kind of mutual advantage made famous by Thomas Hobbes's theory of justice.[26] Justice as reciprocity means that people with different conceptions of the good should seek a set of rules that offers each person the prospect of doing better than any of them could expect from pursuing the good individually without constraints. According to Barry, this form of justice will prove to be unstable since people will violate the rules agreed upon whenever it is in their self-interest to do so, that is, whenever it proves to be to their advantage. The dilemma, then, is that Rawls apparently subscribes to two competing views of justice: justice as reciprocity – which reflects the bargaining strengths of the parties – and justice as impartiality – which arrives at principles that cannot reasonably be rejected by anybody seeking agreement on fair grounds with another. The significance of Barry's conclusion remains unclear, however, because it is open to doubt whether justice as reciprocity does in fact have the stability problems that Barry suggests, particularly when the constraints of Rawls's original position are taken into account. To see how Rawls addresses these issues, we should further examine the particulars of justice as fairness.

Rawls proceeds on the belief that justice is the primary and indispensable virtue against which the laws and institutions of society must be assessed (1971: 3). Given the indispensable status of social justice, a society's laws and institutions must be reformed or abolished if they are unjust, even though they may be good or proper according to some other criteria. According to Rawls, a society is a relatively self-sufficient association of individuals who generally acknowledge certain rules of conduct and generally act in accordance with those rules. These rules specify a system of cooperation organized to advance the good of those involved. Society, therefore, should be conceived as 'a cooperative venture for mutual advantage' (1971: 4). Yet society involves both shared common interests and conflicts of interests among its members. As both Hobbes and Locke recognized in their theories of justice as mutual advantage or reciprocity, an identity of interests exists because social cooperation makes possible a better life for each person in society than they would have outside of society. Conflict of interests arise from the fact that people disagree over how the benefits and burdens of social cooperation are to be divided, and incompatible claims to larger rather than smaller shares of benefits arise. Thus, social life presents a decision theoretic problem as the problem of justice: while all the members of society gain from cooperation, those same members will disagree over the form the cooperation should take. Contrary to Barry's claim about the absence of disagreement in Rawls's model, it is precisely conflict of interest that gives rise to the question of justice. In Rawls's contract theory the basic aim of justice is to transform disagreement into agreement on rules and guiding principles of social organization, through a fair deliberative process.[27]

What Rawls calls the 'basic structure of society' is the primary subject of justice. The basic structure of society is the complex consisting of the major political, social and economic institutions of society. The basic structure also includes the manner in which these institutions assign fundamental rights and duties, distribute the division of advantages and burdens that arise through social cooperation, influence life prospects and affect the hopes, ambitions and realized abilities of the members of society (1971: 7). Because the basic structure of society is the primary subject of justice, the most fundamental principles of justice are designed to regulate the distribution of fundamental rights and duties, advantages and burdens, assigned to individuals by the rules of society.

As Barry has noted, Rawls's theory is notable because of its special focus on the systematic functioning of institutions within a social structure.[28] For Rawls the basic structure of society is to be the result of the application of principles of justice, insofar as the major institutions of society are schematically regulated by those principles. By introducing the idea of the basic structure of society, Rawls recognizes that 'societies have patterns of inequality that persist over time and systematic ways of allocating people to positions within their hierarchies of power, status and money'.[29] Because of these structural allocations of advantages and disadvantages, principles of justice cannot be considered independently of the basic structure, as this would leave unaffected many aspects of the basic structure responsible for arbitrary inequalities. A fundamental aim of justice as fairness is to ensure the existence of a just system of institutions.

Rawls gives a number of reasons for his claim that the primary subject of justice is the basic structure of society. One argument that highlights the importance of the basic structure concerns what Rawls calls 'fair equality of opportunity'. Suppose that a society is free and social conditions are fair at a certain time. It is possible that a series of exchanges and agreements might be made, each component of which – when viewed alone – seems free and fair, and yet the unintended, accumulated result of this series might eventually alter institutions and opportunities so that conditions for free and fair agreements no longer obtain. For example, a series of agreements – each of which seem free and fair when viewed alone – might, together with historical and social contingencies, lead to a state in which fair equality of opportunity no longer exists.

In order to understand fully, however, what Rawls means by fair equality of opportunity, it is necessary to distinguish 'fair' equality of opportunity from 'formal' equality of opportunity (1971: 83–9). Formal equality exists when no laws unequally restrict the opportunities of anyone to acquire wealth, income or powers of office. However, formal equality of opportunity does not concern itself with inequalities of life prospects that stem from unequal starting places in society. Thus, under a scheme of formal equality of opportunity, if two equally motivated and equally talented individuals start from unequal social positions, it is quite likely that they will achieve unequal levels of wealth, income or powers of office. Consequently, persons with equal talents and motivations will not have equal life prospects or expectations.

In contrast, fair equality of opportunity exists when persons with equal talents, abilities and motivations have the same life prospects or expectations of attaining positions involving certain levels of income, wealth and powers of office, regardless of the social position into which each is born (1971: 73). This requires certain institutions designed to mitigate the influence of social position on individual attainment and thus to equalize life prospects regarding the attainment of income, wealth or the powers of office for individuals with similar abilities and motivation. If, for example, two similarly talented and motivated individuals happened to be born into radically different circumstances, such that one of them had access to adequate educational and medical facilities while the other did not, the resulting disparity in life prospects could be lessened by the equal provision of basic education and healthcare. What this means for Rawls is that the basic structure generates, in conjunction with natural and social contingencies, conditions which can be the source of what seem to be significant injustices. Consequently, the basic structure must itself be regulated to eliminate as much as possible such injustices.

Robert Nozick disagrees with Rawls on this point, and claims that an absence of fair equality of opportunity is merely unfortunate, not unjust. Nozick contends that there can be no right to fair equality of opportunity since such a right would violate the more fundamental right to property. This is because, as he sees it, fair equality of opportunity can be achieved only by worsening the situation of those with the greater opportunity, or by improving the situation of those with less opportunity. In either case, resources must be taken from those better off, thereby violating their property rights. Thus, Nozick concludes that improving the situation of those with less opportunity can only be accomplished through voluntary assistance and not through a scheme of distributive justice worked out in the basic structure.[30] Clearly Rawls would object that recognizing property rights does not necessarily conflict with also recognizing fair constraints or limits to such rights, particularly when rights of ownership threaten fair opportunity. Indeed, this is precisely one of the issues the parties in the original position debate, namely, what ought to be the principles of distribution regulating the production and acquisition of goods.

Another possible response to Rawls on this point is to suggest that rules could be devised to regulate each of the series of agreements and transactions made in society so as to ensure that free and fair background conditions are maintained, but without requiring constant attention to background institutions. Rawls replies to this response that the consequences of acts leading to unfair background conditions are usually unforeseeable either because the consequences are so far in the future or because the causal connection is so indirect, thus, such rules cannot be formulated since the necessary information is not available. According to Rawls, therefore, any theory which does not concern itself in a fundamental way with the operation of the basic structure of society will be inadequate as a theory of justice. This is because such a theory will operate at the wrong level of generality by failing to cover the most fundamental injustices, namely, those generated by the basic structure in conjunction with natural and social contingencies.

Rawls offers another reason for taking the basic structure as the primary subject of justice (1971: 160). The basic structure influences the desires, ambitions, hopes, abilities and talents of individuals. Even if some of these, such as talents, have a genetic component, each is still influenced by the basic structure since genetically based attributes can be realized and hindered in a variety of ways by existing social conditions. This basic structure thus ought to be an object of serious concern. Any theory which does not deal in a fundamental way with the basic structure neglects an important influence in our lives, an influence we would surely hope is in accord with the demands of justice.

As a third reason, Rawls observes that the basic structure is the most likely source of a number of the most significant social and economic inequalities, some of which have very pervasive effects throughout society. For instance, these inequalities lead to conditions in which some have lesser life prospects than others due solely to their social origins, as described above. Since the effects of the basic structure are so significant, and since these effects can include what seem to be some of the deepest injustices (such as a lack of fair equality of opportunity), a theory of justice ought to concern itself in a fundamental way with the basic structure of society.

Given these reasons, the basic structure of society plays a central role in Rawls's conception of justice. It should be noted that Rawls distinguishes the terms 'concept of justice' and 'conception of justice' (1971: 5). The question 'What is justice?' poses the issue of which principles are the correct principles of justice. It also conveys a desire to identify the purpose of justice, that is, the role which principles of justice play in society. A *conception* of justice consists of a particular set of principles of social justice. The *concept* of justice is specified 'by the role which these different sets of principles, these different conceptions, have in common' (1971: 5). In Rawls's view, this role consists in the assignment of fundamental rights and duties and the determination of a 'proper distribution of the benefits and burdens of

social cooperation' (1971: 5). Thus, justice provides the most fundamental standard we have for the resolution of the various conflicts of
interest that go with organized human social life. Various *conceptions*
of justice ought to be evaluated in terms of how well they fill this role.

Rawls divides his theory of justice into two parts. The first part to
be developed is ideal theory (1971: 245). In an ideal theory, one
assumes strict compliance and then works out the principles of justice
that would characterize a well-ordered society existing under circumstances favourable to the functioning of such a society. Strict compliance obtains when everyone acts justly and does his or her part in
upholding just institutions. Ideal theory thus gives us an account of
what a perfectly just society would be like, that is, it presents a social
ideal. Rawls is concerned primarily with working out the ideal part of
the theory of justice.

After constructing ideal theory, one completes the theory of justice
by constructing non-ideal theory (1971: 245–6). In non-ideal theory,
one assumes partial compliance and less favourable circumstances.
There are two parts to non-ideal theory. The first part covers the
principles for governing adjustments to ideal theory that are required
because of natural limitations and historical contingencies. The
second part, called partial compliance theory, consists of principles
for handling injustices. Here, principles of punishment, civil dis-
obedience, revolution and just war are worked out.

Ideal and non-ideal theory together fit into a complete theory of
justice in the following manner. Ideal theory presents a conception of
a perfectly just society against which the existing society is judged. To
the extent that the existing society diverges from perfect justice, injustice exists. Non-ideal theory then comes into play as a guide to the
remedying of injustice. Since Rawls's main concern is with ideal
theory, strict compliance and favourable conditions are assumed in
the original position. In other words, the principles chosen in the
original position belong to ideal theory and provide a definition of a
perfectly just scheme of social cooperation. The point of developing
such a theory is to provide a guide for social reform, an ideal for
which we can aim (1971: 245). It will be important to remember
throughout our analysis Rawls's explicit focus on ideal theory as a
regulative model, and in particular when we come to consider his
account of human rights in the law of peoples.

We have seen that Rawls's principles of justice require a thorough
regulation of the entire basic structure of society. Rawls characterizes

his approach to the derivation of the principles of justice from the original position in terms of 'pure procedural justice'. He argues that three types of theories of justice should be distinguished:

1. In *perfect* procedural justice, there exists an independent criterion for what counts as a fair or right outcome, defined prior to and separately from the procedure to be followed. Furthermore, it is possible to devise a procedure which will guarantee the desired outcome. (1971: 85)

2. In *imperfect* procedural justice, there exists an independent criterion for what is to count as a fair or right outcome, defined prior to and separately from the procedure to be followed. However, it is not possible to devise a procedure which will guarantee the desired outcome. (1971: 85)

3. In *pure* procedural justice, there is no independent criterion for the right result. Instead, there is a correct or fair procedure which is such that, whatever the outcome that results, it will be right or fair. (1971: 86)

As an example of perfect procedural justice, Rawls considers a case where a number of people must divide a cake between themselves (1971: 85). The independent criterion of a fair division is, simply, equal pieces for each person. The basic procedure guaranteed to lead to this is to let one person divide the cake and get the last piece, the others choosing their pieces first. As an example of imperfect procedural justice, Rawls mentions a criminal trial. Although an independent standard specifying the correct result obviously exists, no procedure is available to guarantee this result (1971: 85). As an example of pure procedural justice, Rawls refers to a game consisting of a series of fair gambles. In such a case, we have no criterion for the distribution of winnings after the betting has taken place. But if all individual bets have been technically fair, then the outcome is fair as well (1971: 86). Justice as fairness, then, involves pure procedural justice in a fundamental way. Rawls develops principles that aim to ensure that the *process* by which the basic structure operates is a fair process. However, no independent criterion for the proper social outcome is specified.

The definition of the original position, it will be recalled, characterizes the terms of a problem of rational decision. The terms of a rational decision problem must include a conception of value as an assumption about motivation and so the definition of the original position must include an account of what counts as good. However, this raises a problem for Rawls. In justice as fairness, the concept of right is supposed to be prior to the concept of good, which means in part that a necessary condition for something's being good is that it fits into activities consistent with the principles of right already established (1971: 396). Thus, Rawls must work out a theory of right before he works out a theory of good and then the theory of right will be used in the formulation of the theory of good. Yet the definition of the original position is used to determine the theory of right and, as noted, that definition requires a conception of good. So, the problem is that Rawls needs a conception of right in order fully to characterize a conception of good, but he needs a conception of good in order to determine a conception of right.

Rawls's solution is to construct what he calls a 'thin' theory of the good (1971: 395 ff.). The thin theory of the good is used to establish a motivational assumption for the purposes of the original position, and the account of the original position is then used to derive a theory of right. Rawls specifies that the parties in the original position possess a thin theory of the good, in that there are certain things that the parties would rationally want, no matter what else they may want. In other words, the parties in the original position will know that they want or desire these things to serve as their all-purpose means to their personal ends in life. Given this starting-point, once the theory of right is derived then a 'full' theory of the good may be constructed within the constraints of the principles of right. So, the thin theory of the good is used by Rawls in his derivation of the theory of right while any full theory of the good makes essential use of the theory of right, the theory of right being prior to and built into the full theory of the good.

The thin theory consists of the bare essentials of a theory of the good, including a notion of self-realization which extends back to Aristotle. It is essentially an attempt by Rawls to identify certain standard features of what it is that rational persons want or desire in realizing their goals in life. Rawls appeals to the so-called 'Aristotelian Principle' in characterizing the satisfaction of desire relevant to our life plans. This principle states that 'other things [being] equal, human beings enjoy the exercise of their realized capacities (their innate or trained abilities), and this enjoyment increases the more the capacity is realized' (1971: 426). This principle, Rawls holds, will undoubtedly influence the reasoning of those in the original position when it comes to the choice of principles of justice, insofar as it colours their understanding of what is good for human beings, especially with respect to self-realization (1971: 84). The goods that any rational human being is presumed to want regardless of his or her plan of life or place in society are what Rawls calls the 'primary goods'.

Brian Barry contends that the Aristotelian Principle is problematic, because it is both a dubious empirical generalization and an assumed constitutive definition of rationality. In other words, it is not entirely clear that all persons everywhere would in fact be motivated to pursue their good in the way the Aristotelian Principle claims that they would. Moreover, if the Aristotelian Principle is true it would set strict limits between rational and irrational plans of life, indeed rationality itself would have to be defined in terms of the principle. Barry suggests that the principle is 'false for most people most of the time' since it would appear that the majority of people prefer 'eating, drinking, making love or watching television' to pursuing more complex activities.[31] One might accuse Barry of making an unwarranted empirical generalization himself with this claim, but more importantly I think Barry reads the Aristotelian Principle too strongly. The principle does not state that the goods being pursued and enjoyed are the same for each and every person, rather a person's good will be defined from the perspective of the rational plan for *that* person. Underlying this point, when it comes to filling out Rawls's thin theory of the good, is that such pursuit and enjoyment are a consequence of shared capacities which reveal the need for specifying certain things which are means to a wide range of ends. In this way the Aristotelian Principle ties into Rawls's notion of primary goods.

Rawls goes on to define his thin theory of the good with reference to three stages. The first stage provides an explanation of what we mean when we say that some object is good in relation to a shared set of interests and circumstances. The second stage provides an explanation of what we mean when we say that something is good for a certain person when our judgement makes no evaluation of the way the person is living his or her life. Such a definition of good is morally neutral. The third stage is the one that most concerns Rawls, as it provides an explanation of what we mean when we say that something is good for a person insofar as that person's plan of life is itself rational. At this stage moral evaluation is introduced since the definition of good is extended to cover the person herself, and the assessment of her purposes, causes and life plan. The third stage thus presupposes principles of right and justice. According to the three-stage definition, then, a thin, yet objective notion of the human good seeks to identify that which properly satisfies what 'is rational for someone with a rational plan of life to want' (1971: 399).

Among the things that qualify as human goods, Rawls includes the primary goods. These are goods that are necessary for the implementation of any rational life plan; with a greater number of primary goods a person can generally be assured of a greater likelihood of success in carrying out his or her plan no matter what that plan is. Thus, primary goods are goods which it is rational to want no matter what one's rational plan of life. Primary goods are those things needed in order to pursue our life goals, irrespective of the differences that exist between individuals' plans of life. Primary goods are divided by Rawls into two categories. *Social* primary goods, so named because they are directly distributed by social institutions, include rights and liberties, powers and opportunities, income and wealth, and the bases of self-respect. *Natural* primary goods arise from nature and are thus not directly distributed by social institutions, although they are influenced by the basic structure. Included in this category are health, vigour, intelligence, imagination and natural talents (1971: 62).

Rawls offers several arguments in support of his account of primary goods, and these arguments find their full force in his conclusion that what is to count as necessary for the execution of any rational life plan relies upon the general facts of social interdependency. The facts of social interdependency concern those values that are not only good for those enjoying them but which also tend to enhance the good of others as well (1971: 425). Such socially interdependent values will naturally be encouraged in any well-ordered society, and the fact of interdependency provides reason to include these values in any long-term plan of life. For this reason, social interdependency is reinforced by the deliberations of participants in the original position, since their aim is to determine the just distribution of social primary goods through the properly regulated institutions of the basic structure of society. All parties in the original position want to ensure that they have the best possible access to the social primary goods. Because their deliberations occur behind the veil of ignorance, and thus they are unaware of where they will end up in society, the participants will choose those principles which promote equally the good of every person in society.

Rawls observes that we naturally distinguish, in principle, between claims of liberty and right on the one hand and the value of an increase in total social welfare on the other hand (1971: 27–8). Furthermore, he says, we give a certain priority to claims of liberty and right over considerations of social welfare. That is, each person is naturally presumed to have 'an inviolability founded on justice or, as some say, on natural right, which even the welfare of everyone else cannot override' (1971: 28).

Rawls aims, in constructing justice as fairness, to develop a theory which takes account of this 'common sense conviction', that is, that claims of right take a certain priority over considerations of social welfare. Thus:

> In justice as fairness . . . persons accept in advance a principle of equal liberty and they do this without a knowledge of their more particular ends. They implicitly agree, therefore, to conform their conceptions of their good to what the principles of justice require. (1971: 31)

The principles of right that justice as fairness contains place limits upon which satisfactions have value and upon what is to count as a reasonable conception of the good; they therefore serve as constraints upon the principles of good. In this sense, the principles of right are prior to the principles of good. On this view, social policy does not simply take individuals' wants and aims for granted and then seek the most efficient way to fulfil those wants and aims. Rather, a just social system defines the scope within which persons must develop their wants, aims and life plans. Such an approach is 'characteristic of natural rights views (the contractarian tradition) in comparison with the theory of utility' (1971: 32).

The theory of right is used in the definition of the moral virtues found in the full theory of the good. A good person, a person of moral worth, is defined as one who possesses to a higher degree than average 'the broadly based features of moral character that it is rational for the persons in the original position to want in one another' (1971: 437). Thus, moral worth is judged in terms of 'broadly based' properties, that is, properties it is rational to want in a person no matter what social role she fills.

Along with the veil of ignorance, the theory of right is also used by Rawls as a kind of restriction on the parties in the original position. Rawls does not claim that the formal constraints are implied by the concept of right, nor does he claim that they are self-evident or that they follow from the meaning of morality. Rather, Rawls holds that, given the role the principles of right must play, namely, adjudicating the claims persons make on social institutions and on each other through the assignment of basic rights and duties determining the division of social advantages, it is reasonable to impose the conditions of the formal constraints on the choice of conceptions of justice. Five constraints are offered by Rawls:

1. Moral principles, and thus principles of social justice, must be general principles since principles of justice must be capable of serving as a public charter of a well-ordered society in perpetuity.

2. The principles of justice should be public, which means that they must be suitable for use as a public conception of justice.

3. Principles should provide an ordering of conflicting claims that can or that are likely to arise.

4. The principles should serve adequately as a final court of appeal in practical reasoning; there will be no higher standards for the adjudication of disputes concerning claims.

5. The principles must be universal in application. That is, they must be understood and followed by every moral agent and they must hold for a given moral agent simply in virtue of the fact that she is a moral agent.

This last constraint is significant. Rawls's definition of moral person-ality involves two features: (i) a moral agent is capable of having a conception of the good, and she normally realizes this capacity in the normal course of development, and (ii) a moral agent has a sense of justice, that is, the 'desire to apply and act upon the principles of justice' (1971: 505). Moral personality singles out the kind of beings that are bound by the principles of justice. Rawls notes that this idea may be used to provide an interpretation of the traditional idea of natural rights. Claims of right that follow from the principles of justice are based upon the possession of moral personality. Justice as fairness holds that certain fundamental rights are 'assigned in the first instance to persons' and 'are given a special weight' such that 'the system of equal liberties is absolute practically speaking under favorable conditions' (1971: 505–6, n. 30). I will return to the issue of rights in Chapter 2.

In Rawls's conception of justice as fairness, then, the original position is a hypothetical state of affairs which provides for a way of thinking about the question of social justice. The purpose of the original position is to provide for agreement on the fair terms or principles of justice. These principles will regulate the social cooperation and behaviour of citizens in political society. However, the principles of justice will be fair only if the conditions under which they are chosen are fair. Pure procedural justice is incorporated into the original position, along with the veil of ignorance, in order to ensure that the principles chosen are the result of a fair procedure. The principles chosen through the deliberations of the participants in the original position must now be described.

The two principles of justice

After setting out the definition of the original position, Rawls argues that a two-tiered set of principles would be chosen by the hypothetical parties in the original position. The first tier of the two-tiered structure is summarized by Rawls in the form of the following principle, referred to as the 'general conception' of justice: 'All social values – liberty and opportunity, income and wealth, and the bases of self-respect – are to be distributed equally unless an unequal distribution of any, or all, of these values is to everyone's advantage' (1971: 62).

The general conception of justice applies only at early stages of economic development which allow for neither the effective establishment nor the effective exercise of basic liberties (1971: 542). The general conception allows a trade-off of social values such as liberties and equality of opportunity for, perhaps, improvements in economic well-being, provided that (a) the quality of civilization is enhanced in such a way that all benefit, and (b) the improvement moves society closer to a state of development where equal liberty and opportunity can be enjoyed by all as specified in the special conception of justice (discussed below).

The idea here is that, at very low levels of economic development, the marginal value of further economic and social advantages is so relative to the interests of liberty – since the liberties cannot be effectively exercised anyway – that it is rational to allow the stated trade-offs. Rawls argues that, as the economic development of civilization continues, the marginal value of further economic and social benefits diminishes relative to the interests of liberty so that a point is reached beyond which it becomes irrational – from the perspective of the original position – to allow liberty to be traded off for the sake of greater material benefits. Consequently, a new conception of justice would be chosen to govern a society which had advanced to a level of economic development capable of supporting rights and liberties that can be effectively exercised (1971: 542). Thus, the general conception of justice is superseded in favour of the 'special conception' with which Rawls develops his theory of justice as fairness. The special conception of justice constitutes the second of the two tiers, and is expressed in two principles of justice that Rawls argues would be chosen in the original position:

(1) First Principle:
Each person is to have an equal right to the most extensive total system of equal basic liberties compatible with a similar system of liberty for all.
(2) Second Principle:
Social and economic inequalities are to be arranged so that they are both:
(a) to the greatest benefit of the least advantaged, and consistent with the just savings principle, and (b) attached to offices and positions open to all under conditions of fair equality of opportunity. (1971: 302)

In the first principle, Rawls speaks of a 'system' of liberties, which suggests that the various liberties are components affecting one another within a complex network. The reason the principle is framed in terms of a system of equal liberties is because Rawls holds that basic liberties cannot be evaluated singly. Rather, they must be evaluated as a whole since the character of one liberty normally depends upon the specification of other liberties (1971: 203). For example, if freedom of speech is defined too broadly, then property rights might be endangered if certain forms of expression which incite vandalism and rioting are permissible. Although it is true that a greater liberty is by and large preferable to a lesser liberty, this only holds for the system of liberty as a whole and does not hold for each individual liberty. Another reason Rawls gives for the claim that the character of a liberty depends upon the specification of other liberties is the observation that, when individual liberties are left unrestricted, they 'collide' with one another. For instance, without rules of order in a convention, freedom of speech loses its value. The regulation of liberty is necessary for its wider realization. Thus, liberties must be balanced in a give-and-take process until a systematic maximum of total liberty is reached – subject to the constraint that all individuals have the same liberties.

The first principle of justice thus guarantees an equal liberty to each person. Rawls illustrates how the argument for equal liberty from the original position would proceed by taking the example of the liberty of conscience. The reasoning in this case is then generalized to the other freedoms. The parties do not know what their philosophical, religious or moral convictions are, or whether they even have any such convictions. Furthermore, they do not know whether their philosophical, religious or moral attitudes are in the majority or the minority. Thus, they will not want to take chances concerning their liberty of conscience by, for instance, permitting the majority religion to suppress other views (1971: 207). Nor would the parties consent to a utilitarian principle, for their freedom of conscience would then be subject to the 'calculus of social interests' and might be restricted if such an action maximizes utility. Consequently, equal liberty of conscience is the only principle the parties will acknowledge in order to prevent subordination of some persons' conception of the good to that of others.

Rawls goes on to derive a limitation to this principle: the maintenance of public order is understood as a necessary condition for any person's achieving his or her ends, no matter what those ends might be. Thus, from the standpoint of the representative citizen, all have an interest in public order and security, and this common interest limits the principle of liberty of conscience, that is, when it is reasonably expected that the public order will be damaged, liberty of conscience can be restricted. And this gives us a principle of toleration: different moral and religious views are to be tolerated until the point is reached at which the public order is threatened. 'The government's right to maintain public order and security', Rawls observes, 'is an enabling right, a right which the government must have if it is to carry out its duty of impartially supporting the conditions necessary for everyone's pursuit of his interests' (1971: 212).

It is clear that Rawls treats civil liberty and the 'rule of law' as closely associated. Liberty is 'a complex of rights and duties defined by institutions' (1971: 219). The specific civil liberties Rawls identifies as constitutive of liberty are gathered in the following list:

> The basic liberties of citizens are, roughly speaking, political liberty (the right to vote and to be eligible for public office) together with freedom of

speech and assembly; liberty of conscience and freedom of thought; freedom of the person along with the right to hold (personal) property; and freedom from arbitrary arrest and seizure as defined by the rule of law. (1971: 61)

The rule of law is essentially formal justice or justice as regularity, in other words, the ideal of 'regular and impartial administration of public rules' applied to the legal system (1971: 235). The relation between the rule of law and civil liberty is expressed by the observation that, without the rule of law, civil liberties cannot be secure. This relationship has practical consequences with respect to efforts to translate the principles of justice chosen by parties to the original position into constitutional, legislative and judicial policy.

Stressing the connection between liberty and the rule of law, Rawls points out several precepts that regulate their interaction. First is the basic principle that ought implies can. Given this precept, actions required or forbidden by rules of law should be ones that persons can reasonably be expected to do or avoid and, moreover, those who enact laws and give orders must do so in good faith. In addition, impossibility of performance should be recognized as either a defence or at least a mitigating circumstance. Without this precept, a legal system would almost certainly be an intolerable burden on liberty.

Another precept to which Rawls appeals holds that similar cases must be treated similarly. The principle of consistency, that like decisions be rendered in like cases, limits the discretion of judges and figures in authority, and forces them to justify the distinctions they make between people when rendering their decisions. A third precept Rawls mentions is that there is no offence without a law. This requires 'that laws be known and expressly promulgated', 'that their meaning be clearly defined', that laws be general and not be used to harm particular individuals, that the more severe offences be strictly construed, and that penal laws should not be retroactive (1971: 238). Finally, Rawls appeals to the precept of natural justice. A conscientious effort must be made to determine guilt and innocence and impose correct penalties. Thus, orderly trials and hearings, the correct application of rules of evidence, the independence and impartiality of judges and other elements of due process reasonably designed to establish the truth are required (1971: 239). Rawls rightly argues that, without the rule of law, our liberties are uncertain and insecure. In order to attain confidence in the exercise of their liberties, then, the members of a well-ordered society will require the rule of law.

The second principle of justice that Rawls argues would be chosen in the original position focuses on the matter of 'social and economic inequalities'. Rawls is here referring to inequalities in the following social primary goods: income, wealth, opportunities and powers of office. Liberty is not included in this list since it is treated by the first principle of justice.

The term 'least advantaged' in clause (a) of the second principle requires explanation. When principles refer to persons, Rawls notes, the reference is to 'representative persons' holding various representative social positions. For the purpose of generating a theory of justice it is not necessary to consider things from the point of view of each representative person from each social position. This is because an assessment of the competing claims of thousands of different social positions is obviously impossible. A complete theory of justice must therefore single out certain social positions as more basic than others and as providing an 'appropriate standpoint for judging the social system' (1971: 96).

Rawls supposes that each person holds two social positions, that of equal citizenship and that specified by a place in the distribution of income and wealth. The position of equal citizenship is defined in terms of the rights and liberties required by the first principle and also in terms of the fair equality of opportunity provided by the principle of fair equality of opportunity. Equal citizenship, Rawls points out, provides a 'general point of view' from which to judge a social system (1971: 98).

The number of representative positions in the distribution of income and wealth is problematic, but clause (a) of the second principle focuses upon the position of the least advantaged and this requires only the representative least well-off person. Rawls suggests two possible ways of characterizing this position. First, one might take the average income of an unskilled worker and count as least advantaged all those with the average income of this group, or less. The expectation of the least advantaged would then be equal to the average income and wealth of this group. Second, one might count as least advantaged all those with less than half the median income and wealth.

Clause (a) of the second principle of justice is known as the 'difference principle' and allows inequalities in wealth, income and powers of office only *if* these work to the advantage of the least well-off members of society, as measured by reference to an index of social primary goods and a measure of long-run expectations. The extent of the inequalities allowed would be decided, presumably, at the legislative stage, since a great deal of information about society, economic incentives and so on is required for this task, which the veil of ignorance excludes from consideration (1971: 285).

The difference principle is to be viewed in its most basic sense as a requirement that social and economic inequalities are to be evaluated in terms of their impact on the least well-off. Rawls notes, however, that there are several senses in which the expectations of each representative person are raised by the operation of the difference principle (1971: 80). First, it seems clear that each representative person's expectations are raised by the operation of the difference principle in comparison to an initial arrangement of absolutely strict equality, that is, one involving equal shares of the benefits of social cooperation. In addition, expectations might be chain-connected, which means that if an advantage has the effect of raising the expectations of the representative worst-off then it also raises the expectations of all representative positions in between (1971: 79). This does not entail that all effects upon all levels always move together, for nothing is said of cases where the least advantaged do not gain while others do. Second, it is also possible that expectations might be close-knit. This means that it is impossible to raise or lower the expectations of any representative person without raising or lowering the expectations of every other representative person, especially the least well-off (1971: 80). In such a case, all persons generally benefit by the operation of the difference principle in the sense that each person's expectations are raised.

Yet what if the expectations are not close-knit? The representative least advantaged is not affected by some changes in the expectations of the representative best-off, although others are. Thus, providing incentives to certain well-off individuals raises the expectations, say, of the middle class but leaves the expectations of the worst-off unchanged. In order to cover such possibilities, Rawls proposes what he calls the lexical difference principle. This is the general principle of which the difference principle constitutes merely a simplified form:

> [I]n a basic structure with n relevant representatives, first maximize the welfare of the worst-off representative man; second, for equal welfare of the worst-off representative, maximize the welfare of the second worst-off representative man, and so on until the last case which is, for equal welfare

of all the preceding n–1 representatives, maximize the welfare of the best-off representative man. (1971: 83)

Clause (a) of the difference principle also makes reference to the just savings principle. This principle represents a solution to the complex problem of justice between generations. The life of a people is a scheme of cooperation spread out across time and intergenerational relations ought to be governed by the same conception of justice that regulates relations between contemporaries (1971: 289). Thus, a principle of just savings must be chosen from the original position, specifying how the burden of capital accumulation and of raising standards of development is to be shared between generations. In the original position, no generation has stronger claims than any other. The parties to the original position ask what is reasonable for members of adjacent generations to expect of each other, and seek to balance how much at each stage they would be willing to save for their immediate descendants against what they feel entitled to claim of their immediate predecessors. Clause (a) thus requires that the operation of the difference principle be consistent with the just savings principle. By this, Rawls means that the just savings principle acts as a constraint on the application of the difference principle. The expectations of the least well-off in a given generation are to be maximized subject to the constraint that the just amount of savings has been set aside (1971: 292).

Clause (b) of the difference principle requires that fair equality of opportunity be established. As I pointed out earlier, the principle of fair equality of opportunity requires the establishment of various institutions whose purpose is to ensure that similarly endowed and motivated individuals have similar life prospects, regardless of the social circumstances of birth.

Next, Rawls devises two priority rules that apply to the two principles of justice. The purpose of the priority rules is to solve the priority problem which plagues intuitionist theories of ethics. Intuitionism, as Rawls understands it, is the doctrine that there exists a plurality of unranked principles from which all other ethical principles and judgements derive. In cases where the various principles conflict and give contrary directives, the intuitionist requires that we balance the principles against each other by intuition. Thus, the family of first principles is not 'prioritized' and there is no set procedure for resolving ethical problems. Utilitarianism avoids the priority problem by reducing all moral principles to a single, fundamental first principle, namely, the principle of utility.[32] Rawls avoids the priority problem by specifying the two priority rules. Without such rules, we would have no precise way to balance the satisfaction of both of Rawls's principles of justice. The first priority rule states:

> The principles of justice are to be ranked in lexical order and therefore liberty can be restricted only for the sake of liberty. There are two cases:
> (a) a less extensive liberty must strengthen the total system of liberty shared by all;
> (b) a less than equal liberty must be acceptable to those with the lesser liberty. (1971: 302)

The first priority rule, which secures the priority of liberty, places the two principles of justice in a serial or lexical order, with the first principle lexically prior to the second. This means that a society must satisfy the first principle before the second principle comes into play. Therefore, a departure from the institutions of equal liberty – required by the first principle – cannot be justified by a resulting increase in social and economic advantages or by increased fair equality of opportunity. A lexical order prohibits the balancing of principles. It functions like a sequence of constrained maximizing principles: 1>2a>2b. Any principle is maximized given the constraint that the preceding principle is fully satisfied (1971: 43).

As an example of what Rawls has in mind with clause (a) of the first priority rule, consider the following. It might be determined that our total system of liberties is stronger if no private individual has the liberty to possess weapons of mass destruction, such as bombs or chemical and biological weapons. Similarly, our system of liberties might be strengthened if private individuals are not allowed to make public declarations which incite others to engage in indiscriminate acts of violence and destruction, even if they do so purely for their own amusement. In these cases, while our total system of liberties is restricted, the remaining liberties are much more secure so that our total system of liberty is strengthened. Without the restriction, none of our other liberties would be as secure.

Clause (b) of the first priority rule requires that, in order to justify an unequal liberty, one must take up the perspective of a representative person having the lesser liberty and one must prove that the inequality in liberty would be accepted by the less favoured individuals 'in return for the greater protection of their other liberties that results from this restriction' (1971: 231). This qualification, that the unequal liberty must be acceptable only in return for the strengthening of the remaining liberties, is important. For without the qualification it sounds as if an unequal liberty is justifiable if it is acceptable as a means to any other end, whereas the first priority rule ensures that liberty may be restricted only for the sake of liberty.

The second priority rule identified by Rawls states:

> The second principle of justice is lexically prior to the principle of efficiency and to that of maximizing the sum of advantages; and fair opportunity is prior to the difference principle. There are two cases:
>
>   (a) an inequality of opportunity must enhance the opportunity of those with the lesser opportunity;
>
>   (b) an excessive rate of saving must on balance mitigate the burden of those bearing this hardship. (1971: 302–3)

The principle of efficiency is the Pareto optimality criterion of welfare economics. According to this criterion, a social arrangement is optimal or efficient when it is impossible to change it without making at least one person worse off. The principle that Rawls mentions requiring the maximization of the sum of advantages is simply the principle of utility.

By specifying that the principle of fair opportunity is lexically prior to the difference principle, Rawls is requiring that the principle of fair equality of opportunity be fully satisfied before the difference principle comes into play. Thus, the expectations of the least well-off are maximized subject to the constraint that the institutions required for fair equality of opportunity are fully funded and operating properly. By specifying that the difference principle is prior to the principle of efficiency, Rawls is requiring that the difference principle be fully satisfied before officials seek to move the economy towards its Pareto frontier. By specifying that the difference principle is prior to the principle of utility, Rawls is requiring that society must first fully satisfy the difference principle before attempting to promote total or average utility.

This last point brings into view Rawls's critique of the aggregative character of utilitarianism. As a teleological theory, utilitarianism holds that, in order to determine the right action at the social level, the interests of different individuals have to be aggregated or added together, with the aim of producing the greatest amount of happiness or satisfaction overall. But this assumes that there is a social entity that is able to make such decisions in the same way as single individual agents. Rawls argues that the two principles of justice are preferable to utilitarianism insofar as they form a right-based theory that rejects the aggregative character of utilitarian calculations. On the basis of such calculations it is conceivable that an individual's interests will be overridden or sacrificed for the greater good of society, that is, for the sake of a greater average of advantages to everyone. Yet a satisfactory theory of justice should maintain that individuals may not be sacrificed for the presumed good of others. In other words, a theory of justice must embody the Kantian principle that individuals are ends and not merely means,[33] and the idea that individuals possess rights and liberties which may not be violated. The rights of individuals place constraints or limits around the kinds of actions or goals that may be pursued. Rawls argues that the two principles allow the parties to guarantee their basic rights and in doing so also to insure themselves against the severe and unacceptable deprivation of social primary goods that utilitarianism would allow.

2 • The Basic Rights and Liberties

The language of moral rights is the language of justice, and whoever takes justice seriously must accept that there exist moral rights. (G. A. Cohen, 'Freedom, Justice, and Capitalism', 297)

The goal of the preceding chapter was to provide a brief yet coherent survey of contractarianism and its normative concerns, with special reference to the central place it accords to individual rights. This survey was then related to Rawls's contractarian theory of justice and its basic principles.

In the current chapter the primary features of Rawls's theory of justice will be developed in such a way as to bring out the conceptual and substantive claims made about rights in that theory. First, the emphasis Rawls places, in both *A Theory of Justice* and his later *Political Liberalism*, on the social primary goods of basic rights and liberties is elaborated. The next section considers the relationship between social contract theory and the theory of rights, in particular of natural rights, which has informed the development of modern human rights discourse. The final section discusses how Rawls's views on the basic rights and liberties are capable of being interpreted as descriptions of basic *human* rights and liberties, and responds to some criticisms of Rawls's theory raised by Michael Sandel.

Rawls on the basic rights and liberties

The aim in Chapter 1 was to present the distinctive moral and political principles which form the core of Rawls's conception of justice. This section will now focus on what Rawls has to say about the basic liberties and rights, which allows us to consider the connection between ethical principles and social institutions in Rawls's theory. As Rawls recognizes, a satisfactory ethical theory consists of a system of principles that explains our considered judgements in the sense that the theory shows us how our judgements are implied by the operation of a specific set of normative statements plus the relevant factual judgements (1971: 46 ff.). This set of statements thus serves to unify and systematize our considered moral judgements, that is, judgements reached after due consideration in reflective equilibrium. Furthermore, such a system of principles serves to provide guidance in areas where we have no considered judgements. In such cases, we apply the principles because they yield plausible judgements in other areas about which we are more sure.

Individuals normally develop a sense of justice once they reach a sufficient maturity. They display a skill in judging things just and unjust and in giving reasons for these judgements. Rawls suggests that we view moral philosophy as an attempt at describing this moral capacity. A conception of justice describes our moral capacity when the judgements that we make and the reasons that we give are actually in accord with that conception. Of course we should only be concerned with explaining those moral judgements in which our moral capacity is displayed with the least amount of distortion. Thus, theory development involves a process of give and take between theory and considered judgement. The theoretical limit to this process of theory construction is a state of affairs in which theories and considered judgements have been revised back and forth until the best possible fit has been achieved. Rawls calls this process, of testing whether proposed principles of justice fit with our considered judgements, 'reflective equilibrium' (1971: 48).

As described by Rawls (1971: 48–51), the method of reflective equilibrium is employed when we take our unprocessed moral intuitions and subject them to a process of rational critique. When we consider questions of social justice, we begin with pre-reflective, intuitive judgements about what might count as possible answers or solutions to those questions. These intuitive judgements provide the starting-points for our deliberations, and during our deliberations we place them in the context of a coherent theory which supports and justifies them. We then test this theory against alternative theories as well as against relevant facts, revising our initial judgements and the theory until we have a consistent and coherent theory. While this process may never come to a definite conclusion, it is possible to arrive at a reflective equilibrium between our considered moral judgements and our moral theory, leading to the formation of firm principles.

Rawls argues that the principles of justice which he derives from the original position best unify our considered judgements in reflective equilibrium, in the sense that those principles constitute the best fit between theory and considered judgements as mentioned above. In other words, the reflective equilibrium argument purports to uncover the highest-level principles that underlie our considered judgements in reflective equilibrium. These principles provide 'a theory of the moral sentiments' which explicates the 'principles governing our moral powers, or, more specifically, our sense of justice' (1971: 51). Thus, the principles determined in this way, tested by their congruence with our considered judgements in reflective equilibrium, constitute the convictions underlying our moral faculties. Because Rawls is concerned with the normative implications of the contractarian method, as manifested by the principles of justice as fairness, he aims to show that 'a conception of justice cannot be deduced from self-evident premises or conditions on principles; instead its justification is a matter of the mutual support of many considerations, of everything fitting together into one coherent view' (1971: 21).

Onora O'Neill questions whether it is even possible to arrive at such a coherent view, given what she takes to be Rawls's unfortunate dependence upon abstract starting-points. She asks: 'Can a process of Reflective Equilibrium, which tests proposed principles of justice (chosen in the Original Position) against our "considered moral judgements" . . . offer a justification which does not appeal to ideal-ized conceptions of the human subject, of reason, or of action?'[1] O'Neill worries that some theorists, including Rawls, pass beyond abstracting from known truths and engage in idealization. Idealiza-tion means to ascribe 'predicates – often seen as enhanced, "ideal" predicates – that are false of the case in hand, and so denies predicates that are true of that case'.[2] O'Neill considers Rawls's characterization of the choice situation modelled by the original position to be an example of idealization, in part because of his claim that human reasoning is capable of making adjustments to considered moral judgements through the process of reflective equilibrium.

Without rehearsing O'Neill's extensive arguments for her own competing conception of practical reasoning, we can nevertheless address the concern she raises about Rawls's supposedly idealized account of agents and their capacity for reason. As we have seen, Rawls's proposed method of reflective equilibrium is part of the process by which the parties in the original position are able to arrive at considered moral judgements. O'Neill questions whether it is possible to arrive at considered judgements if the process of reflective equilibrium unrealistically idealizes the ability of agents to 'cleanse' their pre-reflective, intuitive judgements of particularistic values or perceptions. However, we might ask why it should be assumed that agents are *not* capable of eliminating biases from their judgements through reflective equilibrium. Does Rawls genuinely idealize such a capability?

Clearly Rawls intends the original position to serve as a mechanism for processing moral intuitions, arriving at suitably objective claims that can serve as authoritative principles of social justice. Rawls admits that the contract agreed upon contains or rests upon pre-contractual values. This must be the case because the original position is not the sole source of our values, rather it is a means of modelling, evaluating and challenging those values. We cannot begin with a foundation of pure values, but nor are we powerless in the face of those values which confront us. We are able to take a position on those values, to examine them and criticize them, because of our powers of reasoning and deliberation. Our existing values may be corrupt or distorted. Rawls's claim is that these values are only a starting-point, since we must start somewhere, yet we may end with something very different. Although it might not be possible entirely to rid our values of bias and distortion, we need not suppose that we cannot eliminate many of the biases and distortions that would hinder the formulation of suitable principles of justice.

Rawls's theory is based on the view that the capacity for reason is the most potent means for eliminating bias and distortion. Our moral judgements and actions are constrained by the notion of rationality, in terms of the requirement of giving reasons in favour of some judgements and actions over others. In taking some principle as a moral guide, in having a reason for holding some belief, or in proposing some action, we take ourselves to be justified in believing or acting the way we do. The judgements which are used to guide and evaluate our beliefs and actions depend, to greater or lesser degrees, upon justificatory reasons (although our justifications may be mistaken or illegitimate), and the requirement for justification provides a means for eliminating bias and distortion. This is especially so because of the public nature of justification. Justification requires that the reasons for our beliefs and actions be offered to others and, ultimately, that those reasons make sense to others. There is no guarantee that our deliberations will resolve all moral disagreements, but having to test our justifications enables us reasonably to correct them for bias and distortion. Indeed, the capacity to reason, shared by the parties in the original position, plays a central role in bringing about agreement on suitable principles of justice through the testing and correcting process of reflective equilibrium. Reflective equilibrium, as well as other theoretical devices of practical reason such as the veil of ignorance, allows for the continuous filtering of the bias and distortion which worried O'Neill, and for the revising of our judgements and theories.[3] Ronald Dworkin captures the spirit of Rawls's position as follows:

> In the end, however, political theory can make no contribution to how we govern ourselves except by struggling, against all the impulses that drag us back into our own culture, toward generality and some reflective basis for deciding which of our traditional distinctions and discriminations are genuine and which spurious, which contribute to the flourishing of the ideals we want, after reflection, to embrace and which serve only to protect us from the personal costs of that demanding process. We cannot leave justice to convention and anecdote.[4]

Ultimately, Rawls's contractarian argument is intended to demonstrate that the conception of social justice that would be chosen by the parties in the original position (a) is fair, (b) is acceptable from a moral point of view, (c) enables individuals to 'express their natures as free and equal rational beings' (1971: 252), (d) is the most stable conception of justice and (e) fosters self-respect. The role of justice is that of providing an objective standard assigning basic rights and duties, fixing a proper balance between conflicting claims to the advantages of social cooperation, and determining the proper distribution of the burdens of social cooperation.

The two principles of justice, together with the priority rules, guarantee each person an equal liberty, a sphere of activity in which one's claims cannot be neglected or overridden by consequentialist arguments for the sake of a greater benefit to society as a whole (1971: 499). In thus guaranteeing to each person – regardless of social position or natural endowment – such an inviolability, the principles of justice as fairness publicly express a deep concern for the autonomy of each person and enhance the good of each as well. On this point Rawls supports the Kantian ideal of fostering the values of autonomy or freedom.[5] This kind of unconditional concern for autonomy and liberty for each person, expressed by the two principles and priority rules, cannot be guaranteed, for example, by utilitarianism. Under utilitarian justice, the liberties of some must be traded off in favour of the liberties of others, if doing so increases the measure of social welfare.

Rawls mentions a further important factor present in a society regulated by the two principles that is absent in one regulated by the utilitarian conception. This is the fact that the difference principle functions as a principle of fraternity. It manages to function in this way because the difference principle expresses a 'refusal by others to take advantage of accident and happenstance' (1971: 499). In a utilitarian society, the effects of natural and social contingencies are taken as given and fed into the social welfare function. The social outcome is thus influenced by these contingencies; no attempt is made to nullify their effects or to choose institutions that are based upon considerations independent of such factors. However, by agreeing to the difference principle, people choose to structure society around a concern for a rational nature as such, independently of social and natural contingencies. But this affirms each person's good, in a public manner, since a concern for a pure rational nature is a concern for our good. Moreover, by affirming the difference principle, those who are more favoured in the natural lottery choose to gain from their luck only on terms that work for the benefit of those less favoured in that lottery. Those more favoured do not wish to gain unless it benefits the least well-off as well. In contrast, the principle of utility expresses no concern for the good of the least well-off, nor does it express a concern that all benefit from the process of social cooperation.

It seems clear that the two principles of justice, when manifested in the basic structure, express the Kantian imperative that each person is to be treated as an end and never merely as a means. Under justice as fairness, each individual person is treated in accord with the principles she would freely and rationally choose in an initial situation of equality. In this sense, each is treated as an equal and as an end. Furthermore, each is guaranteed an equal liberty, which is also to treat each as an end (1971: 180). Finally, the difference principle provides an additional sense in which each is treated as an end. To treat persons as ends is to agree, Rawls says, 'to forgo those gains which do not contribute to their representative expectations' (1971: 180). To treat people as means, on the contrary, 'is to be prepared to impose upon them lower prospects of life for the sake of higher expectations of others' (1971: 180).

According to Rawls, self-respect and effective social cooperation are both important values that are rational to seek and secure from the standpoint of the original position (1971: 178). Public recognition of the fact that the basic structure satisfies the two principles gives increased support to an individual's self-respect, and leads to a greater effectiveness of social cooperation. Rawls argues that the two types of respect – respect for self and respect for others – are reciprocally self-supporting (1971: 179). That is, those who respect themselves are more likely to respect others and those who respect others are more likely to respect themselves. In addition, the absence of respect of others undermines one's self-respect. Rawls contends that the two principles secure mutual respect among persons because when that basic structure satisfies the two principles, everyone's good is included in a public scheme of mutual benefit. The public affirmation of this fact supports and enhances an individual's self-esteem insofar as it affirms that each person's ends are worthwhile. Public recognition of the fact that the principles treat persons as Kantian 'ends in themselves' ought also to affirm both self-respect and respect for others.

Every ethical theory works with a conception of the person, of course, whether implicitly or explicitly. Rawls's theory is no exception. Rawls's idea is that the members of a well-ordered society are regarded as free and equal moral agents who can contribute to and honour the restraints of social cooperation. Each person desires to take part in the scheme of social cooperation for mutual advantage. Furthermore, each person is viewed as motivated by two highest-order interests.[6]

The first is the interest to realize and exercise the capacity for a sense of right and justice. The sense of justice is an effective desire to comply with the principles of justice as defined by the principles of the public conception, and the desire to act on this conception is generally effective. The sense of justice also implies a desire to conform one's pursuit of the good and the demands one makes on others to public principles of justice which all persons can be reasonably expected to accept.

The second is the interest to realize and exercise a capacity to decide upon, revise and rationally pursue a conception of the good. In addition, persons regard themselves as having a higher-order interest 'in how their other interests, including fundamental interests, are regulated and shaped by the basic structure'.[7] They consider themselves beings capable of choosing their own ends and wish to preserve their liberty in this regard. Furthermore, each feels it legitimate to make claims on others – in the name of the conception of the good – regarding the design of institutions. Finally, each has, and views herself as having, 'a right to equal respect and consideration in determining the principles by which the basic structure of society is to be regulated'.[8] Accordingly, Rawls's theory suggests that the basic liberties of persons are intimately connected with the primary goods of respect, both self-respect and respect for others, and human dignity. Rawls notes that, 'when society follows these principles, everyone's good is included in a scheme of mutual benefit and this public affirmation in institutions of each man's endeavours supports men's self-esteem' (1971: 179).

In the first principle of justice, Rawls argues that all persons have 'an equal right to the most extensive total system of equal basic liberties' (1971: 302). As discussed in the previous chapter, Rawls initially outlines that the 'basic liberties' include political liberty, freedom of speech and assembly, freedom of conscience and thought, freedom from arbitrary arrest and seizure, and freedom of the person.

Clearly, Rawls's outline of the basic liberties retains the same emphasis on civil and political freedoms found in traditional liberal theories of rights. This emphasis is also reflected in the priority principles, which dictate the priority of liberty and hold that liberty may not be sacrificed for other social or economic goods. Rawls explains that this prioritization is necessary in order to distinguish between liberty and the worth of liberty, insofar as socio-economic elements affect 'the worth of liberty, the value to individuals of the rights that the first principle defines' (1971: 204). By this Rawls means that the worth of liberty will be unequal, depending on whether a person is either wealthy or poor, educated or uneducated, and so on, such that persons will place different values on the liberties they hold. Despite this difference in the worth of liberty, however, the first principle of justice guarantees that all persons equally possess the same basic liberties.

This last point, that equality in the worth of the basic liberties is not required even though the basic liberties must be held equally, has been criticized by some. Norman Daniels argues, for instance, that the unequal worth of liberty is unacceptable in the original position. He contends that Rawls's priority principles imply that political liberty is compatible with significant social and economic inequalities. Given this assumption, the priority of liberty is 'a hollow abstraction lacking real application' since it is without the ability effectively to exercise the basic liberties.[9] In other words, if the wealthy have an undue influence on the political process, it is difficult to speak of the presence of equal political liberty. And what effect would this influence have on, say, freedom of expression or conscience?

Rawls is not unaware of this point of criticism. A response suggested by his theory is that, because the interests of different people and their own perceptions of those interests will diverge, so too will the relative value placed upon the basic liberties amongst different persons. Yet the difference in relative value and possible conflicts between liberties does not negate the principled criterion identifying and protecting certain fundamental rights. The basic liberties may have different values for different persons, but the liberties themselves are something to which all individuals are entitled independently of the socio-economic conditions affecting the worth of liberty. Thus, varying social and economic benefits do not suffice to justify a less than equal liberty or the equal possession of basic liberties; one is not entitled to 'more' basic liberties if one is wealthy, nor does one possess 'fewer' basic liberties if one is economically disadvantaged. It should be recalled as well that material inequalities may be compatible with equal rights only so long as those inequalities are licensed by the difference principle, that is, only so long as they work to the greatest benefit of the least well-off members of society. Under this scheme, all persons have the same status with respect to the basic rights and liberties. And, as mentioned previously, liberty is accorded an inviolable status because it provides the most effective social basis for enabling us to realize our plan of life as well as the primary goods of mutual and self-respect:

> [T]he basis for self-esteem in a just society is not then one's income share but the publicly affirmed distribution of fundamental rights and liberties. And this distribution being equal, everyone has a similar and secure status when they meet to conduct the wider affairs of society. (1971: 544)

In a just society then, liberty, not income, must be distributed equally, although the distributive schemes in a just society are to be regulated by the difference principle to prevent too great social and economic inequalities. Given the lexical ordering of the two principles of justice, though, the second principle cannot be satisfied by violating the first principle, which guarantees a right to equal shares of liberty. For Rawls, the principle of equal civil and political liberties is at bottom a normative principle directed towards the moral quality of social existence and the security of individuals' relations with one another. On this basis he asserts an integral connection between fundamental rights and liberties and the moral-political norms of personal autonomy, self-respect and mutual respect. Institutional mechanisms, such as public funding of elections and restrictions on campaign contributions, can be employed to ensure fair value of the political liberties in conjunction with the primary goods, without resorting to inefficient and divisive schemes for the equal distribution of income and wealth.[10]

In *Political Liberalism*, Rawls expands upon his discussion of the place of basic rights in his theory of justice and offers a somewhat revised conception of justice as fairness.[11] Before addressing what else Rawls has to say about rights, then, it will be useful to mention briefly some of the recent developments Rawls's theory of justice has exhibited.

Rawls's revised theory of justice is centred on his claim in *A Theory of Justice* that the two principles of justice would ensure social stability since they would be the guiding moral principles adopted by the members of any well-ordered society. However, Rawls came to view this position as unacceptably idealistic, arguing that the pluralism of moral, religious and philosophical doctrines as a permanent fact of modern society makes it untenable to claim that everyone would adopt the two principles as universal moral truths. In response to this problem, Rawls no longer claims that his theory ought to be regarded as a comprehensive and general moral theory; instead, it ought to be seen as a *political* theory of justice. By this he means that a theory of justice should carry out the practical task of developing solutions to political and public problems within society, or a group of societies. The existence of rival doctrines of the good requires the development of a theory of justice based on those points of agreement or publicly shared ideas that obtain among competing views within our society. Only in this way can stable social unity be achieved in the conditions of pluralism.

Rawls's account of justice assumes a political character, he argues, because he now takes the public political culture of a contemporary democratic society to be the background of his theory. In other words, the ideas from which the political conception of justice is constructed and justified are held by Rawls to be implicit in that public political culture. Many of the important features of Rawls's earlier version are still operative, such as the original position, the idea of a well-ordered society and the basic structure, the notion of social cooperation for reciprocal benefit, and the need to establish a set of principles of justice necessary to achieve such social cooperation. However, these principles are now those most appropriate given that there exists an irreducible pluralism of reasonable comprehensive moral, philosophical and religious doctrines in contemporary society (1996: 36).

Given this condition, Rawls suggests that the principles of justice are not comprehensive moral principles governing all aspects of life; rather, they are the appropriate publicly shared principles for socially distributing primary goods and governing the life of persons in the public domain. Thus, Rawls claims that the pluralism which characterizes contemporary societies is one of the basic circumstances of justice, indeed, the natural outcome in a society which respects basic rights and liberties (1996: 66). It is important to recognize the diversity of contemporary multicultural societies since this diversity often has the potential to destabilize a well-ordered society.

More importantly, critics of Rawls's earlier theory argued, social diversity cannot be overcome simply by the rational selection of a single comprehensive moral doctrine or theory of justice overburdened with metaphysical assumptions. It is for this reason that Rawls's revised theory of justice takes its justification from ideas and institutions found in the public political culture of contemporary democratic societies.[12] Rawls describes the justification involved as one of formulating an 'overlapping consensus', that is, a consensus on a 'freestanding' political conception of justice that exists despite the differences due to the various conflicting religious, philosophical and moral doctrines in contemporary society (1996: 15, 39–40). Presumably, such a consensus provides for the stable unity of political society through the engagement and toleration of social differences without resorting to a comprehensive religious, philosophical or moral doctrine.

An overlapping consensus on justice is political, to Rawls's way of thinking, in that it is based upon public principles of justice rather than private comprehensive doctrines, and thus is neutral because of its independence from such comprehensive doctrines. The goal of an overlapping consensus is to reach agreement on principles of justice in a liberal, pluralistic society in order to achieve stability and equilibrium in the public sphere, while remaining neutral towards the private sphere of each individual's personal affairs and beliefs. Overlapping consensus is necessary to Rawls's revised conception of justice because the function of political philosophy is to construct principles consistent with certain 'intuitive ideas' – primarily that of citizens as free and equal persons and of a well-ordered society as a fair system of cooperation over time – found in the common public political culture of democratic society. Justice as fairness is thus conceived in reference to a political culture which shares a liberal ideal of citizenship, namely, of persons as free, rational and equal. Rawls's concern that his earlier conception of justice as fairness amounted to a comprehensive doctrine is thereby eased by putting forward a revised conception appropriate for a modern liberal democracy, but *not necessarily* appropriate for other forms of political society. This last point has serious implications for an account of universal human rights and will be examined further with regard to international justice in Chapters 3 and 4.

Because the political conception of justice relies on the requirement of impartiality to comprehensive doctrines, the veil of ignorance is still employed at the stage of the original position. Consequently, information concerning substantive conceptions of the good must be bracketed by the parties to the original position, if agreement (overlapping consensus) on the principles of justice is to be reached. Thomas Nagel questions, however, whether the necessity of agreement driving Rawls's theory here provides sufficient reason for the parties to exclude knowledge of substantive conceptions of the good. He insists that 'the demand for agreement . . . must be grounded in something more basic'.[13] Nagel suggests the need for 'a kind of epistemological restraint' through which one's convictions are to be regarded 'merely as beliefs' in the context of the public domain, while they may be treated as truths in the context of the private domain.[14] Epistemological restraint would then arrive at the requirement of neutrality by holding that, even though one is absolutely convinced of the truth of one's personal religious or moral doctrines, one would refrain from advancing those doctrines as bases for the principles of a political conception of justice since they could be reasonably rejected by others holding different conceptions of the good. Although Nagel and Rawls take somewhat different routes, they both arrive at the same place, as is evidenced by Rawls's statement that 'it is vital to the idea of political liberalism that we may with perfect consistency hold that it would be unreasonable to use political power to enforce our own comprehensive view, which we must, of course, affirm as either reasonable or true' (1996: 138).[15]

To the problem, then, of arriving at legitimate principles to regulate social interaction given the diversity of contemporary societies, Rawls responds with two somewhat revised principles of justice, which read as follows:

> a. Each person has an equal right to a fully adequate scheme of equal basic liberties which is compatible with a similar scheme of liberties for all.
> b. Social and economic inequalities are to satisfy two conditions. First, they must be attached to offices and positions open to all under conditions of fair equality of opportunity; and second, they must be to the greatest benefit of the least advantaged members of society. (1996: 291)

The first principle of justice, which is most relevant to the present discussion, is revised to read 'a fully adequate scheme of equal basic liberties' rather than 'the most extensive total system of equal basic liberties'.[16] Rawls makes this change because the criterion of the earlier version is 'purely quantitative and does not distinguish some cases as more significant than others' (1996: 331). He then identifies two fundamental cases in which the basic liberties, now firmly identified as specific rights and freedoms that are to be constitutionally guaranteed, help to secure certain essential social conditions for human activity. The first is connected with developing and exercising a sense of justice, while the second is connected with forming, revising and pursuing a conception of the good.[17] Rawls refers to each of these activities in terms of 'moral powers' that are developed and exercised given the appropriate social and institutional conditions or primary goods. Rawls provides the following revised list of primary goods (1996: 308):

> a. The basic liberties, which are: 'freedom of thought and liberty of conscience; the political liberties and freedom of association, as well as the freedoms specified by the liberty and integrity of the person; and finally the rights and liberties covered by the rule of law'. (1996, 291)
> b. Freedom of movement and free choice of occupation against a diverse background of opportunities.
> c. Powers and prerogatives of offices and positions of responsibilities.
> d. Income and wealth, understood broadly as all-purpose means.
> e. The social bases of self-respect.

Rawls offers several arguments in support of the fully adequate scheme of basic liberties and rights which focus on the political conception of the person and the two fundamental moral powers. First, Rawls argues that the political liberties (such as the right to vote, freedom to organize politically, freedom of speech and press) and freedom of thought are primary goods necessary to the development and use of the capacity for a sense of justice (1996: 334). Clearly, people will not be able to develop their moral sense of justice and apply it to the basic structure of society if they are denied freedom of political participation and freedom of thought and expression. Second, freedom of thought, liberty of the person (such as freedom of religious practice, freedom of movement, freedom from arbitrary interference or arrest) and the political liberties are also needed if people are to be able to pursue and realize their particular conception of the good over a complete life (1996: 335).

Freedom of conscience is a particularly important example, since a person's ability to exercise his or her moral powers would be severely violated if he or she were forced into accepting different or new moral, religious and philosophical convictions, or was not allowed to freely develop new or different moral, religious and philosophical convictions. In addition, from the perspective of the original position, the parties do not know whether their beliefs will be those of a minority or a majority within society. Thus, it is reasonable for the parties to choose the most secure guarantee of freedom of conscience that is possible in order to protect their equality in either case.

Taken as a whole, the basic liberties and rights effectively advance mutual and self-respect insofar as they provide normative conditions for how people regard and treat one another in political society: 'By publicly affirming the basic liberties citizens in a well-ordered society express their mutual respect for one another as reasonable and trustworthy, as well as their recognition of the worth all citizens attach to their way of life' (1996: 319). From the perspective of Rawls's revised theory, then, the basic rights and liberties comprise a scheme intended to protect each person's interest in living cooperatively with other persons. Such a scheme also ensures that each person is able to live as free and equal, on terms of mutual respect and reciprocal benefit, under a stable framework of basic political and economic institutions organized by a shared set of principles of justice.

One might question, however, how Rawls arrives at his account as to the basis of the basic rights and liberties, since he fails clearly to address the nature of these rights other than to describe them as 'fundamental'. Ronald Dworkin, for example, has argued that Rawls's theory of justice presupposes the basic right of individuals to equal concern and respect, so that his theory is essentially right-based.[18] According to Dworkin, such 'background' moral rights are distinguishable from 'institutional' or positive-law rights and are akin to the traditional notion of natural rights. Dworkin actually embraces this perspective and suggests that Rawls's original position be seen as modelling what he regards as the fundamental natural right all persons have to equal concern and respect. If Dworkin's argument is correct, however, would this not present a problem for Rawls's contractarian claim that the standards of justice as fairness are derived from a rational choice procedure?[19] While I do think that Rawls 'presupposes' certain basic rights, I do not think that move is fatal to his contractarian theory.[20]

Recall that, in *A Theory of Justice*, Rawls noted that 'it is appropriate to call . . . the rights that justice protects' natural rights (1971: 505, n. 30). In addition, Rawls argued that human beings are equally entitled to fundamental liberties and are 'owed all the guarantees of justice' because of their 'capacity for moral personality' (1971: 507, 505). What this suggests is that, even though the contractarian mechanism is used to derive principles of justice from an agreement between parties to the original position, the parties to the agreements are not themselves completely devoid of certain characteristics. The description of the parties in the original position identifies certain attributes referred to by Rawls as the capacities of moral personality, that is, capacities of humans as 'free and equal' moral persons. As a deontological theory, Rawls's contractarian account of justice therefore seeks to provide right principles 'about the way basic social institutions should be arranged to conform to the freedom and equality of citizens as moral persons'.[21] Parties in the original position are not blank slates; they are 'model-conceptions' of individuals who agree to the chosen principles of justice precisely because those principles accord with their representation as free and equal moral persons.

This last point returns us to our previous discussion of the two moral powers or capacities and the two highest-order interests identified by Rawls as corresponding to the conception of moral personhood. While Rawls's inspiration is decidedly Kantian in this respect, there are further aspects of his revised theory of justice which help us to find answers to the question raised above by Dworkin. First, given Rawls's characterization of his theory as political rather than metaphysical, he emphasizes that he is not starting from assumed a priori principles; rather, he is drawing on 'certain fundamental ideas seen as implicit in the public political culture of a democratic society . . . seen as a fund of implicitly shared ideas and principles' (1996: 13–14). Rawls emphasizes that his theory is constructed from the political conceptions already held by those living in a democratic culture, for the purpose of securing political agreement in spite of substantive differences that people may have with regard to philosophy, religion and morality. Second, then, Rawls insists that his theory applies only to the basic structure of society, that is, to a society's main political, economic and social institutions. While Rawls's theory does not rest on a single comprehensive doctrine, it seeks to provide a conception of justice upon which adherents of different doctrines can converge or overlap despite their differences in matters that do not involve the public political culture. Justice as fairness thus presents a reasonable interpretation of the political ideas and traditions of a democratic culture.

Rawls mentions a number of fundamental ideas that are drawn upon in constructing his theory, such as that of society as a fair system of cooperation over time, but for present purposes we are concerned primarily with the idea 'of citizens (those engaged in cooperation) as free and equal persons' (1996: 14). As mentioned above, the idea of citizens as free and equal persons is to be understood as a model-conception drawn up from the historically developed shared understanding of moral personhood found in our public political culture. In other words, members of democratic societies are regarded as free and equal moral persons in that, as conveyed by Rawls, they possess a capacity for an effective sense of justice and a capacity to form, revise and pursue a conception of the good, complemented by the highest-order interests in developing and exercising these moral powers. The principles of justice are constructed by Rawls in such a way as to reflect the values of the conception of the person implicit in a democratic public political culture. The principles of justice articulated by Rawls would be agreed to because the members of such a culture favour the political ideals of freedom, equality and the autonomy of moral persons.

Three responses are now available to the problem posed earlier by Dworkin's reading of Rawls's account of rights. First, Rawls's contractarian theory is contextualized by the implicitly shared ideas and principles of a democratic political culture. This context provides the background for the original position, the parties in the original position and the principles of right and justice. Second, that background of implicitly shared ideas and principles includes the conception of free and equal moral persons which is fundamental to democratic public political culture. Thus, Rawls does not presuppose a metaphysical notion of the essential human self *per se*, although communitarian critics such as Michael Sandel have taken Rawls to task on this point. Rather, he pulls together the fundamental characteristics of how the members of a democratic society view themselves and each other, that is, he constructs a model-conception of our political self-understandings that have developed historically around the notion of moral personhood. Third, as a corollary to this shared conception of moral personhood, the democratic public political tradition has affirmed the idea of certain basic, inalienable rights and liberties possessed equally by all members of society that ought to be protected by political and legal institutions. Rawls's principles of justice reflect this affirmation and the conviction that such rights and liberties have a special status by virtue of their attachment to the political meaning of free and equal moral persons.

It seems safe to say in response to the issue raised by Dworkin, then, that Rawls does not sacrifice his claim to a contractarian argument merely because he contextualizes his theory with existing social values and practices. This is so because he does provide a political (or practical) rather than metaphysical justification for his account of the basic rights and liberties in modern pluralist societies, and this justification depends upon the mechanism of agreement. Whether these basic rights ought to be characterized as traditional 'natural' rights in some deep metaphysical sense is, I think, unnecessary, given the thrust of Rawls's political conception of justice as fairness.

It would perhaps be more useful to regard them simply as *human* rights, without the metaphysical baggage associated with traditional natural rights, since such rights are treated as the socially recognized and protected claims of all moral persons. By this I mean that Rawls conceives of basic rights as natural rights insofar as they are universal and unconditional, yet in order to satisfy the actualization of social justice these rights *must also* be elaborated in the form of socio-political institutions, including the rule of law. Thus, for Rawls, such rights are like a two-sided coin: they are not merely conventional or positive rights that can be 'taken away' arbitrarily (although they can be violated), but nor do they have a determinate existence unless they are realized and protected in the basic structure of political society.

This last point is also made by Rex Martin, who writes that 'For Rawls all natural or fundamental rights, insofar as they are rights, strictly conceived, are necessarily embedded in the basic structure of society'.[22] It is this feature which distinguishes Rawls's conception of basic rights as 'natural' from the classic natural rights theories, and leads me to suggest that the basic rights are better referred to as human rights. The adjective 'human' does not suggest any deep metaphysical commitments as does the adjective 'natural', nor does it necessarily appeal to any particular religious doctrine that may conflict with some competing doctrine. One might interpret human rights from a religious or deeply metaphysical perspective, of course, but one might also regard them in a purely secular fashion. In either case, the idea of human rights is able to generate and sustain a broad sharability within and across pluralist societies on the claim that any and all human beings have the moral status or value associated with right-holders, that is, moral persons entitled to basic human rights.

Such thinkers as David Hume, Jeremy Bentham and Karl Marx criticized the idea of natural rights. They argued that rights can make sense only if they are regarded as the result of political legislation, sovereign rule and positive law. Positivist legal theory, for instance, came to view rights as presuppositions of domestic and international law rather than as imprescriptible natural rights. Criticisms of natural rights theory tend to focus on the claim that such rights are 'self-evident', pointing to the epistemological difficulty of determining norms that are deduced in some way from an objective, independent moral reality. Another criticism commonly levelled at natural rights theory is that it presupposes a more or less static human 'essence' as the foundation for such rights. However, it is not certain that natural rights must be read in such a strong metaphysical sense. Moreover, the critic of natural rights faces the difficult problem of explaining the obvious moral deficiencies of many existing legal systems and of the positive rights generated by those systems, without having recourse to any source of justification other than already established political authority and the systematic injustices possibly embodied therein. My examination of Rawls will pursue the possibility of conceiving basic human rights as terms of agreement that rational actors would choose in the original position. From this perspective, human rights can be seen as arising by virtue of the human ability to exercise rational choice, such that certain social practices are included within the notion of human rights, including the rule of law, although such rights are not simply reducible to legal rights as such.[23]

Contractarian theory and human rights

The philosophical and political dialogue on human rights has been greatly influenced by the natural rights tradition associated with classical and modern contractarianism. Although the natural rights perspective has often been criticized by various competing theories, it is nevertheless generally regarded as the primary precursor of contemporary human rights doctrine and remains an important concept in philosophy, politics and law. In the aftermath of the Second World War, natural rights theory became central to the renewed attempt to protect humanity from the atrocities promulgated by unrestrained political machinations and iniquitous laws divorced from critical ethical and moral foundations.

As we have seen, to some degree the classical social contract theorists all share a desire to protect the interests, well-being and rights of individual persons. Their view is that the various rights naturally possessed by persons are irrevocable elements essential to a scheme of social justice. In other words, if all individuals equally possess certain fundamental rights, then the consensual moral and political framework of the social contract is concerned to protect those rights, as justice demands. Thus, the contractarian scheme of social cooperation in the pursuit of justice rests, to a great extent, on the view that there are certain fundamental rights which are basic features of a just social order. Such rights are properly called 'human' rights because they prescribe a minimum definition of what it means to be human in society.[24]

The influence of the idea of natural rights is evident in contemporary human rights theory and law. For instance, the Universal Declaration of Human Rights (UDHR) begins by stating: '*Whereas* recognition of the inherent dignity and of the equal and inalienable rights of all members of the human family is the foundation of freedom, justice, and peace in the world . . .' Article 1 of the same document asserts: 'All humans are born free and equal in dignity and rights. They are endowed with reason and conscience and should act towards one another in a spirit of brotherhood.'[25] As employed in contract theory, natural rights embody aspects of both negative freedoms, that is, freedom from government intervention in the quest for human dignity, and positive freedoms, that is, rights to just governmental intervention in the quest for human dignity. Negative freedoms roughly correspond to the civil and political rights that are often referred to as 'first generation' human rights, while positive freedoms are said to belong to the 'second generation' of economic, social and cultural rights.[26] From the survey given thus far, it is possible to identify four basic concepts from the contractarian tradition which have informed the contemporary idea of human rights, as expressed in the Universal Declaration of Human Rights:

1. The equality, dignity, and worth of each individual (Article 1).
2. The right of liberty to pursue the quest for human dignity against the abuse of political authority (Articles 2–21).
3. The right to basic necessities in order to ensure an existence worthy of human equality and dignity (Articles 22–7).
4. The obligations and responsibilities of individuals, states, and the international order to ensure these rights for all (Articles 28–30).

These basic conceptual and normative points have been formalized in a number of conventions and declarations in what is collectively referred to as the International Bill of Human Rights. The International Bill of Human Rights consists of the human rights provisions of the United Nations Charter of 1945, the Universal Declaration of Human Rights of 1948 and the two Covenants of 1966 on Civil and Political Rights and on Economic, Social and Cultural Rights. In the Covenants, which are treaties that legislate what the Universal Declaration has declared, states undertake to respect and ensure the following rights: to life and personal integrity and security; to freedom from torture and cruel, inhuman and degrading treatment or punishment; to freedom from coercion, slavery and forced labour; to due process of law and to a humane and working penal system; to freedom to travel within and outside one's country; to freedom of thought, conscience, religion, expression, assembly and association; and to take part in the conduct of government and public affairs (including the right to vote and be elected). The dominant themes in the Covenant on Civil and Political Rights are equality (equal treatment, equal protection of the law, equality of opportunity) and non-discrimination on the bases of race, colour, sex, language, religion, opinion, origin, birth and status. In connection with non-discrimination, members of minorities within states also are granted the rights, in community with other members of their group, to enjoy their culture, practise their religion and use their language.

According to the Covenant on Economic, Social and Cultural Rights, states are supposed to take steps 'individually and through international assistance and cooperation . . . to the maximum of their available resources . . . with a view to achieving progressively full realization . . . by all means, including legislative measures' towards the fulfilment of the following rights: to work; to just and favourable conditions of work, including leisure; to join trade unions and to strike; to social security; to social protection of the family, mothers and children; to an adequate standard of living, including adequate food, clothing, housing, medical care, social services, especially in the events of unemployment, sickness, disability, old age or any other lack of livelihood beyond one's control; to standards of physical and mental health; to education and training; and to take part in the cultural life of the community and benefit from any scientific progress therein. Again, the themes of equality and non-discrimination are dominant in this Covenant.

According to the standards for civil and political, and economic, social and cultural rights laid out in the 1948 Universal Declaration of Human Rights and the 1966 International Human Rights Covenants, human rights are taken to be international and universal. In addition, human rights are thought to be inviolable entitlements; in other words, they are supposed to work as normative trumps, having priority when in conflict with other norms, values or goals. The rights articulated in the International Bill of Human Rights are also viewed as interdependent, and protective of a range of interrelated and equally important categories or generations of goods.[27] Moreover, human rights are thought to imply advantages for individuals and groups, as well as obligations on an individual's society and any other pertinent actor anywhere in the world.

One of the major consequences of holding that human rights are international can be seen in the formal recognition that human rights are both international standards and a matter of international concern, as is any other matter under international law, and are no longer only a matter of individual states' domestic jurisdiction. By adhering to the UN Charter – and virtually all states are now parties to the UN Charter – states are obligated to recognize the internationalization of human rights. Not only is the Universal Declaration considered an authoritative interpretation of the rights provisions of the Charter, it is also considered customary law since it is claimed in principle that all governments must now ensure the enjoyment of all the rights of the Declaration, irrespective of whether they are parties to any other formal agreements. To put it another way, the universality of recognition and obligation on the part of every state and the universality of the applicability of rights standards to every human being are presumed in international human rights law.

With respect to the character and purpose of the International Bill of Human Rights, it aims not only to help establish the legal, political and economic climates in which individual freedom and equal dignity can flourish, but also to help protect the individual against governmental excesses everywhere. Following the massive atrocities committed during the Second World War, it was argued that existing national protections for rights were deficient and that additional, international protection was necessary. It was believed that some of the gross violations of rights carried out during the war period might have been prevented had an international system of protection been in place. Given the international nature of human rights, however, it is still the case that human rights are to be implemented as rights enjoyed under the constitutional-legal system of domestic society. Indeed, one of the primary reasons that an international law of human rights was promulgated was to induce states to rearrange their constitutional-legal systems in order to achieve the domestic guarantee of basic human rights. The aim of international human rights law, then, is to secure the universal acceptance of the whole range of rights and the substantive, universal enjoyment of normative standards in their integrity.[28] When differences between national and international standards do exist, the latter are supposed to supplement national rights and in that way secure the same rights for all persons even though they live within different domestic systems.

When we reflect upon human rights abuses carried out in various countries around the world, we are characteristically torn between two potentially contradictory ethical concerns. On the one hand, we have strong, deep-seated intuitions that certain behaviour, carried out by nations other than our own is, nevertheless, morally reprehensible. In juxtaposition is our simultaneous recognition of the value of cultural pluralism, coupled with an acknowledgement of a dismal history of Western colonialism and unfounded moral condescension. The tension between these two sentiments has resulted in the contemporary dispute regarding the moral foundation and nature of human rights. For the most part the dispute centres on the different positions advanced by cultural relativists and by universalists. On the one hand, cultural relativists contend that an individual's human rights are exclusively determined by his or her culture's traditions and contingent norms while, on the other hand, universalists insist that despite a wide diversity of cultures, every human being qua person possesses certain inalienable rights universally held against a state or culture.

Cultural relativism, generally, is the thesis that 'culture is the sole source of the validity of a moral right or rule'.[29] It is a political, often philosophical, conviction which results from a great variety of sources, some anthropological, others sceptical.[30] Relativism is, in no small part, a backlash against eighteenth- and nineteenth-century notions of rationality and enlightenment. While there has always been a current of moral relativism throughout the history of Western philosophy, it did not attain its contemporary stature of acceptance until well into the twentieth century and after the two world wars. The apparent senselessness of the world wars, coupled with their unprecedented levels of human loss and social destruction, irreparably broke much of the West's historical confidence in its moral and social superiority. Philosophers in both the analytic and continental schools became increasingly sceptical of traditional moral and religious thought, and enlightenment notions of universal reason. At the same time, an increase in Western interaction with foreign nations and cultures resulted in a greater scepticism toward the applicability and international relevance of supposedly European ethical norms.

Against this background, cultural relativism has entered into the debates concerning international human rights in a diversity of forms. There are, in the first place, anthropological observations that, as a matter of fact, the various cultures of the world have sometimes radically different ethical norms. To what reason, some ask, might we appeal for the belief that our moral systems are better than those of other nations or cultures? Other relativists concede the possibility of universal morality, but believe it is epistemically impossible to determine what rights or duties such a moral system would entail. Lacking any potential knowledge, we should, and in fact must, content ourselves with whatever rights (if any) are provided in the context of our particular culture. Finally, there are several radical relativists who, perhaps paradoxically, argue that the very notion of human rights is inescapably *immoral*, in that the imposition of human rights is destructive of non-Western cultures.[31]

Cultural relativists thus believe, to varying degrees, that culture forms the only legitimate basis for assessing the validity of any code of conduct.[32] Hence, whether an individual can exercise any particular right will ultimately depend upon whether, and to what extent, the protection of that right will conflict with that individual's native culture. In response, human rights proponents typically assert that, irrespective of culture, international norms are either universal imperatives derived from the status of being human or rules of conduct explicitly consented to.[33] A universalist might argue, for example, that while it is clearly true that culture and upbringing determine, in different ways and to various extents, our self-conception and societal roles, there remain, regardless of cultural input, certain features common to all human beings, ranging from the ability to experience pain to the capacity rationally to form conceptions of the good (although the conceptions themselves vary).

So, when a universalist claims of an individual that she has a human right, he might mean that 'She ought to be treated in such-and-such a manner' because all human beings have certain common interests or moral powers that can be violated regardless of the culture in question. A universalist also might argue that the attitude of the cultural relativist, though perhaps motivated by a well-intentioned tolerance of cultural differences, is naively romantic, stereotypical and ultimately discriminatory. It degrades the intelligence of 'non-Western' people and refuses them a place in the international community.[34] Finally, a universalist may counter that, although one can in principle agree that respect and tolerance towards different manners of organizing social life are sound goals, in practice, the catchword of 'difference' is often appropriated by state élites for use against their own populations. Thomas Nagel makes this last argument when he calls for the need to resist the 'cynical appeals to cultural relativism with which authoritarian regimes defend the cruelties they use to stay in power'.[35]

I agree with Nagel's position and, without entering into an extended discussion of this debate, I believe that cultural relativism is ethically and politically more problematic than useful. I should clarify, however, that this book is not intended to be an examination of theories of cultural pluralism and universalism *per se*, and it will therefore engage with the issues surrounding these theories only insofar as they arise in my treatment of Rawls's work in relation to his accounts of international justice and human rights. In other words, my purpose here is not to offer a theory or justification of human rights solely in response to the universalism/relativism debate but, in the first instance, to assume the principles contained in the major instruments of international human rights law as my starting-point and then examine how well Rawls's remarks on international justice and human rights satisfy those principles.

Social and cultural pluralism is, naturally, an issue to be addressed by any suitable contemporary account of human rights, but it is not clear that relativism of the type mentioned above is the only possible consequence of trying to frame human rights in ways congenial to diverse cultures and traditions. As we have seen, Rawls speaks, for instance, of the social bases of self-respect as a primary good of social justice, that is, as a way of showing equal respect and consideration towards diverse individuals and their interests. Others, such as Will Kymlicka, have argued that protecting those 'social bases' might entail the granting of special rights to minority cultures, for disadvantage with respect to the primary good of cultural membership affects the individual distribution of other benefits and burdens, which is the concern of liberal democratic justice.[36] In *The Law of Peoples*, Rawls goes further and speaks of the need to tolerate 'other reasonable ways of ordering society', that is, other communities 'organized by comprehensive doctrines, provided their political and social institutions meet certain conditions' such as protecting basic human rights. This approach, he suggests, is very much in keeping with liberal democratic ideals. In Chapter 4 we will be concerned with evaluating Rawls's claim.

Furthermore, the moral concern with community and cultural pluralism is, in fact, expressed in the international human rights instruments themselves. The International Bill of Human Rights recognizes a number of human rights that must be exercised by individuals as members of different racial, ethnic and religious groups, in the understanding that membership and participation in those groups are essential to a life of dignity. Thus, the right of individuals in community with others to practise and observe their religion is an integral part of freedom of religion and might forbid, as expressed in the Declaration on the Elimination of Intolerance and Discrimination based on Religion or Belief, the establishment of measures on the part of the state whose effects are the impairment of that right. Of special importance are the cultural rights of minority cultures within multinational states; thus, Article 27 of the Covenant on Civil and Political rights ensures to members of those cultures in community with others the right to preserve their distinctive language, religion and, ultimately, their 'way of life'.

Because of the range of human rights protected in the major international human rights instruments, we can draw the conclusion that the framers of these agreements believed that cultural and individual rights are not necessarily at odds. The difficulty facing both the relativist and universalist views is that, if either is taken too abstractly, the result is the denial of important elements of our humanity. The relativist ends up overlooking the value of individuality while the universalist ends up overlooking the necessarily social nature of every human being. I think it is for these reasons, therefore, that human rights have best come to be defined as those moral rights that *every* individual possesses as a human being, that is, merely by virtue of being human, even though individuals live in different cultures.[37] Yet because humans are necessarily social creatures, the human rights of individuals must be realized within a scheme of social cooperation with other persons. In a clear indication of the influence of the contractarian tradition, human rights are further defined as the moral rights held by human beings vis-à-vis the state, those 'ethical liberties, claims, powers and immunities' of the individual which cannot be justly expropriated by any political power and which ought to be guaranteed by domestic and international law.[38]

Human rights, then, are generally understood to mean those fundamental rights that human beings mutually recognize and grant one another in order to guarantee a life that meets the necessary conditions of dignity, liberty and respect across *all* cultures. This does not preclude recognizing and respecting the diverse interests and values of individuals and groups, yet at the same time it means protecting those interests – such as obtaining the means of subsistence necessary for a life of dignity, and not being arbitrarily arrested, imprisoned and tortured – that can be reasonably regarded as common to all persons wherever and whenever they happen to exist. Human rights have thus been recognized as being of paramount importance to matters of social justice.

As I have suggested thus far, Rawls's theory of justice can be seen as making a substantive contribution to the enquiry into an adequate basis for a philosophy of human rights. Seeking to pose an alternative to the consequentialist tradition, Rawls offers a contractarian conception of justice as fairness which provides that all social primary goods, such as rights, liberties, opportunities and self-respect, are those things that all rational persons are presumed to want. For Rawls, injustice is a result of inequalities of these primary goods, such that the respect and human dignity of persons is unjustifiably violated. As I hope to demonstrate in the remaining chapters of this book, Rawls's theory of justice places on the philosophical and political agenda the realization that philosophy can help articulate notions of a just society and, moreover, a just world order in which human rights are regarded as an essential outcome of justice. Whether Rawls himself articulates such a clear vision of global justice and human rights is the central problem to be examined in the following chapters.

Rawls, rights and individualism

I have argued that the account of basic individual rights formulated within the framework of the political conception of justice as fairness can be referred to by a vocabulary of human rights rather than classical natural rights. This is because Rawls conceives of such rights in terms of our publicly justified convictions of the characteristics of moral personhood and not as deep metaphysical truths. In this way, the ethical-political theory advanced by Rawls is firmly entrenched in the liberal tradition even though it challenges some of the foundationalist assumptions of that tradition. As Thomas Nagel recognizes, 'Liberalism takes various forms, but they all include a system of individual rights against interference of certain kinds, together with limited positive requirements of mutual aid, all institutionalized and enforced under the rule of law in a democratic regime.'[39] In the present section I want to examine further the broader contours of Rawls's political liberalism and especially the issue of social pluralism, which was itself a difficulty recognized by classical liberalism. The discussion will then be tied back into that of the basic rights and liberties by way of a few remarks on Michael Sandel's communitarian critique of Rawls's theory.

One of the many complaints levelled against liberal political philosophy is that its commitment to individualism, supposedly grounded on mistaken metaphysical premises, necessarily results in insufficient attention being given to the fact that individuals are embedded in and never detached from the communal, social and cultural relations that contribute to forming the individual's identity and moral linkages.[40] These criticisms, at least in regards to Rawls's work, were no doubt principally inspired by his ideas of the veil of ignorance with an 'unencumbered self' placed in the original position, allegedly 'independent of its contingent wants and aims'.[41] One of the most vocal critics of liberal individualism has been Michael Sandel, who writes:

> What is denied to the unencumbered self is the possibility of membership in any community bound by moral ties antecedent to choice; he cannot belong to any community where the self itself could be at stake. Such a community – call it constitutive as against merely cooperative – would engage the identity as well as the interests of the participants, and so implicate its members in a citizenship more thorough-going than the unencumbered self can know.[42]

However, Sandel's objection misses the practical aim towards which Rawls is working, namely, 'to provide a more secure and acceptable basis for constitutional principles and basic rights and liberties'.[43] This is not an easy task, as Rawls well understands. He recognizes the fact that individuals are situated in communities, and that the diversity of those settings also implies 'a diversity of doctrines and [a] plurality of conflicting, and indeed, incommensurable, conceptions of the good affirmed by the members of existing' communities.[44] The fact that there are different settings constitutive of moral ties, identities and interests motivates Rawls to undertake the serious practical task of elaborating a non-metaphysical conception of justice that steers clear of controversial religious, moral or metaphysical doctrines. Individuals embodying different frameworks of values do not always agree or cooperate in a reasonable manner over what should be the political principles of a democratic polity nor how those principles will be implemented and realized in political, social and economic life. Thus Rawls is not fabricating an abstract individual that can assume a transcendent kind of justice, because the aim of the political conception of justice as fairness is practical in that it 'can serve as the basis of informed and willing political agreement between citizens viewed as free and equal persons'.[45]

As I argued in the first section of this chapter, taking the view that citizens are to be regarded as free and equal in no way suggests that they are somehow miraculously unencumbered with their constitutive identities or comprehensive doctrines. Rawls's endeavour to recast the social contract in terms of an overlapping consensus requires negotiating the empirical contingencies of individual difference, social dissensus and histories that are the all-encompassing framework in which we are embedded as social beings. Yet, as Rawls states,

> the reason why the original position must abstract from and not be affected by the contingencies of the social world is that the conditions for a fair agreement on the principles of political justice between free and equal persons must eliminate the bargaining advantages which inevitably arise within background institutions of any society as the result of cumulative, social, historical, and natural tendencies.[46]

In other words, Rawls is not concerned with eliminating the causes of dissensus but in practically navigating the effects in such a way as to 'shape into one coherent view the deeper bases of agreement embedded in the public political culture of a constitutional regime and acceptable to its most firmly held considered convictions'.[47]

In his argument, Rawls presupposes the general fact that a democratic political culture contains certain fundamental intuitive ideas concerning rights and liberties that can be worked up into a political conception of justice suitable for a democratic constitutional regime. We can also grant that, for any public political agreements to be achieved, many of the fundamental intuitive ideas must also have found their way, albeit perhaps somewhat altered, into the background doctrines of civil society. The original position only serves to model what Rawls considers fair conditions whereby free and equal citizens can elaborate the terms of social cooperation in the case of the basic structure of society. In this manner, a framework could be secured enabling individuals to pursue both private and cooperative goods over a complete life. Against this, Sandel's argument that Rawls's individual could not experience either a constitutive community or a deeply meaningful citizenship begins to lose its plausibility.

However, Sandel is also troubled about the priority Rawls places on universal rights insofar as such rights set limits on permissible ways of life. Sandel is concerned that the 'universalizing logic of rights' has displaced direct political life from smaller fora of participation to the universal, comprehensive dimension of the state. This he considers to be the supposedly dangerous contemporary predicament of the 'unencumbered self'. Sandel offers the following description of the current political situation as he perceives it:

> [I]t is a striking feature of the welfare state that it offers a powerful promise of individual rights, and also demands of its citizens a high measure of mutual engagement. But the self-image that attends the rights cannot sustain the engagement.
>
> As bearers of rights, where rights are trumps, we think of ourselves as freely choosing, individual selves, unbound by obligations antecedent to rights, or to agreements we make . . .
>
> In our public life, we are more entangled, but less attached, than ever before. It is as though the unencumbered self presupposed by the liberal ethic had begun to come true – less liberated than disempowered, entangled in a network of obligations and involvements unassociated with any act of the will, and yet unmediated by those common identifications or expansive self-definitions that would make them tolerable. As the scale of social and political organization has become more comprehensive, the terms of our collective identity have become more fragmented, and the forms of political life have outrun the common purpose needed to sustain them.[48]

Sandel paints a grim tableau of life in a liberal democratic polity, but his reflections are part nostalgic fiction and part misconstrual of the landscape in which we live. The nostalgic fiction is implicit in the above characterization of liberal democracies as an ensnaring matrix of abstracted rights, obligations and entanglements that disempower individuals from being able to exercise will-governed acts of genuine meaning entwined with collective identities and common purposes. According to Sandel, true individuality cannot be experienced in the alienating, fragmentary spaces of the all-encompassing welfare state where we are compelled by rationalized obligations to engage with other individuals. Instead, the saving grace that lies within Sandel's denunciation of liberalism is some unnamed living solidarity of persons in a community defined by antecedent moral bonds and common purposes that create a 'true' local political life. In that association, rights are not necessary as trumps against others because they would be irrelevant in such a community of self-sustaining mutual aid and respect. But just where does Sandel's counter-example exist? Sandel's criticism clearly misses the sources of fragmentation and disempowerment to which he should be directing his attention, such as unequal and unjust economic development and consumption, decaying urban spaces, degraded environments, extensive movements of populations, social and familial violence and so forth, which cannot be so conveniently blamed on liberalism. It is also fair to say that Sandel fails to appreciate that the invention of universal human rights has proven to be one of the most effective tools for addressing assaults on human well-being and dignity.

Rawls's priority of right clearly is an essential element in his political conception of justice as fairness in that 'the principles of (political) justice set limits to permissible ways of life; hence the claims citizens make to pursue ends that transgress those limits have no weight'.[49] John Stuart Mill succinctly explained the purpose of such a political morality in the well-known third chapter of his *On Liberty*:

> That mankind are not infallible; that their truths, for the most part, are only half-truths; that unity of opinion, unless resulting from the fullest and freest comparison of opposite opinions, is not desirable, and diversity not an evil, but a good, until mankind are much more capable than at the present of recognizing all the sides of the truth, are principles applicable to men's modes of action, not less than to their opinions.[50]

In minimal terms, rights can be considered as deliberately considered rules in an informal or formal rule-governed system which protect certain claims of right-holders by imposing reciprocal duties. However, I believe that this does not fully convey the sense of mutuality, solidarity and reciprocity implicit to the concept of human rights, nor does it capture the importance Rawls gives to the complementarity between the right and the good. Human rights should be understood both as positive principles invoked by moral persons to aid and cooperate with other individuals in securing, protecting and promoting the full realization of fundamental rights and liberties, and as negative principles not to impede or coerce other individuals from participating in securing, protecting and promoting the conditions in which individuals will be enabled fully to develop their moral powers. As Rawls puts it:

> [T]he equal liberties and freedom of speech and thought enable us to develop and exercise these powers by participating in society's political life

and by assessing the justice and effectiveness of its laws and social policies; and liberty of conscience and freedom of association enable us to develop and exercise our moral powers in forming, revising, and rationally pursuing our conceptions of the good that belong to our comprehensive doctrines, and affirming them as such.[51]

Clearly, Rawls is concerned with establishing that his political conception of justice elaborated through political liberalism is not a comprehensive doctrine embracing the whole of life and defining the moral boundaries for each kind of relation in which we are engaged. For political liberalism to attain that kind of totalizing insinuation into a democratic pluralistic civil society, 'only the oppressive use of state power' could be used to 'maintain a continuing affirmation of one comprehensive . . . doctrine'.[52] Rawls believes that a constitutional democratic state should be grounded in the fundamental intuitive idea of society as a fair system of cooperation between free and equal persons who are fully cooperating members of that society over a complete life. Rawls's version of the social contract is replete with the importance of participation, cooperation, civility, tolerance, mutual and self-respect: terms that no doubt Sandel would consider as exemplary of social relations in his meaningful, non-contractarian community. But one of the important differences between them is that Rawls stresses the importance of individuals having the appropriate conditions of basic rights and liberties to make the important deliberations and decisions which affect their lives. To develop and exercise one's full moral powers, a setting is needed where individual action and social cooperation are 'guided by publicly recognized rules and procedures which those who are cooperating accept and regard as properly regulating their conduct'.[53]

Rawls, of course, sees these rules and procedures as based on the principles of justice as fairness. In order for political liberalism to justify its principles as a legitimating framework for the basic structure of a democratic polity, a reciprocal tolerance is needed between those principles and other religious, philosophical or moral comprehensive doctrines. This reciprocal tolerance is a necessary feature of Rawls's well-ordered society where there is 'a public understanding not only about the kinds of claims it is appropriate for citizens to make when questions of political justice arise, but also about how such claims are to be supported'.[54] The key to such tolerance is revealed in Rawls's notion that the right and the good are complementary, and provide that nexus for finding 'a shared idea of citizen's good that is appropriate for political purposes . . . that is independent of any particular comprehensive doctrine and hence may be the focus of an overlapping consensus'.[55]

The right and the good are complementary in the sense that publicly affirmed rules and regulations covering permissible and impermissible actions do not force a single metaphysical good on all individuals, but contribute to public conditions being secured and promoted that enable each person to pursue his or her conception of the good, either singularly or in community, as long as it does not transgress the limit of permissibility. As Rawls explains,

> permissible comprehensive conceptions of the good, however distinct their content and their related religious and philosophical doctrines, require for their advancement roughly the same primary goods, that is, the same basic rights, liberties, and opportunities, as well as the same all-purpose means such as income and wealth, all of which are secured by the same social bases of self-respect.[56]

Sandel's criticism that the 'universalizing logic of rights' is somehow the cause of alienation and fragmentation overlooks the good that has been achieved through the post-Second World War human rights system, especially when combined with democratic practices. It also overlooks the fact that human beings all over the planet who, on a daily basis, face illiberal regimes and practices and yet aspire to be the moral subjects of human rights can appeal to those rights to protect their well-being and dignity. One might go so far as to say it is evident that comprehensive doctrines which only minimally, or do not at all, embrace the kinds of principles espoused in Rawls's political liberalism have taken unfair advantage of political, social and economic relations in such a fashion as to undermine the stability of human rights as the primary core of justice as fairness.

The two principles of justice seek to enable all persons, regardless of their identities or histories, to benefit equally from the scheme of basic (human) rights and liberties, and provide a limiting restraint to inequalities through an ethic of sharing the burdens of inequalities more equally. Since we are indeed situated in particular social contexts that are constitutive of our diverse characters, values and goods, Rawls's rights and principles of justice serve as a threshold of dignity which should guide our relations with other persons and give us the permissible latitude to choose how we will lead our lives. However, Sandel argues that these terms of the social contract by 'their very arbitrariness' of imposing 'entanglements' of rights and claims and the imposition of a 'false' ethic of sharing are remote from the particular moral ties that constitute the real bonds, where sharing is something more than the redistribution of resources for the public good of a 'concatenated collectivity'.[57] But why should we consider that human rights or an ethic of sharing the burdens of inequalities are somehow disingenuous compared to what might exist in some romanticized 'traditional' community? Do rights, liberties or an ethic of sharing resources to secure citizens' fundamental needs fail some test of substantiality whereby they cannot serve as basic values constitutive of who we are as human beings engaged in both common and private purposes?

Sandel in fact fails to provide any plausible reason to accept that some traditional constitutive community which regards 'commonality' as fundamental could provide the conditions by which a human being can fully develop his or her moral powers as an individual and citizen in a multi-ethnic culture. Indeed, the modern struggle for human rights and freedoms has been principally against the prejudices of traditions that discriminate against 'otherness' and deny claims to equal rights. Human rights as part of a society's constitutional framework also place obligations on legislative majorities to respect and protect those rights regardless of the particularities that differentiate us as human beings. This is where Sandel and other communitarians misunderstand what the liberal individual is and the role that human rights play in today's pluralist political and civil societies. Human rights do not serve as the identification of a single, unchanging nature for all human beings. They are, instead, political and ethical principles that human beings have worked out for treating each other's well-being and dignity while respecting the differences that otherwise distinguish them.[58] Thus, as Thomas Nagel recognizes, the 'radical communitarian view that nothing in personal life is beyond the legitimate control of the community if its dominant values are at stake is the main contemporary threat to human rights'.[59]

The centrality of civil and political rights to sustaining this project of obtaining human well-being is of great ethical importance. Freedom of expression, belief, conscience, religion, association, equality before the law and security of persons all contribute a dynamic component to a political society by the very fact that the individuals constituting it are *empowered* via political principles with moral import. When combined with the cultivation of just and fair conditions supportive of social cooperation and individual choice, reciprocally complementary experiences of self- and mutual respect are bound to make both public and private lives substantially more meaningful and connected. If this is the case, Rawls notes, differences and diversity can then be accepted as a healthy state of public democratic culture.[60] It is through these practices and principles realized within our lives that a democratic political society can generate commitments cooperatively to justify its principles. This is done by addressing the affairs that are important to our lives as members of that society and by legitimating its constitutional stability through protecting individual rights and liberties. Rawls's justice as fairness and the priority of right serve not only as non-metaphysical principles for securing the conditions necessary for human dignity, but also for establishing fair rules and conditions of cooperation and participation so that different individuals can work out the everyday essentials of living together.[61]

It is true, however, that another difficulty, which I have purposely avoided up to this point, is presented with Rawls's theory of basic rights and liberties. Rawls's political conception of justice draws upon the public political culture of Western democratic societies. Consequently, Rawls stipulates that one of the basic assumptions upon which the application of his conception to the basic structure of society rests is the following:

> I assume that the basic structure is that of a closed society: that is, we are to regard it as self-contained and as having no relations with other societies . . . That a society is closed is a considerable abstraction, justified only because it enables us to focus on certain main questions free from distracting details. At some point a political conception of justice must address the just relations between peoples, or the law of peoples, as I shall say. (1996: 12)

The theory of justice that I have analysed up to this point is thus meant by Rawls to address the issue of justice within a single society. As Rawls admits, this leaves issues of international justice out of the picture. Despite this omission, it is certain that the questions of international justice and human rights are at the heart of the problems with which Rawls's political philosophy is at the end concerned. This is particularly apparent in Rawls's focus on the basic rights and liberties of persons in today's culturally diverse societies. But does Rawls's assumption that his theory is constructed in terms of a 'closed' liberal democratic society negate the possibility that principles of political right are applicable across the boundaries of diverse political cultures? To address this question, what must be examined next is how well Rawls's theory succeeds in developing a conception of international justice consonant with the domestic conception of justice and, ultimately, with the notion of universal human rights.

II • The International Dimensions of Justice as Fairness

3 • From Domestic to International Justice

If we really do believe that all human beings are created equal and endowed with certain inalienable rights, we are morally required to think about what that conception requires us to do with and for the rest of the world. (Martha Nussbaum, 'Patriotism and Cosmopolitanism', 13)

Although the discussion in the previous chapter made clear that Rawls's theory of justice contains a central role for basic human rights, it has not yet been established that Rawls provides the kind of extension of justice as fairness to an international level that must be regarded as a corollary to the modern conception of human rights. Over the course of the next two chapters I intend to establish that Rawls's work does indeed allow for that extension. I will also argue, however, that Rawls unnecessarily limits the range of that extension and therefore fails to provide an adequate account of human rights within his own theory of international justice.

The purpose of the present chapter is to explore how the domestic theory of justice as fairness presented in *A Theory of Justice* might be expanded into the international domain and thus provide the framework of a theory of international justice that is both consistent with Rawls's overall treatment of justice and yet also develops some of those areas that remain untreated by Rawls. Doing so will bring out some of the conceptual difficulties and practical consequences of extending justice as fairness on an international scale. The next chapter will then carry the discussion forward into the context of Rawls's most recent thoughts on international justice and human rights.

To begin with, I shall review what Rawls has to say about international justice in *A Theory of Justice* and then, over the course of the chapter, I shall flesh out those rather sparse remarks into what I hope is a more revealing discussion of international justice as fairness. In the next section, I draw attention to two fundamental problems in Rawls's account of international justice: first, the priority of the domestic original position over the international original position;

and, second, the analogy he draws between individuals and states. I then examine several arguments concerning a Rawlsian version of global justice as they relate to the issue of diversity or social pluralism. This leads to a discussion of the principle of self-determination and how certain difficulties with this principle problematize the law of nations scheme endorsed by Rawls. In the final section, I consider the possibility of extending Rawls's two principles of justice to a global scale and some criticisms that might be raised against this move.

Rawls's account of international justice

In *A Theory of Justice*, Rawls divides the problem of social justice into three stages: that concerning the justice of domestic institutions; that concerning individuals; and that concerning international justice and the conduct of states (1971: 377). In the first two stages, the primary subject of justice is essentially the basic structure of domestic society, that is, the way in which the major social institutions distribute fundamental rights and duties and determine the division of advantages from social cooperation. In the previous chapters I discussed how the principles of justice, in light of which the basic structure of society can be evaluated, are specified by means of Rawls's hypothetical social contract and rational choice procedure.

According to Rawls, once the principles of justice as they apply to the basic structure of domestic society and to individuals have been derived, one may then extend the interpretation of the original position and 'think of the parties as representatives of different nations' choosing together the fundamental principles of justice to adjudicate conflicting claims among states (1971: 378). Those parties to the international original position are, as were those to the domestic original position, represented as rational (choosing among principles by reference to the interests of their nations as defined by the principles of justice already acknowledged), as situated symmetrically and equally, and as deciding for appropriate reasons. The parties know nothing about the particular circumstances of their own society, its power and strength in comparison with other societies, nor do these representatives know their place in their own society. However, Rawls suggests that the parties do know that nation-states are the historical reality of the day and that nation-states, like individuals in society, will have conflicts of interest (1971: 108 ff., 378). 'This original position', writes Rawls, 'is fair between nations; it nullifies the contingencies and biases of historical fate' (1971: 378). I will argue in the sections which follow that the international original position offered by Rawls does not in fact nullify certain significant historical contingencies and biases, and that his theory is thus flawed. This flaw is carried over by Rawls into his later conception of the law of peoples.

As Rawls's aim at this point is a very short account of international justice, the nations so represented need to choose principles to order their interactions and to adjudicate any conflicting claims between parties. Before the principles of justice that would be chosen under this model can be indicated, however, it is first necessary briefly to describe the formal constraints of right that would apply to the choice procedure of the parties. The first constraint on the parties is that any set of possible principles of international justice must be narrowed such that their derivation is consistent with the institutional and individual principles of justice already chosen in the domestic context of justice as fairness. Just as the individual and social institutional principles of the domestic context together had to form a coherent conception of justice as fairness, so too are international principles supposed to conform to the previously established conception of justice.

The second constraint is based upon one of the conditions of the rationality of the parties. According to the condition of strict compliance, the principles finally acknowledged will constitute the basis for an ideal theory of international justice. In Rawls's words, strict compliance means that 'the parties can rely on each other to understand and act in accordance with whatever principles are finally agreed to. Once principles are acknowledged the parties can depend on one another to conform to them' (1971: 145). This constraint allows for the parties to concentrate on selecting those principles of reciprocal advantage for well-ordered nations that will become the foundation for the basic institutions of a well-ordered society of nations.

Given these first two constraints, the parties can now consider the principles to be chosen with respect to the matter of international relations. In Rawls's opinion, the 'familiar principles' of international law, or what he refers to as the law of nations, would be chosen under this scenario (1971: 378). The first principle of international justice to be chosen is apparent given the conception of the parties as free and equal. This is the basic principle of equality: 'Independent peoples organized as states have certain fundamental equal rights' (1971: 378). This principle analogizes the status of individuals as free and equal to the status of states as free and equal as well. The principle of equality is the consequence of the transfer of the moral status of individuals to nation-states, based upon the characterization of the parties to the international original position as representatives of states. Rawls remarks that the principle of equality between nations, that is, the idea that the fundamental rights and obligations of all nations are the same, is a long-standing principle of international law, indeed is the 'basic principle of the law of nations' (1971: 378).[1] The principle of equality seems required, of course, by the very structure of the original position and the constraints outlined above, since it is fundamental to establishing reciprocal relationships for mutual advantage and co-operation. Rawls's point here is that international law would not retain its legitimacy and force if nations were not treated equally under it.

The second principle to be chosen is that of self-determination, that is, 'the right of a people to settle its own affairs without the intervention of foreign powers' (1971: 378). This principle means that each nation's conception of the good, being protected by the principle of equality, is deemed legitimate and of equal worth. Because the particularities of specific conceptions of the good are unknown behind the veil of ignorance, the parties could not reasonably agree to a principle which would allow the ranking of differing conceptions, thereby putting their own nation's conception of the good in jeopardy. Any other principle permitting one nation's predominance over or interference in the internal affairs of another state, due solely to differing conceptions of the good, could not be allowed and would violate the principle of equality. Rawls claims that the principle of self-determination thus carries with it a right to non-intervention and a right to self-defence, with the latter right implying principles of just war (*jus ad bellum* and *jus in bello*). Rawls's brevity on the connection between self-determination and non-intervention leaves much to be desired, since he seems not to consider that the right to be free from foreign interference can operate so as to preclude humanitarian intervention or even investigation into the so-called internal affairs of a sovereign state, in the event of unjust violence or abuses of human rights on the part of that state.[2] Rawls would reply, of course, that his comments on self-determination are given with the assumption that more-or-less just states are in view under an ideal theory of justice as fairness and strict compliance. I return to this matter below.

The third principle acknowledged by the parties in the original position is the basic principle of obligation, traditionally known as the principle of *pacta sunt servanda* ('treaties are to be observed'), which means that states must carry out their treaty obligations in good faith and without exception (1971: 378). This principle is needed if the international order is to be given a structure based on reciprocity. It can be viewed as encompassing the individual analogue of fairness, combined with the duty of mutual respect, already acknowledged at the domestic level. Consequently, nations must acknowledge and take responsibility for their international claims and actions. The principle of obligation thereby establishes the contours of reciprocity in international relations.

According to Rawls, then, these three principles (and their corollaries) taken together form a foundation for erecting a basic structure of international justice. These principles are intended to represent the final stage of a coherent theory of justice as fairness when aligned with the previously derived principles of individuals and domestic social institutions. Although the discussion of international justice provided by Rawls in *A Theory of Justice* is clearly minimalist (two pages out of a book of nearly 600 pages) in comparison to his treatment of justice as fairness at the domestic level, Rawls nevertheless indicates an expectation that his domestic theory can be extended so as to cover international affairs. Rawls himself admits, however, that *A Theory of Justice* 'does not pursue these larger matters' (1989, 252). In the sections that follow I discuss a number of problematic assumptions contained in Rawls's theory of international justice and propose several changes to his theory that would, I think, result in a fuller conception of international justice which nevertheless retains its Rawlsian character.[3] In the next section, I address some of the difficulties presented by Rawls's account of the international original position.

The international original position

Rawls characterizes the international original position as follows:

> Let us assume that we have already derived the principles of justice as these apply to societies as units and to the basic structure. Imagine also that the

various principles of natural duty and of obligation that apply to individuals have been adopted . . . Now at this point one may extend the interpretation of the original position and think of the parties as representatives of different nations who must choose together the fundamental principles to adjudicate conflicting claims among states . . . Once again the contracting parties, in this case representatives of states, are allowed only enough knowledge to make a rational choice to protect their interests but not so much that the more fortunate among them can take advantage of their special situation . . . Justice between states is determined by the principles that would be chosen in the original position so interpreted. (1971: 377–8)

As was discussed previously, the original position (both domestic and international) is considered fair by Rawls insofar as it 'nullifies the contingencies and biases of historical fate' (1971: 378). The point in ideal theory of nullifying the effects of specific historical contingencies is to ensure that the parties to the original position will not exploit such contingencies to their own advantage when it comes to the choice of principles of international justice. The question that I will examine here, however, is whether the original position and the veil of ignorance limitations portrayed by Rawls actually meet that desired purpose.

Thomas Pogge argues that in *A Theory of Justice* Rawls does not distinguish between two possible readings of his account of how the contractarian choice procedure is to apply at the international level.[4] On one possible reading (R_1) the parties to the international original position *represent persons* from the different societies; on another possible reading (R_2) the parties to the original position *represent states*. In both cases, of course, the international original position is utilized only after the principles of justice have been chosen at the domestic level.

It seems clear that these two readings can be put forward as competing accounts of the international original position. However, I am not as sure as Pogge is that R_1 is to be found in Rawls's own comments. I would argue that Rawls obviously intends the parties to the international original position no longer to be mutually disinterested persons. Rather, given Rawls's insistence that the international original position only comes into play subsequent to the establishment of domestic societies as closed units at an earlier stage, it is certain that the participants are literally, in Rawls's words, 'representatives of different nations' and 'representatives of states' (1971: 378). Consequently, I think the parties are to be understood in Rawls's own account as representatives of nation-states, and not of persons, in an initial situation where they are to choose principles for structuring the relations between states.

Pogge's claim that two possible readings of Rawls's description of the international original position can be found in *A Theory of Justice* thus appears unfounded. It does nevertheless point to what I think are the two fundamental flaws of that very description: first, the priority of the domestic choice situation over the international choice situation and, second, the analogy employed between individuals and states. More specifically, I am concerned that each of these features in Rawls's theory undermines the attempt to establish a genuinely fair choice situation from which principles of international justice can be derived in ideal theory.

The problem with Rawls's prioritization of the domestic over the international choice situation is that it negates the ethical advantages gained through the utilization of the veil of ignorance. Rawls concedes that the parties to the international original position 'know nothing about the particular circumstances of their own society, its power and strength in comparison with other nations' (1971: 378). However, the parties do know a most important fact, namely, that the societies of the participants are nation-states and the parties are to serve only as representatives of those states. This is problematic because the idea and existence of the nation-state is a uniquely modern, historically contingent factor. As such, it is not the only possible perspective from which to approach the selection of ideal principles of international justice. In other words, Rawls assumes without justification that international justice is concerned *only* with relationships between states (reading R_2) and not relationships between persons who reside in various societies (reading R_1).

This problem is exacerbated by Rawls's presupposition that the domestic principles of justice apply to societies that are 'self-contained national communit[ies]' or 'more or less self-sufficient association[s] of persons' (1971: 457, 458). While Rawls insists that the priority of the domestic over the international choice situations is intended to guarantee that the parties to the international original position are states that have already adopted domestic principles of justice, there is no similar guarantee that the parties will be willing to extend the same principles to others when it comes to dealing with one another solely as sovereign states. In setting up the international original position as he does, Rawls unnecessarily burdens it with the type of contingent historical features abstracted from the domestic original position. In the international original position the veil of ignorance fails to screen out the particular features of the situation which threaten the possibility of a fair agreement between free and equal *persons*. If domestic societies are conceived as more or less self-contained or self-sufficient states, what motivation might they have for agreeing to principles of global justice that are intended to apply to all persons in all places? The model of an interstate system in which each state is committed only to ensuring justice within its own border falls well short of the idea of an international society based upon equal rights and liberties for all persons, wherever those persons might happen to reside at any given time.

In Rawls's description of the international original position, in which the parties represent the interests of particular states as against people in other states, the basic rights and liberties extend up to but not necessarily beyond the national level. Extending the idea of a fair agreement between free and equal persons to an agreement on principles of international justice, in a hypothetical choice situation that asks what the parties could or would agree to, requires a more stringent veil of ignorance so that the original position is not distorted by 'contingent historical advantages and accidental influences from the past', such as the particular political form of the nation-state.[5] Because the principles of a fair agreement are supposed to be binding from the present into the future, pre-existing features and circumstances should not be allowed to affect the agreement.

The problem of prioritizing the domestic over the international is further reflected in the analogy Rawls draws between individuals and states. In particular, Rawls analogizes the interests, equality and autonomy of persons with the interests, equality and sovereignty of states (1971: 378). In this way he apparently derives a convenient device for shifting the identities of the parties to the original position. In the domestic original position, the participants are individual persons; while in the international original position, the participants are representatives of states. In both cases the parties are conceived of as 'free and equal' and having similar interests. There are, however, significant differences between the two types of participants which I believe would have a negative impact on the principles of justice that ultimately would be chosen. Moreover, it is not clear to me just how the participants can move from their status as individuals to that of state representatives unless Rawls incorporates several unnecessary assumptions into his theory.

In the domestic choice situation, of course, the aim is to select those principles that will guarantee individuals an equal or equitable share of those social primary goods necessary in a just and well-ordered society. The principles of justice adopted are therefore those that are in the best interest of individuals, within a situation in which the constraints of having a political morality are enforced. As a result, the domestic original position is said to represent fair conditions among free and equal moral persons, that is, persons who possess the capacity to exercise their moral powers with respect to how a just society ought to be organized.

In the international choice situation described by Rawls the aim and method of ideal theory appears to be relegated to a secondary status behind the dictates of a realist view of international politics. The realist school of international relations theory emphasizes the nation-state as the primary actor in the international system. Thus in Rawls's realist-inclined international original position the participants are no longer moral persons, rather they are fully formed nation-states, or more accurately the representatives of those states. The problem here, I want to argue, is that this move changes the entire complexion of a Rawlsian-based ideal theory of justice. This is because Rawls overdetermines the characteristics of the international original position. The question is not left open as to what type of system of international justice will be adopted by the participants to the original position, since Rawls has already defined those participants as nation-states and has already indicated that international justice is relevant only insofar as it can 'adjudicate conflicting claims among states' (1971: 378).

Consequently, the interest that is to be taken into consideration by each contracting party when selecting the principles of international justice is the 'national interest' of the state apparatus, which does not necessarily coincide with the interests of moral persons (1971: 379). To repeat the point more bluntly, the representatives of states who function as parties to the international original position are there primarily to 'protect their [nation's] interests' (1971: 378). This is a dominant theme of realism.[6] It is little wonder then that Rawls observes that 'there would be no surprises' among the principles of international justice adopted in such a choice situation, since the principles would be the 'familiar ones' of the traditional law of nations (1971: 378). Yet it is not at all apparent to me that if the participants to the original position were moral persons such as those conceived in Rawls's domestic theory of justice, they would in fact adopt such all-too-familiar principles.

I would argue that the concept of international justice differs from that of domestic justice insofar as it refers to a set of moral and political principles that transcend the narrow interests defined by a nation-state's historically contingent borders. It is from this perspective that Rawls's account of international justice succumbs to the present-day dictates of realism in international politics. And yet an ideal theory of international justice should be concerned not so much with what is but with what ought to be, not so much with adopting familiar rules of political realism but with articulating principles with which to evaluate those existing rules and suggest goals for transforming them. An ideal theory of international justice must be, in the end, about how the world *ought* to be organized.

The need for a global original position

In the argument that has been offered thus far, I have suggested that Rawls's description of the international original position is flawed because, first, Rawls prioritizes domestic justice above international justice and, second, he replaces the interests of persons with those of states in the choice situation and thereby assumes that the interests are analogous. More must be said, however, about how these features of the international original position result in principles of international justice that do not, in important respects, live up to the rigorous standards of domestic justice proposed by Rawls. In this section I consider some of the principles of international justice that Rawls claims would be adopted by the parties to the international original position as modelled in *A Theory of Justice*, and show how these principles are deficient for purposes of constructing a robust theory of international justice.

Here I will return to Pogge's contention that Rawls does not clearly distinguish between two possible readings of his account of the international original position. While Pogge may overstate Rawls's confusion on this point, the two different interpretations of the international original position provide the rationale for extending our analysis. Pogge's criticisms of Rawls's views on international justice are grounded in Rawls's endorsement of the so-called 'familiar principles' of international law and thus to reading R_2. On reading R_1, it will be recalled, the global parties represent persons from the different societies; on reading R_2 they represent states. Pogge rightly argues that the endorsement of a conventional version of the law of nations goes against important Rawlsian commitments, specifically the need to focus on the basic structure of society as well as the moral conception of persons. Such commitments, Pogge suggests, are absent not only from R_2 but also from R_1.

Pogge proposes that the absence of a single world government is not the fundamental problem facing international justice. Instead, the weakness of international law is due to the fact that states presently operate within a realist political system in which international relations are based upon *modus vivendi* agreements. As defined by Rawls, a *modus vivendi* is a purely instrumental agreement founded upon compromise and exhaustion (1996: xli). The parties to a *modus vivendi* support its establishment and continuation not because they believe it to be either the ideal agreement for all concerned or the most desirable agreement from a partisan perspective, but rather because they have exhausted all efforts to secure a voluntary or coerced obedience to their respective comprehensive views. Consequently, the parties conclude that a *modus vivendi* offers the best possible temporary option. Under a *modus vivendi*, toleration of conflicting religious, moral and philosophical views is simply the result of an inconclusive distribution of power, that is, no single party commands sufficient power to suppress opposing and competing views.[7] Because the parties involved believe that the agreement holds no particular intrinsic value for them, apart from its ability to secure short-term political stability, they will abandon it when they believe they are in a position to do so and use their power to try to force others to obey the precepts of their particular comprehensive doctrine. Thus, the stability of a *modus vivendi* is extremely tenuous and even illusory, since it depends upon 'circumstances remaining such as not to upset the fortunate convergence of interests' (1996: 147). Subject to the vagaries of circumstance and fortune, a *modus vivendi* is unable to secure the kind of stability needed to establish and maintain a well-ordered society (domestic and international).

In a realist international system, then, states are concerned only to further their own interests and interstate relations are carried out only on prudential grounds in order to accommodate otherwise 'irresolv-able' disagreements or differences. In such a system, relatively weak international institutions are the result of governmental practices based on prudential, rather than moral, reasons informed by the current distribution of power and states' attempts to maintain their relative ranking.[8] Realists contend that states rarely join or comply with regimes that are not in their national interest, defined by the need to acquire, maintain and exercise power. As Hans Morgenthau puts it, 'The main signpost that helps political realism to find its way through the landscape of international politics is the concept of interest defined in terms of power.'[9] As a result, finding a moral reason to support some part of this international order – for instance, international human rights agreements – is very difficult, since such agreements can be seen as just another step in self-interested prud-ential behaviour rather than a commitment to the global common good.

Given an intergovernmental *modus vivendi*, assurance and stability problems in international relations are acute. In a *modus vivendi*, even though prudential equilibrium is necessary – all parties must have a reason to participate on the going terms – the terms of such equilibrium are not. The competition over the balance of power and over the terms of the *modus vivendi* is unrestrained and unlimited. Despite the fact that a *modus vivendi* is a very malleable arrangement, perhaps preventing an all-out war in the long run (the malleability of the terms accommodates changes in the power and situation of the parties), it is precisely this malleability which fosters short-term instability and detachment from higher-order moral values. For instance, the prudentially determined survival of a nation's own values, as well as ensuring that a decline in power and a deterioration in the terms do not occur, takes precedence over the short-term instantiation of higher-order moral values. Seen through the lens of political realism, ethical constraints upon the pursuit of power in the present might well be viewed as signalling defeat in the future and the long-term eradication of one's own values. Thus, no party's values are adequately reflected in its external conduct, its decisions about com-pliance, or the terms of the *modus vivendi*.

In a *modus vivendi*, effective mechanisms of adjudication and enforcement become impossible. Each party fears that it will be dominated by those who dislike its way of life and domestic institu-tions. Thus, those mechanisms will be dependent upon the strongest governments' temporary bargain and not the rule of law. Further-more, international treaties will not be honoured when the benefit of non-compliance is considerable; international treaties are perceived as reflecting self-interested bargaining, with no higher ethical standing. And parties assume others to be ready to reinterpret treaties or abrogate them as well when it is to their benefit to do so.

Finally, an intergovernmental *modus vivendi* is unsatisfactory on at least three related counts. First, such a framework is insensitive to the fate of others in the poorest or weakest societies. A party's bargaining power is a function of the distribution of military and economic strength; a concern for deprived foreigners and for universal human needs is perceived as putting a nation's own bargaining position in jeopardy. Second, an intergovernmental *modus vivendi* embodies little concern for the treatment of persons within their own societies. Within this system, a party's interest in controlling its own population outweighs its interest in those abroad. Third, a party in the *modus vivendi* framework is relatively unconcerned about the treatment of persons at the hands of allied governments or governments that are operating within its sphere of influence. A basic feature of the *modus vivendi* framework is that each major power has special claims to those regions which are more essential economically or strategically to its security than to that of the next major power. In a world structured around the dictates of political realism, changes of govern-ment, political systems and economies in that sphere of influence frequently occur without significant resistance or objection motivated by ethical concerns.[10]

Given the realist paradigm of international politics as a struggle for power, it can be argued that Rawls's description of the international original position is deficient in that it leads him to endorse the traditional principles of the law of nations, principles that are burdened with the realist presumptions of a *modus vivendi* system. An international system based on such principles is better characterized not in terms of global justice, but in terms of global instability marked by the rise and fall of great powers, the pursuit of narrow self-interests and indifference towards the interests of persons who happen to reside outside of a nation-state's own borders. For the realist, the world is an anarchical system that does not reward state cooperation but rather the enhancement of state power. The principles of such an anarchical system are grounded on prudential rather than moral reasons, a situation that is hardly fitting for an ideal theory of justice.[11]

Pogge argues that the principles of international law assumed by Rawls are inadequate for dealing with contemporary issues of distributive justice; even an intergovernmental system in which each state is committed to ensuring justice within its borders (as Rawls wants) will degenerate into a *modus vivendi* if it is based only upon such principles. In R_2, in which the parties to the original position are representatives of states, the right to political equality, fair equality of opportunity and the difference principle extends up to but not beyond the national level. Since in R_2 the global background justice is assessed by how it tends to affect the domestic justice of states, especially the least just, the reading still allows for indefinite international inequalities. Those international inequalities, plus the fact that Rawls's two principles of justice need not be fulfilled at the global level, translate into enormous inequalities among the members of different communities, in regard to political rights, opportunities and socioeconomic means. In R_1, in which the parties are representing persons, the principles chosen make the position of the least advantaged individual globally the criterion of international justice (since, given the veil of ignorance, the parties do not know the place of their society among others, nor do they know their place in their own society). However, in Rawls's model, the domestic choice situation takes precedence over the selection of principles in the international choice situation and, given this precedence, even the criterion that would be chosen in R_1 cannot be fulfilled.

Under both R_1 and R_2, the priority of the domestic choice situation assumes that the favoured model of a just national basic structure can be developed without paying attention to its international environment, in other words, that principles of domestic justice can simply be complemented with international rules intended to prevent global injustice. Yet this is insufficient in that merely adding rules to an initial situation that favours the individual nation-state cannot accommodate the fact of a plurality of nations and the ramifications of their actions taken collectively. Moreover, if an international scheme is to endure, it must engender in national populations a moral allegiance to and compliance with the system of norms and laws of that scheme. The ability to engender such allegiance will partly depend on the domestic institutional organization of societies. What this means is that deliberation on national institutions and the construction of models for them are to be conducted from the beginning with a focus on considerations of the stability and functioning of the basic structure of global society, that is, together with the preferred ideal of a global basic structure. Pogge explains that:

> Since national and global basic structures strongly affect each other's stability and are closely interrelated in their effects upon individual lives, we should think about our basic social institutions *in general* and from a global point of view, thereby aiming for an integrated solution, a just and stable institutional scheme preserving a distribution of basic rights, opportunities, and index goods that is fair both globally and within each nation. Such an institutional scheme, if constructed along Rawlsian lines at all, would be developed through a single unified original position global in scope.[12]

A single unified global original position affords those reflecting upon the two principles of domestic justice the constrained standpoint of persons who are both insiders and outsiders of different national societies. Indeed, a single global original position raises the question of whether nation-states would either play a role to begin with in the procedure, or even be selected as a possible outcome of the procedure. The global original position thus subjects the institution of the modern nation-state in its present form to moral scrutiny.[13] In contrast to the approach adopted by Rawls, Pogge points out that, while the institutions of a supposedly isolated state might be justified by reference to its least advantaged members (even by the communal life they protect for all its members), a system of sovereign states requires a *global* examination and justification. In a greatly interdependent world one cannot decide whether competitive markets, private ownership of the means of production and other such institutions are to be governed by the domestic criterion of the initial choice situation or the global criterion of the international choice situation, because in such a world it is impossible to maintain the sharp distinction between national and international institutions that both R$_1$ and R$_2$ maintain.

The point made by Pogge illustrates clearly one of the concerns I have suggested about Rawls's remarks on international justice, namely, that they are not attuned to the increasingly globalized character of world society. International relations are coming more and more to resemble domestic society in several respects relevant to the justification of principles of social justice, yet Rawls assumes that states are more-or-less 'self-sufficient' or 'self-contained'. The self-sufficiency thesis takes for granted that the nations of the world interact only in marginal ways, if at all. As Onora O'Neill observes, this assumption 'assumes predicates which are false of all existing human societies'.[14] The traditional principles of international law presuppose that, at least in non-ideal theory, each society's external behaviour is controlled solely by its domestic principles of justice. Agreement on principles for the law of nations is made only to provide states with security regarding other states' behaviour or to consolidate their positions of power. But what if the world as a whole fits the description of a scheme of cooperation under the circumstances of justice?

While the interrelationships between globalization and social justice are complex, it is none the less possible to recognize that the contemporary world fits the description of a global scheme of cooperation. There exists interdependent economic (as well as political, social and cultural) activity that produces substantial aggregate benefits, and a pattern in which international and transnational institutions (multinational corporations, international and transnational trade and investment, property rights over national territories and their resources) distribute those benefits as well as burdens. However, as Charles Beitz recognizes,

> it is easier to demonstrate that a pattern of global interdependence exists and that it yields substantial aggregate benefits, than to say with certainty how those benefits are distributed under existing institutions and practices or what burdens those institutions and practices impose on participants.[15]

Despite this lack of certainty, some general observations are possible.

Global interdependence, as it now functions in a *modus vivendi* framework, widens the gap between rich and poor countries, generates political inequality and inequality of opportunities among the members of different countries and, domestically, widens the gap between the upper and the lower income classes.[16] The process of globalization carries with it significant interdependencies, including a reduction of barriers to the flow of goods, services, finance, people and communications. This process also entails increasing gaps in economic, social and political standards within and between states, which must be addressed by the international society of states. Given the interdependencies of peoples throughout the world generated by globalization, principles of social justice ought to apply globally. The shared fates and interests of persons extend beyond political boundaries, as economic, social, cultural and political life becomes increasingly global. These considerations lead to the conclusion that, in a world where state boundaries do not constitute the limits of social cooperation, Rawls's confinement of principles of distributive justice to the domestic sphere has the effect of taxing poor countries and poor classes therein. In characterizing the principles of international justice as the familiar rules of the law of nations, Rawls sacrifices strong consideration of the distributive aspect (of substantive goods) of international justice to the notion of simple conformity to the common or established rules of international affairs. This is a serious omission given the necessity of having both principles of justice as fairness in place in Rawls's domestic conception.

The two principles of justice, when given domestic preference within a realist framework, might then justify wealthy nations in permanently denying assistance to the poorest countries in the world, generating gross inequalities in lifestyles and prospects for the future. However, if we are to define social justice in global terms, that is, as providing universal access to the social primary goods, then principles of domestic justice will be genuinely just only if they are consistent with principles of global justice. Principles of global justice therefore must be considered from the start and not treated as a mere afterthought. Because of our global interdependence, Beitz contends that Rawls's difference principle ought to hold globally and that a resource redistribution principle would have to apply to the uneven and morally arbitrary distribution of the earth's natural resources.[17]

It might be argued, however, that the types of global interdependence evidenced primarily by the transactions of the present world system are not a sufficient foundation upon which to build a Rawlsian model of international justice. In particular, the steadily growing recognition of cultural diversity and the distinctiveness of many peoples' identities have often led to sentiments that run counter to a sense of global or even national solidarity. Considerations of social cooperation at the domestic level are problematic enough given the now well-entrenched fact of social pluralism. Even as the world becomes increasingly global along economic lines, it may still be the case that the nation-state and the lines of association formed through national culture and national language retain their primacy.

One way to approach this matter is through a discussion of the notion of self-determination, which Rawls suggests is one of the familiar principles chosen by the parties to the international original position. Yet Rawls has little to say about self-determination, other than that he understands it to mean 'the right of a people to settle its own affairs without the intervention of foreign powers' (1971: 378). What does it really mean, though, when Rawls invokes the right of 'a people' to 'settle its own affairs'? Such a claim could imply a democratic determination of public policy by the equally free members of a political community (that is, by individual persons as citizens), or it could refer to the policies pursued by a state (that is, 'a people') without recourse to democratic and public decision-making procedures. While the latter situation might conflict with the requirements of Rawls's version of *domestic* justice, it is less certain that it would conflict with Rawls's version of *international* justice.

A further problem arises when Rawls analogizes the 'equal rights of citizens' with the 'equal rights' of states (1971: 378). Surely it would be wrong to intervene in the affairs of a person who, possessing basic rights and liberties, exercises those same rights and liberties in pursuit of his or her vision of the good, as long as that pursuit does not negate the equal rights and liberties of others.[18] However, can the same be said of a state? Rawls seems to be claiming that the members of a political community should be able freely to choose the framework and policies constituting their community, without outside interference. But if a state, in pursuing its national interest, violates the equal rights of some of its own citizens, should it be free from the intervention of foreign powers as Rawls suggests? Can the state be regarded as so insular when it comes to issues of social justice? I do not think a satisfactory answer can be given on the basis of Rawls's model which – while attempting to analogize the interests and rights of states and persons – elevates the interests of states over that of persons in the case of international justice. The fact of the matter is that, in the realist law of nations model endorsed by Rawls, states and persons are not analogous, since the state reigns supreme. Consequently, it will be worthwhile to say something further about the subject of self-determination in order to illuminate some of the tensions contained in Rawls's treatment of international justice.

The problem of self-determination

The principle of national self-determination has a significant genealogy in the political thought and practice of the Enlightenment. One can argue that intimations of this idea emerged in the political writings of Marsilius of Padua, where he made the distinction between the *universitas civium* (the people) and the *pars principans* (the ruler) in his theory of the autonomous state, with the legitimacy of the ruler resting on the sovereignty of the people.[19] This idea was later taken up by Machiavelli in his considerations on the most appropriate and stable form of government, which Machiavelli believed to be a type of civic republicanism legitimated by popular support and sovereignty. Johann Gottfried von Herder also contributed to the doctrine of the right of national self-determination, in his claim that the state is the embodiment and protector of the nation and its culture.[20] The famous revolutions of the eighteenth century, however, charged into new political terrain by overturning the divine right of monarchical sovereignty and replacing it with the sovereign will of the people. Both the American and French Revolutions ushered in radical political rearrangements based on the participation of the people who determined through their will the form of government and political institutions by which they would be governed.

The stirring opening of the Declaration of Independence of the United States of America set a new precedent by which national self-determination attained its inalienable status as a principle or right:

> When in the Course of human events, it becomes necessary for one people to dissolve the political bands which have connected them with another, and to assume among the powers of the earth, the separate and equal station to which the Laws of Nature and of Nature's God entitle them, a decent respect to the opinions of mankind requires that they should declare the causes which impel them to the separation. – We hold these truths to be self-evident, that all men are created equal, that they are endowed by their Creator with certain unalienable Rights, that among these rights are Life, Liberty, and the pursuit of Happiness. – That to secure these rights, Governments are instituted among Men, deriving their just powers from the consent of the governed, – That whenever any Form of Government becomes destructive of these ends, it is the Right of the People to alter or to abolish it; and institute new Government . . .

The implications of this document, conjoined with Enlightenment political thought concerning civil society, government and rights, are still struggled over, appealed to and claimed as legitimate bases for altering political associations that do not fulfil the political, economic, social and cultural aspirations of a people. As the Preamble of the US Constitution declared, 'We the People' have the right and responsibility to determine the appropriate form of popular rule. The affirmation of popular sovereignty and freedom from external domination established the consequential value of political decisions that are subject to and decided by the inhabitants of a specific territory: 'The value of national self-government is the value of entrusting the general political power over a group and its members to the group.'[21]

Just as self-determination is a key element in the US Constitution, it is also central to the United Nations Charter, which can be considered the founding instrument of the modern doctrine of self-determination. It is possible to read in the Charter's opening phrase 'We the Peoples of the United Nations' the same justification of popular sovereignty as the legitimate basis of state or government authority. This phrase underscores the importance placed on the UN's role in fostering self-determination, human rights and peace between peoples as developed in Articles 1 and 55. Article 1.2 states that the members of the UN are 'to develop friendly relations among nations based on respect for the principle of equal rights and self-deter-mination of peoples', while Article 55 declares that

> with a view to the creation of conditions of stability and well-being, which are necessary for peaceful and friendly relations among nations based on respect for the principle of equal rights and self-determination of peoples, the United Nations shall promote . . . universal respect for, and observance of, human rights and fundamental freedoms . . .

The language of the Charter presents a significant evolution of the political ideals developed during the Enlightenment, by directly linking self-determination with universal human rights and fundamental freedoms. More importantly, it also recognizes that there is an intrinsic connection between those rights and freedoms, and creating and sustaining the necessary conditions both for domestic well-being, stability and peace of peoples, and for global stability and peaceful relations between peoples.[22]

Therefore, while self-determination has been linked to the realiza-tion of human rights, particularly by decolonization movements after the Second World War, it has also been regarded as conceptually and normatively problematic, since it is a right that has been codified in international law by *established* states.[23] In the modern international system states derive their sovereignty from other states. Sovereignty is not an attribute of the state *per se*, but is attributed to the state by other states or rulers of states.[24] The rise of the nation-state and the notions of sovereignty and power associated with it in the modern international system essentially began with the Treaty of Westphalia in 1648. Within this system the claim to a right of national self-determination has been one of the most potent doctrines of the modern era, insofar as it assists in legitimating the existence of independent sovereign states.

Yet, if the right of national self-determination is a positive right, created and sustained by existing states, it becomes difficult to see how such a right can be exercised, since it would presume that states allow the secession of their territories inhabited by distinct national groups. In other words, a genuinely universal right of self-determination would require a state to recognize the legitimacy of its own dissolution. Rupert Emerson, in his book *Self-Determination Revisited in the Era of Decolonization*, nicely captures the contradiction contained in the doctrine of self-determination: 'My right to self-determination against those who oppress me is obviously unimpeachable, but your claim to exercise such a right against me is wholly inadmissible.'[25] Emerson's insight into this paradox of self-determination exemplifies the still dangerous tensions that exist between claims for self-determination and the legal sanctity of an existing territorial arrangement as embodied in a sovereign state. Political and legal thinkers who have addressed the notion of self-determination generally assume, then, that existing state arrangements serve as the ultimate precedents by which claims to self-determination are to be evaluated.

The rapid process of decolonization following the Second World War was instrumental in establishing the contemporary political and legal right that a people have to freedom from external or foreign control over their political institutions, affairs and everyday lives. This right to national self-determination was articulated in the 1960 UN Declaration on the Granting of Independence to Colonial Countries and Peoples, which states that:

1. The subjugation of peoples to alien subjugation, domination and exploitation constitutes a denial of fundamental human rights, is contrary to the Charter of the United Nations and is an impediment to the promotion of world peace and co-operation.

2. All peoples have the right to self-determination; by virtue of that right they freely determine their political status and freely pursue their economic, social and cultural development.

Several paragraphs later (para. 6), however, the Declaration asserts that 'Any attempt at the partial or total disruption of the national unity and the territorial integrity of the country is incompatible with the purposes and principles of the Charter of the United Nations'. This statement reflects the conviction within international law that 'a people's' right to self-determination is conceived within the framework of the modern sovereign state, whose integrity and unity are fundamental.[26] This approach, which favours the territorial control of existing nation-states, has led to many injustices in multi-ethnic states where governmental power is controlled and exercised by one group of people while other groups are subjugated or marginalized. In such situations human rights are often filtered through the apparatus of a state power defined by a dominant group, giving rise to a kind of 'tyranny of the majority' such as Mill warned of in *On Liberty*. Human rights then become dependent on the vicissitudes of a domestic legal-political system, giving rise to normative confusion when pleas for outside intervention are raised in the event of domestic abuses by a majority against the rights of a minority. This situation underscores some of the vulnerability of Rawls's notion of international justice, which is subordinated to the statist principles of the traditional law of nations.

A further tension is revealed, then, when we consider that the doctrine of national self-determination is connected to the principle of non-intervention, both of which ultimately derive from and protect the principle of state sovereignty. A classic definition of sovereignty states that 'there is a final and absolute political authority in the political community', which takes precedence over any other possible type of authority elsewhere.[27] The doctrine of self-determination and the principle of non-intervention are, at bottom, intended to protect all of those matters viewed as coming under the purview of the domestic jurisdiction of states.

I have also pointed out, however, that a paradox resides in the current international system: on the one hand, the principles of sovereignty, self-determination and non-intervention are regarded as necessary to constrain the 'external' power and actions of states, and thereby produce international peace and stability; on the other hand, the principles also restrict the progression of international peace and stability by placing the 'internal' power and actions of states off-limits to outside interference.[28] Yet the domestic and foreign affairs of states are not so neatly separated and when internal crises result that threaten regional or global peace and stability (or simply one particular power's supposed national interests), political contortions are often needed to justify responses such as humanitarian intervention. Indeed, the gradual influence of the idea of human rights in international relations in recent years has increased the legitimacy of intervention into the internal affairs of other states and, consequently, has challenged the conventional realist valorizations of sovereignty and individual state interests.[29]

The tension between national self-determination and the identities of those persons living within a state's territory has generated conceptual confusion between what is 'a people' and what is 'the state', and thus made the adjudication of rights and duties around self-determination ambiguous and difficult. As Hurst Hannum remarks,

> Perhaps no other contemporary norm of international law has been as vigorously promoted or widely accepted as the right of all peoples to self-determination. Yet the meaning and content of that right remain as vague and imprecise as when they were first enunciated by President Woodrow Wilson and others at Versailles.[30]

While self-determination has been held up as a fundamental right, the troubling question of 'What does self-determination mean?' still persists. Answering this question is particularly challenging when the history of implementing the right to self-determination shows that it consistently clashes with the bias towards state sovereignty that has settled into international political-legal practice. The conceptual confusion between the state as 'a legal and political organization with the power to require obedience and loyalty from its citizens' and the people 'as a community . . . whose members are bound together by a sense of solidarity, a common culture, a national consciousness' has only contributed to contradictory and divergent interpretations of the meaning of the right to self-determination and to the moral and legal evaluation of nationalistic claims.[31]

The controversies surrounding the ambiguity of the doctrine of self-determination have therefore been of special concern in the recent period that has seen a tremendous growth of ethnic nationalism.

Since the end of the cold war, new life has been given to a diverse spectrum of ethnic aspirations for nation and state building around the world. Multi-ethnic tensions across Africa, Asia and the Middle East have generated numerous conflicts fuelled by aspirations for self-determination and freedom from what are considered oppressive regimes. These regimes are often controlled by an ethnic group which has unfairly employed the institutions and apparatuses of the state for capturing power, control and resources to the detriment of other ethnic groups. Civil war, genocide, ethnic cleansing and violent suppression of minority-rights movements characterize conditions in the former Yugoslavia, Rwanda, East Timor, Kosovo, Burma, Chechnya, Armenia, Azerbaijan and Somalia, to name only a few. The forceful resurgence of ethno-national aspirations is the contemporary stage where the drama of self-determination is once again being played out, especially when the right to self-determination clashes with the rights of state sovereignty and the internationally recognized moratorium against secession.

Within the contemporary international system and the structure of international law, discussions concerning international justice generally make reference to the state as the political and legal agent and representative of the citizens of the state. As James Crawford argues,

> [r]eferences to the State, the basic unit of international law, involve a reference to the social fact of a territorial community of persons with a certain political organization, in other words, a reference to a collectivity. In this sense, international law rules that confer rights on States confer collective rights.[32]

But interpretations of international law have also established a rule that, because states are the political and legal agents of a community of people and collective rights are first conferred on the state, the government's interests and rights stand first even if the government's actions diverge from the popular interests or demands of the citizens. Thus, the tensions unique to the concept of self-determination are especially apparent between what has come to be delineated as the external and internal dimensions of self-determination. While the external dimension defines the right of 'a people' (state) to be free from outside interference, thereby demarcating certain aspects of relations between peoples or relations between states, the internal dimension implies the right of 'a people' (ethno-national group) to assert its will over and, if need be, against the government that supposedly represents its interests. The conventional law of nations, as well as Rawls's account of international justice, is prepared to recognize only external self-determination within the modern context of sovereign states. Yet contemporary world events have increasingly focused on issues of internal self-determination, particularly in the case of minority groups or indigenous peoples within existing but contested territorial arrangements. In each case, however, the right of self-determination is invoked on behalf of 'a people'.

One of the most pressing of current problems, then, is that the right of a people to self-determination lacks a precise definition of what constitutes 'a people', especially in our contemporary multi-ethnic (or multicultural) societies. For many political and legal theorists the operative assumption has been that 'a people' shared a common political identity. This assumption is found in the interpretation of Articles 1 and 55 of the UN Charter by the German jurist Hans Kelsen. Kelsen leaned towards interpreting the term 'peoples' as simply referring to the state, that is, the national government.[33] Kelsen and others contributed to equating a political-legal symmetry between the state and the people, where the two terms were understood as being synonymous and interchangeable. In many regards, this interpretation can be understood as an interpolation of the Enlightenment political principle of the popular sovereignty of citizens as the ground of state legitimacy and authority. From this perspective, it is plausible to argue that the people are coterminous with the state. This argument supports the conventional law of nations approach to international affairs adopted by Rawls in *A Theory of Justice* and, as we will see, in *The Law of Peoples*.

Yet is the identification of a nation-state with a people either an accurate reflection of today's multi-ethnic societies or a viable political, philosophical and legal ideal? Consider, for example, that the political reality in many, especially postcolonial, societies is that the definition of a people is grounded on an exclusivist sense of community that has led to ethnically based definitions of sovereignty. Ethnic sovereignty is then linked to a contiguous political ideology that is understood in terms of some type of ethnic nationalism, which usually identifies the 'members of an ethnically defined national grouping' as sharing common 'physical characteristics, culture, religion, language, and . . . ancestry'.[34] Yet, if the right to internal self-determination is reduced to exclusivist ethnic definitions of sovereignty, it might not be possible for external self-determination to succeed plausibly within the established international system since that system is threatened by a state's domestic instability.[35] The fact of pluralism, when given the broad sweep implied by the doctrine of national self-determination, thus challenges the simplistic picture of international society endorsed by Rawls. In the postcolonial and pluralist world, self-determination does not simply buttress the territorial borders of established autonomous states against outside interference; instead, it can be the very means to challenge the legitimacy of statehood.[36]

Recognition of this dilemma raises the question of how states might harmonize domestic rules and institutions with international norms and practices. In order to effect such harmonization states may have to trade the traditional concept of sovereignty for a more integrated association with international institutions and regimes, subordinating state autonomy to the ideals and values needed for the cooperative pursuit of collective or global good. For example, Pogge speaks of 'another way for a shared institutional scheme to emerge and be sustained even while its participants have divergent interests and values'. In this alternative scheme, Pogge thinks that the 'central idea is to seek institutions that are based not upon free bargaining informed by the changeable distribution of power but upon some values that are genuinely shared'.[37] Pogge refers to such shared values as 'ultimate' in the sense that they are to be embodied in the institutions regulating the public, political interactions among participants. Since those interactions are, under this scheme, interactions among persons rather than states one need not fear that the exchanges between nations (or cultures) might be well-ordered while their domestic exchanges are not.

Pogge suggests that the predicament confronting the possibility of generating just interstate relations is not that there is no, or too little, value overlap among diverse populations. The problem is that shared values generally have played no role in the standing international institutions, given the realist *modus vivendi* framework and its focus on nationalism and the legitimation of state sovereignty. Unfortunately, Pogge says little about those presumed shared values. Like Rawls, however, Pogge points out that ultimately what is being sought is an overlapping (not strict) consensus upon public (not all-pervasive or comprehensive) values, that is, upon those values which have to do with other persons and with other persons as a matter of justice.[38] For

Pogge, the prerequisite of the embodiment of shared values into 'institutional fixed points' that stand above prudential bargaining (where everything is negotiable) is the moral acceptance on the part of all societies of the 'continued existence of one another and of the values central to their domestic social contracts'.[39] This prerequisite is what Pogge calls the moral acceptance of international pluralism.

Pogge, following Rawls's own example, compares international pluralism within the *modus vivendi* framework to the relations between the plural Christian faiths after the Reformation. Each side long sought to reunify the Church on its own terms, sought to prevail over the other, until a fragile bargain was struck (following the dictum *cuius regio eius religio*, 'each lord may force his religion upon his subjects without outside interference'). This bargain was gradually transformed into a shared value commitment of religious toleration with deference to the individual's freedom of conscience. 'The decisive condition for an analogous transformation in our current world', writes Pogge, is widespread acceptance of international pluralism, 'the idea that knowledgeable and intelligent persons of good will may reasonably favor different forms of (national) social organization'.[40] Yet might it be possible that widespread acceptance of international pluralism can be at odds with an interest in the protection of equal individual freedom and human rights? Is national or cultural autonomy reducible to agreement of a society's main institutions with appropriate principles of international justice?

According to Pogge, wanting one's own political ideal to prevail only contributes to our *modus vivendi* predicament, that is, a lack of assurance on the part of others that one is not seeking to destroy their domestic institutions and, thus, an analogous desire to prevail politically on the part of others as well. International acceptance of international pluralism is a step towards solving this assurance problem: it allows value clusters 'with their coordinated national forms of regime' to be morally accepted and protected against extinction. It also makes possible for every party, once they know that their existence and that of their constitutions are no longer at issue, to focus on the shared global scheme and order their preferences concerning that scheme according to how well it reflects their own values, not simply their survival. As Pogge recognizes, this is a realist argument: it is for the sake of one's own values that one should accept a scheme reflecting a core of overlapping values and thus that one should accept a modification of one's values in the direction of greater mutual tolerance.

Pogge remarks that the international acceptance of international pluralism is not tantamount to agnosticism with respect to the justice of national institutions; it is equivalent to the acceptance of disagreements as *reasonable* disagreements. In a reasonable disagreement, other persons cannot beforehand be assumed 'irrational' or 'deluded' and one cannot assume that one stands to learn nothing from the variety of national regimes and ways of life. Still, the examples of reasonable disagreements at the global level that Pogge offers – whether the means of production should be owned by national governments, private owners, or workers; whether democracy is best achieved through a single party or a multi-party system; whether civil and political or social and economic rights are more important in the reform of institutions – are not the only disagreements that might be encountered. What should be done about regimes that do not accept any democratic form of political participation, or those where the bulk of the population is economically deprived, or where human rights are violated? Does a society whose constitution codifies that only certain classes – religiously or racially defined for example – are to have full rights still count as a society to be respected because of the centrality to them of the values of their social contracts? Can we be sure that such social contracts have much to do with widely and reasonably held values or only with the values of certain élites? These questions will receive more extensive treatment in Chapter 4.

The general point to take from all of this is that the current interstate system does not live up to rigorous standards of global justice. The criticisms being made here, however, are not to be understood as a recommendation that states be abolished (but nor do I foreclose that possibility). Rather, I am arguing that the core of the problem is that state interests and domestic justice are too quickly given priority over global interests and global justice, defined in terms of everyone in the world. This can be seen not only in current interstate practices but also in Rawls's account of international justice, which considers international justice as a kind of afterthought to domestic justice and thereby replicates the realist view of international relations. While Rawls considers international justice to be justice among states, I think that international justice ought to be at least equally about justice among persons, irrespective of what historically contingent state a person happens to be a member of at present.

A further point I am trying to make, then, is that a theory of international justice cannot simply represent or model the kind of international society which currently exists; it ought to say something significant about what kind of international society *might* exist, by contesting existing principles and presenting alternatives. Although I think Rawls fails, in *A Theory of Justice*, to take this further step, the question remains open as to whether his fundamental account of justice can be globally extended in some other way. Is it possible to strike a different balance between domestic justice and global justice than Rawls? In particular, is it possible to offer an account of international justice without it having to follow upon a prior account of domestic justice? In the following section I will argue that the possibility does exist, but only if we take the primary subject of international justice to be persons, not states.

Towards global justice

The discussion carried out thus far of Rawls and international justice has been critical of the view articulated in *A Theory of Justice*. The criticisms advanced, however, have sought to evaluate Rawls's description of international justice from the point of view of Rawls's own theory of domestic justice, especially the centrality accorded there to the moral status of persons and their basic rights and liberties. Now I would like to consider in more detail the need and process of working towards a theory of global justice structured by Rawls's two principles of justice as fairness.

There is some question of whether and how successfully Rawls's two principles of justice can be globally extended. Charles Beitz, following Brian Barry and Thomas Scanlon, argues that the principles can be extended as long as the model of the hypothetical social contract is altered somewhat.[41] First, national boundaries, not being coextensive with the scope of global cooperation, have no fundamental moral significance and therefore do not mark the limits of the obligations of justice. Second, then, it cannot be assumed that the parties to the original position know that they belong to a specific national community and are choosing principles for a nation-state; the veil of ignorance applies to matters of nationality and the principles of justice must be chosen to apply globally. If Rawls's arguments for the two principles are correct, 'there is no reason to think that the content of the principles would change as a result of enlarging the scope of the original position', writes Beitz. 'In particular, if the difference principle . . . would be chosen in the domestic original position, it would be chosen in the global original position as well.'[42] In Beitz's opinion there is no reason to assume that membership in the least-advantaged group will be coextensive with membership in any particular state. Thus, the parties in the international original position are treated as moral persons and not as existing states or representative of states. Starting from this position allows for the possibility of a single global original position rather than the two-stage original position (domestic and then international) offered by Rawls.

If this argument is correct, that is, if the notion of a scheme of global cooperation and a conception of justice given that scheme of cooperation are sufficient to justify modified Rawlsian global justice, then we are led to support a quite different conclusion than that drawn from Rawls. Rawlsian principles of global justice would guarantee to every person in the world the same set of rights, as well as the means to make those rights worthy, irrespective of nationality and culture and of whether they are citizens or outsiders. As citizens of the world all persons would be entitled to the same rights. The universality of human rights would thus be grounded on considerations of a cosmopolitan version of Rawlsian global justice. From a cosmopolitan point of view, all humans are citizens of a single moral order upon which the demands of justice, including global human rights and obligations, are based. Whereas Rawlsian *international* justice would be concerned first with the interests of peoples defined as nation-states, Rawlsian *global* justice would be concerned first with the interests of all individual persons regarded as free and equal and possessing moral powers. The moral claims and interests of states – assuming that such forms of organization would be the outcome of a global original position – would then have to be justified as derivative and not asserted as foundational. Rawlsian global justice thus takes a universalist stance with regard to the moral interests of every person. A cosmopolitan conception of Rawlsian global justice would be shorn of its realist assumptions favouring the interests of states. In the global original position, the parties represent all persons as members of the same world, and take all persons to be the focus of equal moral concern. Any basic structure derived from this original position must satisfy the cosmopolitan criterion of justice.[43]

We have seen that Pogge is also concerned to specify an account of global justice that is better suited to the purpose of recognizing and respecting the moral interests, especially the rights and liberties, of all persons. As discussed in the previous section, Pogge presents a theory of global justice that is informed by, yet different from, Rawls's idea of international justice as presented in *A Theory of Justice*. Pogge claims that, according to his theory:

> [T]he globalized first principle might be viewed as requiring a thin set of basic rights and liberties (analogous to the Universal Declaration of Human Rights . . .), which each national society could, in light of its national conception of domestic justice, 'inflate' and specify into its own bill of rights . . . Similarly, while the global second principle would constrain how societies may arrange their economies, these constraints would be less stringent than Rawls's requirement [in *A Theory of Justice*] that each society must satisfy the difference principle internally.[44]

As the above quotation makes clear, Pogge's emphasis on the moral salience of and the international responsibility for the global basic structure amounts to a defence and development of the Universal Declaration of Human Rights in its most cosmopolitan reading, specifically, as stated in Article 28: 'Everyone is entitled to a social and international order in which the rights and freedoms set forth in this Declaration can be fully realized.' The cosmopolitan order envisioned by Article 28 affirms the existence of fundamental rights and liberties for all persons wherever they may be.

However, a number of pressing questions remain as yet unanswered in our discussion of Rawlsian global justice. Can the description of the original position remain the same at both the domestic and global level? Is the argument that persons are free and equal at the global level reasonable or can it be made reasonable? Are the ideals of a moral community of human beings, that is, of cosmopolitanism, reasonable among and within a framework of nation-states? These questions are significant because it is my intention to defend the applicability and workability of Rawls's modified criterion as regards the global basic structure and its participants. Pogge partly addresses the questions raised above while responding to several objections put forward against the ideal of a Rawlsian world order. Those objections assert that there are special factors in the international realm that make it inappropriate to apply Rawls's criterion to the global structure.

One common objection asserts that the global system is so marginally well-ordered in Rawls's sense that one cannot apply to it a criterion appropriate only to the developed democracies of North America and Europe.[45] In response, it should be remembered that Rawls's notion of a well-ordered society is not descriptive but normative. This means that, when the parties to the original position are said to be choosing a criterion for a well-ordered society, that criterion is supposed to harmonize with and guide towards an ideal of society which, in Rawls's words, 'it seems one would, on due reflection, wish to live in and want to shape our interests and characters'.[46] It does not mean that the criterion is only applicable to actual well-ordered societies, for there is good reason to think that are no such societies in reality. What is important, though, is the normative thrust of the ideal theory Rawls's project offers. Rawls's ideal theory retains a Kantian emphasis on the demands of moral reason and not solely on any empirical fact. In this sense, it is misguided to maintain that a Rawlsian criterion of global justice must change in response to different, arbitrary global conditions. Rawlsian ideal theory suggests that the duty of agents is to act as if the economic, political and legal institutions that one would think, upon due reflection, ought to exist in a just world actually were in place, while also seeking to create those institutions both domestically and globally. The normative ideal provides a regulative principle for the practical pursuit of global justice.

A second, more powerful objection is one that is based on the fact of cultural pluralism. The ideal of a Rawlsian global scheme, the objection goes, may cohere with the traditions and values of one particular culture but it is inappropriate due to the existing diversity of traditions and moral judgements across the world's cultures. If this is so, Rawlsian institutional reform at the global level might well require the imperialistic displacement or at the least the reorganization of cultures in the name of our own values.

I think that, in order to respond to this objection, it is first necessary to present the Rawlsian conception of global justice under the appropriate rationales. Pogge holds, for instance, that Rawls's reluctance to globalize his conception of justice affects only one aspect of such globalization; namely, it reflects the belief that the domestic institutional organization and the assessment of the justice of such organization should perhaps be left to the members of communities whose cultures are different. Yet such an alternative is not available with respect to the global structure. The question of how the global structure should be reformed and assessed cannot be evaded because of the unavoidability of global interaction, nor can it be adequately dealt with except through a background conception of global justice. Rawls's criterion when globalized is not a politically neutral criterion equally congenial to every value and every culture, and thus to every particular form of domestic institutional organization. But, then again, there are no politically neutral criteria of justice. As Rawls himself recognizes, the idea of institutional arrangements under which *all* values and judgements would flourish is an impossibility. Any global scheme can be opposed on the grounds that it is inhospitable to some other way of political life. The question then, though Pogge does not clearly state it, is whether there is a better alternative than a cosmopolitan conception of global justice that takes into account the fact of global interdependence, the importance of global rights and obligations and the ideal of moral persons as free and equal. I believe that there is not a better alternative and that universal respect for all persons as moral beings must provide the basis for a satisfactory scheme of global justice.

Another way of responding to the second objection is to contend that a 'degrees' approach to the legitimation of Rawlsian justice within different communities might be appropriate. Thus, as Pogge points out, many of the protestations against pursuing supposedly culturally biased ideals of justice in the international arena come from advantaged members of Western culture and communities and, one may add, the advantaged members of most communities. Similar protestations generally do not come from those actually living in hunger or oppression. This is not to deny that intercultural diversity in moral judgements may be great; it is simply to point out that one does not know how great it is. Any national government, taken as the representative of 'a people', clearly will be violating rather than expressing the different moral judgements of its own various communities, when it engages in the detention and torture of political prisoners or the denial of civil and political liberties.

Moreover, even communities endorsing different political judgements and different criteria of justice regarding a more just world might still agree on the Rawlsian conception as the first step on the long road to global institutional reorganization. According to Pogge, this possibility is confirmed by the fact that some Third World proposals for global institutional reforms could arguably be favoured by Rawlsian principles. Ironically, such proposals have been resisted by the West on the grounds of toleration of diversity. But resisting reforms demanded by justice as we ourselves understand it, on the ground that others do not really or fully share our convictions, is to take a position which acquiesces to the preservation of existing advantages. At minimum, then, the globalization of Rawls's conception must be the normative benchmark in the assessment of government policies, norms and institutions.

A further response to the objection based on diversity is to argue that the proposal of Rawlsian global justice under appropriate rationales will be followed by consensus. Despite the great intercultural diversity of considered judgements on justice due to the diversity of histories and traditions, what matters at the global level, as at the domestic level, is convergence upon the Rawlsian criterion itself. Such a convergence need not require a particular derivation of or rationale for the criterion. What the objector has to show is more than diversity of considered judgements; he has to show that agreement on and convergence around the criterion of global justice is in fact impossible. It is highly unlikely that this can be done.

In addition, the proposal of global justice can appeal to the notion of reflective equilibrium. Rawls's conception of justice when globalized is, I think, among the best proposals in the light of which an international, cross-cultural moral dialogue on justice can be initiated. The idea of dialogue implies that one deals with objections and counter-proposals from others as they arise; it also implies self-criticism, as the dialogue itself broadens the vision of its participants and requires them to accommodate others and the relevant facts, making their political convictions less parochial.[47] The dialogue on a substantive moral issue of common concern will require others, perhaps including non-liberal disputants, to work out their conceptions of justice and clearly expound the grounds of their disagreement. It is possible, of course, that disagreement will persist and that a global overlapping consensus on Rawlsian global justice will not be reached. However, as Pogge notes, the

> fact of disagreement is no reason not to act in the light of whatever (factual and) moral beliefs we now think are best supported. Our considered judgements support a conception of justice whose scope is universal, even though its present appeal is not.[48]

The point to take from this is that cultural traditions, public institutions and considered judgements have no ultimate moral sanctity based only on their existence; rather, their continued existence requires justification and their value is open to critical scrutiny and change.

The final and probably the most important response to be made is that a globalized version of Rawls's conception of justice offers a good deal of flexibility for incorporating cultural diversity and various forms of association. Unlike the two readings (R_1 and R_2) that Pogge identifies in *A Theory of Justice*, the parties to a global original position are not constrained by any prior Rawlsian criterion of domestic justice. The global parties can *in a single global session* decide how much room to leave for differences in national conceptions of justice and in domestic institutional arrangements. For instance, the globalized first principle of justice may be viewed as requiring the 'thin' set of rights and liberties embodied in the Universal Declaration of Human Rights, which each national society can then augment in its own bill of rights in light of its domestic conception of justice. And the globalized second principle of justice, though constraining how societies may arrange their economies so as not to affect the globally worst share of primary goods, may still allow choices among more-or-less egalitarian forms of domestic organization. As Pogge argues:

> The resulting global institutional ideal would then allow each society a good deal of choice as regards its internal practices (and moral principles), so long as such choices are supported by most of its citizens and are consistent with the basic rights of all human beings, citizens as well as outsiders . . . What matters is that by balancing the liberty interest in collective [domestic] autonomy against other liberty interests, [the globalized conception] goes beyond R_1 and R_2 in the liberal quest to allow for 'opposing religious, philosophical, and moral convictions'.[49]

Pogge's globalization argument amends not only the scope but also the content of Rawls's conception of justice as fairness. Part of amending Rawls's principles of justice consists in specifying the first principle so that it forbids radical social and economic inequalities (avoidably involving extreme poverty).[50] In other words, human rights to a minimum of social and economic benefits are incorporated into the first principle.

As discussed in Chapter 2, lexical priority is defended in Rawls's special conception of justice; the maximin criterion consists of two criteria governing, respectively, those aspects of the basic structure that define and secure the equal liberties of citizenship, and those that produce social and economic inequalities. Each scheme is to receive two scores based, again respectively, on the worst position it generates in terms of rights and liberties and on the worst socio-economic position. Weights are assigned to these scores to make possible the ranking of alternative schemes; in the special conception first score differentials always override second score differentials. Rawls's rationale for prioritizing the satisfaction of the first principle over the second is

> that the interests of liberty . . . become stronger as the conditions for the exercise of the equal freedoms are more fully realized. Beyond some point it becomes and then remains irrational . . . to acknowledge a lesser liberty for the sake of greater material means and amenities of office. (1971: 542)

Underlying Rawls's lexical priority is his distinction between liberty and its worth. The goods under the two principles make different contributions, according to Rawls, to the same supreme value of liberty. The goods under the first principle spell out effective legal freedom or simply 'liberty', while the goods under the second principle (plus effective legal freedom) spell out the worth of this liberty. The question of compensating for a lesser than equal liberty does not arise; that of compensating for a lesser worth of liberty does since, according to Rawls, the capacity of the least fortunate would be even less were they not to accept inequalities whenever the difference principle is satisfied. The usefulness of liberty is specified in terms of an index of primary goods regulated by the second principle. According to the two principles, then, the basic structure is to be arranged so as to maximize the worth of the equal basic liberties to the least advantaged. The demands of social justice reveal the need to include among the rights and liberties protecting the freedom and integrity of the person 'rights to a socioeconomic position that is sufficient to meet the basic social and economic needs of any normal human participant in the relevant social system'.[51]

Pogge's considerations of Rawls's position on international justice are helpful in allowing us to recognize the deficiencies of that position, and also offer us some means of improving upon those deficiencies. It might be further argued, however, that a revised cosmopolitan conception of Rawlsian global justice such as that which I have advocated here – understood as a global scheme that regards every human being as a citizen of a just world community in which all persons have a common moral status – requires domestic liberal democracy of a Rawlsian kind. By this I mean that there exists an equal and quite demanding set of rights, liberties and opportunities for all citizens; those rights and liberties take priority over claims of the general good and of perfectionist values; and also that there are measures ensuring both citizens as well as outsiders the all-purpose means so that those rights and liberties are effectively realized. If it is the case that the effective realization of universal human rights requires a liberal democratic organization of society, is it possible to articulate a scheme of global justice that allows for significant differences in domestic political and institutional frameworks? A question that remains to be examined further, then, is whether the conception of global justice presented here is compatible with the existence of radically different social and political systems that are not committed to the values of democracy and equal rights and liberties. It is to this question that I turn in Chapter 4.

4 • The Problem of Human Rights

The enormous importance of the human rights question derives from the fact that it is closely linked to the two fundamental problems of our times: democracy and peace. (Norberto Bobbio, *The Age of Rights*, 63)

Looking over the arguments of the previous chapter, one might be led to wonder if Rawls's political philosophy has anything of real worth to offer a theory of universal human rights. We started with his minimal extension of justice as fairness to the international level, which, resulting in a traditional law of nations framework, fails to contain a robust human rights principle. Then we saw that Rawls's account of international justice is unnecessarily weak, because of both the priority he assigns to the domestic original position over the international original position and the analogy he draws between individuals and states. Finally, Rawls's conception of justice as fairness seems unable to provide for a conception of global justice unless the priority he gives to the domestic original position is eliminated, a move Rawls is not inclined to make. So what is there of merit in Rawls's work when it comes to prescribing a principle of universal human rights?

In what follows I will try to answer this question through a close examination of what Rawls has to say specifically about human rights within the context of social justice at both the domestic and international levels. In his most recently published work, *The Law of Peoples* (1999), based on an earlier (1993) essay with the same title, Rawls's main task is to respond to some of the criticisms his theory of justice has received from those concerned with the international aspects of social justice, and in particular with universal human rights. Rawls claims that a general liberal theory of justice may be extended internationally and form the basis for a universally recognized basic human rights minimum. Additionally, Rawls suggests that this scheme of international justice, called the 'law of peoples', is an improvement on other liberal theories dealing with human rights because it would be acceptable to non-liberal societies as well as to liberal societies. For Rawls, this acceptability is important because it would help maintain the internal sovereignty of states and thereby contribute to national security.

I will begin this chapter with an examination of Rawls's elaboration of the law of peoples. Rawls utilizes the familiar contractarian choice model of the original position as the procedure with which to construct his newly proposed principles of international justice. He attempts to show that, by a gradual extension of the original position through several stages, the perceived shortcomings of his earlier sparse remarks on international justice would be corrected and improved upon. I argue not only that Rawls's attempt to extend justice as fairness into a global setting goes wrong, but more importantly that his treatment of human rights leads him to the verge of a cultural relativism that is not able to support efforts to strengthen international human rights norms.

This argument is developed in the next section by pointing out two ways that Rawls's theory fails as an account of universal human rights, that is, rights which are the same for all persons everywhere. First, I argue that the theory fails because it assigns different sets of rights to different societies in an attempt to accommodate cultural pluralism. In restricting the set of rights available to persons in non-liberal societies, Rawls undermines his claim that liberal and non-liberal peoples alike would accept the same law of peoples.

Second, I argue that the theory fails because Rawls asserts that persons need not be regarded as free and equal in non-liberal or hierarchical societies. However, since the rights derived in the first liberal original position and those of the 1948 Universal Declaration of Human Rights *are* based on the ideal of persons as free and equal, it is again unlikely that hierarchical societies would in fact endorse the same law of peoples as promulgated by liberal societies. Based on this possibility I suggest that the principle of respect for human rights which Rawls claims is inherent to the law of peoples would require a cosmopolitan ideal of global justice as well as the transformation of hierarchical societies into egalitarian liberal democracies.

This last point raises another issue for discussion. Recent global political events point towards the need to give serious philosophical attention to the relationship between human rights, democracy and peace. While each of these ideals has independently enjoyed expanding recognition since the end of the Second World War, there has also been widespread reluctance to assert a necessary linkage between them. Much of the reluctance stems from the persistent tension that exists in the international system between the universality of human rights and the traditional primacy of state sovereignty. Although the UDHR seeks to establish minimum standards of treatment for the citizens of all states, the claims of sovereignty – including those to non-democratic and illiberal forms of government – have often trumped the practical implementation of rights intended to guarantee those standards. True, the end of the cold war and the decline of some authoritarian regimes in Eastern Europe, Africa, Latin America and Asia have generated greater willingness to speak of the benefits gained by linking democracy and human rights. Yet political reality continues to fall well short of the assertion contained in Article 21 of the UDHR that 'The will of the people shall be the basis of the authority of government'.

Given this situation, I also use the analysis of the law of peoples to argue for the more normatively ambitious claim that international human rights and democratic government require one another. Without denying that this claim entails serious practical and theoretical difficulties that cannot be fully addressed, much less resolved, here, my position is that both democracy and human rights are at risk unless each includes the other. Moreover, it is my contention that world peace provides the substantive context for promoting such deep linkages between democracy and human rights. In the end, just democratic governments and sustainable human rights cannot be realized without stable peace, and a stable peace is made all the more possible by an international system composed of democratic governments committed to human rights for all.

In the following section I further pursue the concept of a human right to peace. Recent years have seen increased debate about the contributions that human rights make to the creation of conditions of peace. However, less attention has been paid to the claim that peace itself is a genuine human right. Whereas some critics argue that a focus on rights results in an overly formal juridical account of peace at the expense of a more robust notion of positive peace, others contend that a legal framework of rights is all that is needed to eliminate violent conflict. In this section I strike a position between these two arguments and articulate a normative defence of the human right to peace embedded within a broader discourse of social justice. I do so by demonstrating that a right to peace is a genuine human right because it satisfies appropriate justificatory tests, including those concerning its scope, the duties it generates and its economic feasibility.

The final section draws together the arguments advanced in Chapters 3 and 4, and proposes a framework for cosmopolitan principles of global justice that builds on the ideas presented in *The Law of Peoples*. This framework includes a strongly universalist principle of human rights, which would require the law of peoples to recognize and support equally the rights of all people.

The argument of the law of peoples

In *The Law of Peoples*, Rawls responds to criticisms of his perceived neglect of international justice in his earlier work. Rawls states that his proposed law of peoples is 'a political conception of right and justice that applies to the principles and norms of international law and practice' (1999: 3). International law is the existing, positive, legal order understood by Rawls according to the law of nations perspective endorsed in *A Theory of Justice*. The law of peoples, as Rawls presents it, is the family of political concepts and principles specifying the content of a liberal conception of justice worked up so as to apply to and evaluate the mutual relations between domestic societies (1999: 3–4). Rawls's idea is to pair liberal ideas of justice, similar to but more general than those of justice as fairness, with the law and the political practices of the international society of peoples, and see whether the latter can be legitimated. In so doing, Rawls's aim is twofold. First, he wants to give an account of the role of human rights and the form of toleration of non-liberal societies that liberalism must extend by means of the law of peoples. Second, he wants to prove that his law of peoples is acceptable to both liberal and 'decent' non-liberal peoples; he wants to prove, in other words, that a society need not be liberal or democratic in order to respect human rights.

Rawls identifies a political conception of international justice as having the following three features (1993: 220 n. 2):

(1) it is framed to apply to basic political, economic, and social institutions; in the case of domestic society, to its basic structure, in the present case to the law and practices of the society of political peoples;

(2) it is presented independently of any particular comprehensive religious, philosophical, or moral doctrine, and though it may be derived from or related to several such doctrines, it is not worked out in that way;

(3) its content is expressed in terms of certain fundamental ideas seen as implicit in the public political culture of a liberal society.

For Rawls, the process of extending liberal ideas of political justice to yield a law of peoples follows from the constructivist approach of the social contract tradition. As in the case of the principles of justice for the basic structure of liberal domestic society, the principles of the law of peoples must be constructed by way of a reasonable procedure in which rational parties would adopt and assent to those principles. Rawls states that the choice procedure is to be modified in order to include the 'Society of Peoples', by which he means 'all those peoples who follow the ideals and principles of the Law of Peoples in their mutual relations' (1999: 3). Thus, the principles chosen must be endorsed on due reflection by the agents to whom they are supposed to apply, in this case 'peoples'. Rawls explains that he uses the term 'peoples' to refer to 'persons and their dependents seen as a corporate body and as organized by their political institutions, which establish the powers of government' (1993: 221, n. 5).

The question that motivates *The Law of Peoples* is, then, how a workable political conception of justice can be applied to the international system, without requiring that all societies be liberal or democratic. Such a concession is necessary, Rawls contends, because the predominant realism of the existing world order privileges state sovereignty. The challenge, of course, is how to reconcile strong state autonomy with the moral obligations generated by human rights. To meet this challenge Rawls envisions a global 'original position' in which representatives of liberal states deliberate in order to select the appropriate principles of justice, first, for themselves domestically and, second, for the international political society of liberal states. The principles derived from this contractual procedure would, Rawls contends, be endorsed on due reflection by the agents to whom they are supposed to apply, in this case liberal 'peoples'.

Although Rawls claims to make a distinction between peoples (or nations) and states, he specifies that the terms of the law of peoples can be accepted and observed only through the exercise of the rights and capacities belonging to states. Peoples are understood by Rawls to refer to collective entities organized through a system of state structures. This is significant because Rawls argues that states are the only actors with the legitimate authority to develop and agree to the law of peoples. Rawls's definition of what constitutes a people in this way approximates to his use of nation-states as the representing parties in the international original position presented in *A Theory of Justice*. Yet this statist framework tends to conflate peoples and states, with the result that state interests potentially can be pursued to the prejudice of individual human rights. Thus, while Rawls begins by rightly assuming no strict correspondence between peoples and states, he ends by subordinating peoples to the organs of the state, seeing them as virtually analogous. Some problems presented by this analogy were discussed in Chapter 3.

Given that perfect isolation is a thing of the past, Rawls notes, every society must have conceptions of how it is related to other societies and how it must conduct itself with respect to them; every society must have principles and ideals that guide its foreign policies towards other peoples. The question for a liberal society is how a conception similar to justice as fairness can be extended to cover that liberal society's relations with both liberal and non-liberal societies and yield a law of peoples that is 'reasonable'. For in the absence of that extension the liberal conception of justice would be historicist, applying only to similar, liberal societies. Rawls suggests that the way to proceed is to defend a constructivist liberal doctrine that is universal in reach, in the sense of giving principles for the most comprehensive of subjects, that is, the society of peoples. Its authority rests on the principles of practical reason adjusted to apply to the subject at hand and on the fact that it can be endorsed upon due reflection by those to whom the principles apply.

The procedure that Rawls proposes to extend the liberal ideas of justice to yield the law of peoples has two stages. The first stage, which includes three steps, is that of ideal or strict compliance theory, and the second stage is that of non-ideal theory. The first step in the first stage of ideal theory is for a liberal society to choose its conception of justice at the domestic level. The second step is to prove that the original position is a device of representation for the case of different and well-ordered *liberal* democratic peoples at the law of peoples level. This amounts to showing that, similar to the account of international justice given in *A Theory of Justice*, representatives of liberal societies in the original position adopt a law of peoples whose content turns out to be almost identical to the standing principles of international law.

The third step in the first stage of ideal theory is to specify the requirements of well-orderedness for *non-liberal* yet decent societies.

This consists of demonstrating that the original position is also a device of representation when used to adopt a law of peoples among what Rawls calls 'hierarchical peoples', and of showing that representatives of hierarchical peoples in the original position would adopt the same law of peoples as that adopted by liberal peoples. Notice that the original position is used only once, at the law of peoples level, for decent hierarchical societies. Rawls contends that 'an original position argument for domestic justice is a liberal idea' and therefore is inapplicable to the case of domestic justice in a decent hierarchical regime (1999: 70).

The second stage of non-ideal theory addresses two actual conditions of states that prevent acceptance of the law of peoples. The first condition is non-compliance, or the simple refusal to comply with the law of peoples, and the second concerns unfavourable historical, economic and social conditions which burden a state so drastically that it is unable to establish any just or decent institutions. The discussion that follows will incorporate some features found in non-ideal theory, while focusing primarily on the issues surrounding ideal theory.

Since we are familiar with the original position as it applies to the domestic level of a liberal society, we can omit discussion of the first step of ideal theory. The second step in Rawls's ideal theory, then, is to demonstrate that the original position is a device of representation for the case of different and well-ordered liberal peoples taken together. Rawls adds that three requirements are essential to setting up this initial original position: (1) the representatives of liberal societies are symmetrically and equally situated; (2) the representatives are to choose among principles for the law of peoples by reference to the interests of their democratic societies; and (3) the representatives do not know certain details (such as the size and population of their territories, the relative strength of the people they represent, the amount of their natural resources and their level of development). Given these requirements, citizens of different liberal democratic societies would agree that the original position models fair conditions under which representatives of societies are to specify a law of liberal peoples (1999: 30–3).

Rawls argues that liberal ideas of justice contain three important elements: (1) a list of basic rights, liberties and opportunities; (2) a priority for those freedoms, especially with respect to claims of the general good and of perfectionist values in general; and (3) measures ensuring each citizen all-purpose means of making those freedoms effective. However, Rawls excludes from the more general liberal idea of justice upon which the law of peoples is to be constructed the strong egalitarian features of his concept of justice as fairness, namely, the principles of the fair value of the political liberties and of fair equality of opportunity, and the difference principle (1993: 51–2).

This contractual procedure is then repeated by non-liberal states with respect to principles of international, but not domestic, justice. The extended contractual procedure for defining the principles of international justice is carried out in order to ascertain whether non-liberal states would accept the same principles as liberal states. Rawls argues that non-liberal states of a certain type would accept the same principles; these states Rawls refers to as 'decent'. More will be said below on these non-liberal states. As a result, he suggests that international consensus can then be achieved on the following principles of justice, or 'law of peoples', between liberal and decent non-liberal states (1999: 37):[1]

1. Peoples are free and independent, and their freedom and independence is to be respected by other peoples.
2. Peoples are to observe treaties and undertakings.
3. Peoples are equal and are parties to the agreements that bind them.
4. Peoples are to observe a duty of non-intervention.
5. Peoples have the right of self-defense but no right to instigate war for reasons other than self-defense.
6. Peoples are to honor human rights.
7. Peoples are to observe certain specified restrictions on the conduct of war.
8. Peoples have a duty to assist other peoples living under unfavorable conditions that prevent their having a just or decent political and social regime.

Given agreement on the principles of the law of peoples, Rawls argues that a 'Society of Peoples' composed of liberal and non-liberal but decent peoples will be formed. The idea of this Society of Peoples is 'realistically utopian' insofar as it follows from principles of international relations and cooperation that can be reasonably affirmed by the diverse peoples of a pluralistic world (1999: 6). Consequently, even though peoples are to honour human rights, Rawls frames the law of peoples in such a way that the standard sovereignty rights of traditional international law remain intact.

It is worthwhile to note that, in many respects, the law of peoples devised by Rawls is similar to the law of nations (*ius gentium*) that Kant develops in order to identify the just arrangement of international society. There are significant differences as well, however, most importantly the more radical transition from the law of nations to cosmopolitan law (*ius cosmopoliticum*) which Kant advocates, but Rawls does not.[2] In his account of public right, Kant approaches the issue of international justice in the first instance by way of domestic or civil right, followed by international right (the law of nations) and then cosmopolitan right.

The Kantian law of nations arises from the international society composed by agreements between sovereign liberal and non-liberal states that are intended to regulate their dealings with one another. The idea here is that the law of nations is generated by the efforts of independent states to overcome to some degree the state of nature and war that exists internationally. The law of nations is constituted by a set of rules made and observed by pre-existing states, that is, states that have domestically or internally left the state of nature. These rules then define how states are related to one another and how their actions are to be constrained in pursuit of their own interests. Thus, the law of nations sets the conditions for establishing a federation of sovereign states, or a league of nations. The principles of Kant's law of nations are contained in a larger set of 'preliminary' and 'definitive' articles described in his essay *Perpetual Peace* (1970: 93–105). Presented through six requirements, the 'Preliminary Articles' are:

1. No conclusion of peace shall be considered valid as such if it was made with a secret reservation of the material for a future war.

2. No independently existing state, whether it be large or small, may be acquired by another state by inheritance, exchange, purchase or gift.

3. Standing armies will gradually be abolished altogether.

4. No national debt shall be contracted in connection with the external affairs of the state.

5. No state shall forcibly interfere in the constitution and government of another state.

6. No state at war with another shall permit such acts of hostility as would make mutual confidence impossible during a future time of peace. Such acts would include the employment of assassins or poisoners, breach of agreements, the instigation of treason within the enemy state, etc.

Kant explains that while three of the preliminary articles require immediate implementation regardless of present circumstances, the implementation of the other three may be temporarily deferred until auspicious circumstances arise. The three most urgent articles – numbers 1, 5 and 6 – require states to honour peace above their own absolute security. Yet, in order to achieve peace, states must recognize the principle of right not only externally but also internally and as a principle of humanity. Consequently, Kant also proposes the three 'Definitive Articles', which are:

1. The civil constitution of every state shall be republican.
2. The right of nations shall be based on a federation of free states.
3. Cosmopolitan right shall be limited to conditions of universal hospitality.

Not all of these articles are considered part of the law of nations. In particular, the six preliminary articles are regarded as the law of nations between liberal and non-liberal states, while the three definitive articles in addition to the six preliminary articles constitute cosmopolitan law. Taking into account only principles two to six of Rawls's law of peoples and the six preliminary articles of Kant's law of nations, it can be said that Rawls and Kant are in close agreement on the scheme of principles needed to regulate the interactions of liberal and non-liberal states. What I will examine in the following sections, however, is how Rawls's and Kant's fuller conceptions of international justice begin to differ when the ideals of human rights and democracy are taken into account from the cosmopolitan perspective suggested in the definitive articles.

In summary, extending the law of peoples to well-ordered hierarchical societies involves proving that a second session of the original position – in which representatives of non-liberal peoples are equally situated, rational and deciding for appropriate reasons – actually models what non-liberal peoples consider to be fair conditions under which to choose a law of peoples. This extension also involves proving that in such a second original position the *same* law of peoples – the same standing principles of international law – as that adopted by liberal peoples would be adopted by non-liberal peoples. An important corollary to the law of peoples, then, is that non-liberal societies are also to honour human rights.

The question that will be the concern for much of the remainder of this chapter is whether non-liberal hierarchical societies, as portrayed by Rawls, can in fact honour human rights. I will argue that it is possible to believe they can only if one adopts a relativistic conception of human rights which grants 'different' human rights to 'different' cultures. I think that Rawls ends up adopting this conception in order to make his law of peoples work, and as a result his theory of international justice as a whole suffers. If human rights are 'different' depending on the social context, are they even recognizable as human or universal rights? It is clear that they are not.

The universality of human rights

Would all non-liberal states accept the principles of Rawls's law of peoples? Tyrannical regimes clearly would be unwilling to endorse many if not all of the principles of justice for the law of peoples. Rawls distinguishes, however, between tyrannical or 'outlaw' states and merely non-liberal governments. The latter, he explains, belong to the same class of well-ordered societies as do liberal states, since they are non-expansionist and their political institutions are organized around a common good conception of justice which honours certain traditional distributions of basic rights and duties. Given these criteria, Rawls argues, it is likely that well-ordered non-liberal societies will in fact endorse the same law of peoples as liberal states. But is this claim accurate? I do not think so, as an examination of Rawls's discussion of well-ordered non-liberal states and of human rights will make clear.

According to Rawls, a non-liberal hierarchical society is characterized by the following factors: its church and state are not separate and combine to form a state religion; its political institutions specify a consultation hierarchy as well as a hierarchy of estates or castes; and its basic social and legal institutions satisfy a conception of justice that expresses an appropriate conception of the common good. If such non-liberal societies are also non-expansionist, then their hierarchy is just and their legal and political systems are legitimate; in short, those societies are 'decent' or 'well-ordered' (1999: 62–72). This well-orderedness, Rawls suggests, ensures the human rights of their citizens. He contends that those societies will therefore have no problem in agreeing to a liberal law of peoples, one of whose main principles is respect for human rights.

A hierarchical society is peaceful and non-expansionist if its religious doctrine, though comprehensive and influential in governmental policy, does not seek to undermine the civic order of, and liberties within, other societies. Its system of law is legitimate if it imposes moral duties on all persons within its territory, guided by a common good idea of justice; if it takes impartially into account the fundamental interests of all members of society; and if judges and administrators sincerely believe and publicly defend that the law is indeed guided by such a common good conception. Another way of further spelling out this last requirement is to say that the political institutions of a well-ordered hierarchical society constitute a reasonable and just consultation hierarchy. Rawls explains:

> They include a family of representatives bodies, or other assemblies, whose task is to look after the important interests of all elements of society. Although in hierarchical societies *persons are not regarded as free and equal citizens,* as they are in liberal societies, they are seen as responsible members of society who can recognize their moral duties and obligations and play their part in social life.
>
> With a consultation hierarchy there is an opportunity for different voices to be heard, not, to be sure, in a way allowed by democratic institutions, but appropriately in view of the religious and philosophical values of the society in question. Thus, individuals *do not* have the right of free speech as in a liberal society; but as members of associations and corporate bodies they have the right at some point in the process of consultation to express political dissent. (1993: 62; my emphasis)[3]

Rawls asserts that, if all of this is the case, a hierarchical society's common good conception of justice secures for all persons certain 'minimum' rights. In Rawls's view, the basic rights recognized by well-ordered hierarchical societies are rights to subsistence and security; to liberty understood as freedom from slavery, involuntary servitude and forced occupations; to formal equality as in 'similar cases must be treated similarly'; and to some personal property. Not included are several of the so-called 'liberal' rights, such as rights to freedom of opinion, expression and the press; to freedom of thought, conscience and religion; to political participation; to democracy; and to rights against discrimination based on religion, ethnicity, race and gender (1999: 65, 78–80).

Rawls defends the exclusion of these so-called liberal rights because hierarchical societies embody traditional cultural practices that do not recognize the value of such rights. Indeed, a state organized according to social hierarchy must necessarily reject the idea of equal individual rights because of the inherent inequalities that structure its cultural arrangements and political institutions. In hierarchical societies the lower castes or classes, and the groups marginalized due to race, ethnicity, gender, religion or political affiliation are not entitled to claim the same rights as those individuals higher up in the hierarchy, and even the rights of those higher up are less demanding than the rights recognized in liberal societies. Thus, even the formal equality included by Rawls can secure equal treatment only among those members of 'similar' groups in hierarchical societies; equality cannot be claimed as an entitlement between 'dissimilar' groups.

Confronted with the problem that in hierarchical societies a state religion or comprehensive doctrine might not admit full and equal liberty of conscience and thought for all, Rawls strikes a compromise in his response. He notes that it is essential to the well-orderedness of hierarchical societies that other religions are not actually persecuted or denied practice, and that the society allows for the right to emigration. Doctrines that deny full and equal freedom of conscience are not reasonable, but, Rawls adds cunningly, they are not unreasonable either. Allowing 'a sufficient measure' of liberty of conscience, though not fully and not equally, lies between the fully reasonable and the unreasonable, which denies it entirely (1999: 73–4). Thus, Rawls circumvents the problem of whether a state religion to which certain privileges attach, and which denies full and equal liberty of thought, might end up affecting the fullness and equality of other fundamental rights as well.

At any rate, the conditions of well-orderedness specified by Rawls (non-expansionism, the legitimacy of the legal system and reasonableness of the hierarchy, and the honouring of human rights) are presented, on the one hand, as the necessary conditions for membership in good standing in a reasonable society of peoples and, on the other hand, as the proof that non-liberal societies can be members in good standing in terms of their own conceptions of social justice.

In order to confirm that an agreement on the part of hierarchical societies on a law of peoples protective of human rights is possible, Rawls argues further that the original position is a device of representation for hierarchical peoples among themselves. Although domestically the conceptions of justice in these societies are not political, nor can they be said to be constructed or justified in a manner consistent with Rawls's political constructivism, it is not unreasonable for these different hierarchical societies to insist that their representatives be rational and equal in making claims against other societies at the second step of the extension. Members of those societies would thus agree that the original position models fair conditions when their representatives: (1) care for the good of their own societies, understood in accordance with their own conceptions; (2) have equality in making claims vis-à-vis other representatives; and (3) care for the benefits of peace, trade and assistance (1993: 64). Also in this case the standards of fairness for trade and other cooperative arrangements focus on how well a society can meet its basic needs, understood in terms of that particular society's cluster of minimum rights and liberties (1999: 42–3).

If this is the case, Rawls continues, representatives of hierarchical societies will agree to the same law of peoples as liberal societies, and hierarchical peoples will honour the law of peoples for the same reasons liberal peoples do. Rawls explains that this is because the law of peoples as derived allows each people to pursue their interests and their conceptions of justice, within certain limits. Thus the limits of the law of peoples apparently coincide with those that hierarchical societies impose upon themselves in terms of their own common good ideas of justice.

I find Rawls's argument unconvincing on this crucial point. Rawls describes his project as one intended to deny that the law of peoples and the principle of respect for human rights are ethnocentric, reflecting and imposing Western values (1993: 69–70; 1999: 65, 68). As a way of furthering this project, we have seen that Rawls divides the original position for the law of peoples into three distinct steps corresponding to predetermined characterizations of contrary political cultures; thus, he is necessarily committed to the distribution of different contents and scopes of freedom and equality. Rawls rationalizes the existence of different and unequal rights standards among liberal and non-liberal peoples, and among members of non-liberal peoples themselves, as a way of leaving undisturbed the 'religious and philosophical values of the society in question' (1993: 62).

However, it is this strict division which is problematic. In liberal democratic societies, claims of the general good and other perfectionist values do not take priority over the freedoms and interests of individual citizens. The law of liberal peoples, and the principle of respect for human rights in particular, must ensure a very demanding set of individual rights, liberties, opportunities and socio-economic means. Rawls is careful to include the fair equality of opportunity and difference principles at the domestic level of liberal societies in order to demonstrate that the liberal law of peoples can ensure that set. Yet he excludes those same principles when extending the law of peoples to non-liberal societies, thus allowing the possibility for indefinite interpeoples inequalities. A common good conception of justice in a hierarchical society must guarantee only a very minimum set of rights to its members, but it also grants a wider set of rights to a few privileged members; and all of these rights are much less demanding than those of a liberal society. The law of hierarchical peoples is therefore a different law from that of liberal peoples. The law of hierarchical peoples ensures only a narrow set of rights, and fewer means to make those rights worthy, than does the law of liberal peoples.

Contrary to Rawls, then, I would argue it is unlikely that liberal societies made up of individuals matching Rawls's political conception of persons – and thus concerned about preserving the worth of a demanding set of rights, liberties and opportunities – would agree to principles of international justice that allow for indefinite inequalities among peoples and to the narrower, unequal set of human rights and means ascribed to non-liberal peoples. In addition, I think it unlikely that hierarchical societies, as described by Rawls, would accept a law of peoples that required the same set of rights, liberties and opportunities as found in liberal societies. In other words, the law of peoples accepted by the parties to the original position would not be the *same* law of peoples for liberal and non-liberal societies. This is the first way in which Rawls's theory fails as an account of universal human rights.

The second way Rawls's theory fails can be seen from a closer examination of his description of human rights. Rawls maintains that several conditions are essential to the agreement he has proposed. The first is that the original position at the second level of the law of peoples does not incorporate a 'liberal' conception of the person as free and equal. The second is that the law of peoples is not worked out through an all-inclusive global original position representing all persons regardless of their society and culture (1999: 82–3). My concern here, however, is that universal human rights are premised on the ideal that *all* persons *are* free and equal, regardless of the society into which they happen to be born, and that the point of human rights is to protect this freedom and equality from the type of discriminatory treatment characteristic of hierarchical societies.

In light of the above conditions, Rawls sums up his rather peculiar conception of human rights. Rawls contends that human rights are different from rights in political liberalism. Human rights, he informs us, 'do not depend on any particular comprehensive religious doctrine or philosophical doctrine of human nature', such as, for example, that human beings are moral persons and have equal worth, or that they have certain particular moral and intellectual powers that entitle them to rights (1999: 68). Nor do human rights require the 'liberal idea that persons are citizens first and have equal basic rights as equal citizens' (1999: 66). Apparently, human rights are assignable only when it is determined what particular society a person is born into, and then *that person's fundamental moral obligations and interests will be different* depending on which type of society happens to be in question, whether liberal or non-liberal. If a person is born into a liberal society then he or she can claim the rights consistent with the status of free and equal persons; if a person is born into a hierarchical society then he or she cannot claim such a status and is granted only a restricted set of rights.

Thus, because those fundamental moral obligations and interests are variable in Rawls's view, human rights need not be the same for all persons everywhere. A member of a hierarchical society need not be considered a person possessing moral powers, and can be denied equal worth on the basis of their contingently acquired membership. Oddly enough, given Rawls's stance to the contrary in *A Theory of Justice*, the arbitrary circumstances of historical and geographical fate are allowed to determine in the law of peoples whether a person is treated equally or unequally.[4] While Rawls's position may be an accurate description of certain non-ideal situations in which people are in fact treated unequally and rendered powerless within their societies, his normative concession to the traditional political realism of international relations seems a far cry from the theory of justice as an ideal moral conception.

Rawls further explains that the non-liberal conception of the person in hierarchical traditions regards persons as first and foremost 'responsible' members of society acting in accordance with their pre-assigned moral duties and obligations, whose minimal rights arise from their prescribed 'place' in society. These minimal rights are referred to as enabling rights, that is, rights enabling persons 'to meet their duties and obligations' as assigned to them by the different groups or castes to which they belong (1999: 68). According to Rawls, it 'does not matter' that rights are understood to hold for persons only as unequal members of estates and corporations, and not as equal individual citizens (1993: 70). What is more important to Rawls is that these so-called basic human rights can be protected (through the imposition of moral rights and duties on persons as members of differentiated groups) in a hierarchical society, without appealing to a comprehensive or political liberalism. He asserts that the minimum rights recognized in hierarchical societies must therefore be referred to as human rights in the same way as the more robust set of rights in liberal societies are referred to as human rights.

Rawls concludes that human rights are a special class of rights with a 'special role' in a reasonable law of peoples; in his view, they are distinct from constitutional rights and the rights of democratic citizenship (1999: 79). To support this conclusion, Rawls offers a limited interpretation of the Universal Declaration of Human Rights. According to his interpretation, human rights 'proper' are only those contained in Articles 3 and 5 of the UDHR, that is, the rights to life, liberty and security, and rights against torture and degrading treatment or punishment, and possibly the other rights listed between Articles 3 and 18 (1999: 80, n. 23). As we have seen, however, Rawls understands the right to liberty and security to apply differently in liberal and hierarchical societies; in hierarchical societies, liberty and security are only minimally and negatively conceived as freedom from slavery, serfdom and forced occupations. The remaining fourteen articles of the UDHR, and apparently the economic, social and cultural rights set out in the International Conventions of 1966, fall outside the realm of human rights 'proper' and their status is left uncertain.

Article 1 of the UDHR, which states that 'All human beings are born free and equal in dignity and rights' is dismissed by Rawls as merely expressing 'liberal aspirations' (1999, 80, n. 23). This move is telling, however, because Rawls's interpretation ignores that Article 1 is the very basis for all of the interdependent rights contained in the UDHR and the Conventions. The principle of equality or non-discrimination, which holds all persons to be free and equal, is typically recognized as the foundational concept of universal human rights in various legislation, judicial interpretation and other international instruments. According to those sources, the purpose of human rights is universally to respect, protect and promote the freedom and equality of *all* persons everywhere. Eugene Kamenka conveys this last point in clear fashion:

Peoples, in other words, are above all people, members of the human race. As such, they are entitled to dignity, respect, and the recognition that they are fully members of the human race. They are not entitled to immunity from outside or internal criticism of their dominant customs, practices and traditions in so far as these are themselves destructive of respect for persons, of moral compassion and the recognition of the moral equality of all people.[5]

Rawls's insistence that human rights are a special class of rights, dissimilar from constitutional and citizens' rights, also ignores two different facts. The first concerns the international character of human rights law, that is, the fact that human rights standards are *international* and not merely local. The second concerns the fact that human rights are rights of the *individual*, there to protect the inviolability of the individual person from domestic and international threats. Human rights theorists insist that human rights are individual rights and that their only 'special' characteristic is that they are claimed when legal and political remedies are not working or have failed.[6] Far from being dissimilar from constitutional and citizens' rights, human rights become redundant or 'self-liquidating' precisely when constitutional and citizens' rights are in place. In other words, human rights should be regarded ultimately as the constitutional rights of individual citizens.

Universal human rights refer, then, to two basic conceptual and normative requirements. First, persons are regarded as free and equal in worth and dignity. Second, they are considered to possess equally certain fundamental rights and obligations needed to ensure an existence worthy of human equality and dignity. Because the representative interests of hierarchical societies as described by Rawls are not those of citizens, much less equal citizens, such societies would not recognize the more robust set of human rights satisfying these two requirements, which is the set of rights granted citizens of liberal societies. Therefore, I contend that they would not accept the same law of peoples as that accepted by liberal societies, and Rawls's theory once again fails as an account of universal human rights.

In contrast to Rawls, then, it is more appropriate to follow Martha Nussbaum in holding that 'a human right, unlike many other rights people may have, derives not from a person's particular situation of privilege or power or skill but, instead, just from the fact of being human'.[7] People are born into and belong to different cultures, but

they have no choice over this fact or the particular common good idea
of justice associated with it, unless the opportunity for choice is
provided through a people's domestic social and political institutions.
Rawls declines to support such opportunities in the case of
hierarchical peoples, and allows the contingencies of where one is
born to determine unequally the human rights to which one has
access.

Human rights, democracy and peace

Let me summarize my argument. Rawls's account of human rights is
unable to meet the standard of universality since it allows for the
possibility of unfair inequality as the result of ascribing a different,
more limited set of rights to persons in hierarchical societies. It is also
unable to meet the standard of universality because Rawls eliminates
the ideal of persons as free and equal from the conception of human
rights, thereby undermining the basic justification for international
human rights norms. Both aspects of his theory lead Rawls to an
unsatisfying version of cultural relativism.

Cultural diversity is clearly an important issue to consider when
addressing the implementation of human rights, since some rights
may not yet be realizable given existing social conditions; for instance,
rights concerning the formation of trade unions and labour strikes
(International Covenant on Economic, Social and Cultural Rights,
Article 8) might not yet be relevant in non-industrial economic contexts. However, it is one thing to hold that certain recognized rights
are not yet realizable in some cultures and therefore that the conditions for their realization have to be created (such as an independent
and impartial judiciary), and another to hold that certain rights are
never appropriate for non-liberal cultures and we ought not to try to
create the conditions for their realization. Holding the latter belief, as
Rawls does, is to treat 'culture' as an essentialist, ahistorical category
forever dividing liberal and non-liberal societies. Moreover, although
Rawls's theory is motivated by a well-intentioned tolerance of cultural
differences, it is ultimately discriminatory since individual persons
living in hierarchical societies are deprived not only of an equal status
in the international community, but also of a philosophical and moral
justification for challenging the inequalities they must endure. This
last point is particularly troubling since Rawls actually overlooks

social pluralism at the level of individuals when he too readily analogizes between (non-liberal) peoples and states; vulnerable and marginalized individuals and groups are thus left at the mercy of varying local standards for their 'human' rights.

I have argued that if this is the case it must be conceded that liberal and non-liberal societies will not endorse the same principle of respect for human rights. Further, I think the distinction Rawls makes between tyrannical (outlaw states or benevolent absolutisms) and merely hierarchical states is not as strong as he suggests. Several points can be drawn from Rawls's account to illustrate this claim, points that have serious implications in the debate about human rights and their connection with democracy and peace. First, in the international system portrayed by Rawls, liberal and non-liberal peoples cannot even claim to enjoy the same set of rights. Rawls indicates that he is committed to the distribution of different sets of rights as a means to maintain the distinctiveness of liberal and non-liberal cultures. In particular, he suggests that the scope and content of human rights are determined relative to the particular values, beliefs and practices of a given culture.

One of the more troubling arguments Rawls makes in favour of this type of relativism is that human rights do not depend upon a conception of all persons having equal moral worth, contra Article 1 of the UDHR. Of course, eliminating such a conception makes it possible for hierarchical societies both to discriminate against certain individuals and to 'honour' basic human rights. But this view seriously threatens an integral element of human rights, namely, their universality. If the contents of human rights are variable in relation to whether the individuals in question are regarded *culturally* as legitimate or illegitimate claimants, this takes away the basis for fulfilling those rights for all persons. The result would be not only different sets of 'domestic' and 'international' human rights, but 'domestic' rights would themselves vary according to hierarchical classifications: men have more rights than women, whites more than non-whites, and so on. The extreme inequalities in human rights across and within cultures that Rawls's theory allows degrades the understanding that such rights are concerned with protecting and realizing the dignity and worth of all human beings.

Second, Rawls's stance illustrates the somewhat fashionable perspective of what Ken Booth has recently called the tyranny of cultural essentialism or 'culturalism'.[8] Culturalism is the tendency to reduce complex social and political factors into a reified totality called 'culture', which is then allowed to trump philosophical, ethical and policy controversies concerning human rights. Culturalism is evident in Rawls's law of peoples, for instance, when he assigns an unequal set of rights to hierarchical societies on the assumption that other 'liberal' rights would never be accepted by those societies. In doing so Rawls treats culture as a timeless essence, something without history and processes of change. This in turn leads to a privileging of traditionalism, which is central to hierarchical societies that construct political authority upon persistent patterns and forms of sub-ordination, such as the unequal status and treatment of women in many Islamic societies, or that of 'untouchables' in India's entrenched caste system.

Third, the combined effects of relativism, culturalism and tradi-tionalism undermine recognition of the importance of democratic governance. Recall that, for Rawls, agreement on the principles of the law of peoples, including human rights, is reached by representatives of liberal and non-liberal states. Yet it should be asked whether the representatives in each case are similarly legitimate. In the case of liberal states, citizens are already regarded as free and equal and are able to exercise their individual rights within a democratic political system so as to influence public policy. The requirements of trans-parency, accountability and participation guarantee at least a reason-able possibility that citizens' interests will be suitably represented when it comes to assertions about international human rights and their domestic guarantees. In the case of non-liberal hierarchical states, their members are not regarded as free and equal and they do not enjoy democratic rights. They are unable to influence public policy through participatory mechanisms nor do they have the opportunity to select political representation. As a result, it is unlikely that representatives of non-liberal states – most likely élites who benefit from the advantages of traditionally unequal power structures – would adequately represent the needs and interests of those societies' members.

This non-egalitarian position is overlooked, however, by a cultural-ism that erases the distinctions that exist in non-liberal states between the privileged and powerful and the oppressed and powerless who have no voice. In such situations, who speaks for those not at the top of the hierarchy? Given the opportunity, would the oppressed accept the restricted set of rights endorsed by 'their' so-called representatives?

The institutionalized discrimination, oppression and denial of demo-cracy characteristic of non-liberal hierarchical states discredits, I think, the moral and political legitimacy of their representation.[9] Because these conditions negate the possibility for intersubjective justification of moral and political principles, the claims of hierarchical states with respect to international agreements on equal human rights should be regarded as illegitimate as well. Thus, the line Rawls draws between tyrannical and hierarchical states begins to blur, which undermines his claim that the law of peoples represents a framework for international justice, human rights and security.

All of this suggests that if the law of peoples does not provide adequate recognition for universal human rights, it also fails to support the sort of global political culture that is required in order to secure conditions of genuine lasting peace. It should be recalled that the UDHR begins by stating that 'recognition of the inherent dignity and of the equal and inalienable rights of all members of the human family is the foundation of freedom, justice *and* peace in the world' (Preamble; my emphasis). Existing human rights documents are clear in asserting that their ultimate purpose is to support efforts to raise domestic standards of protection and thus create the conditions necessary for the implementation of the full range of rights proclaimed in the Universal Declaration of Human Rights and the International Conventions. Only by doing so can it be said that strong steps are being taken to secure the basic conditions of peaceful coexistence domestically and internationally. Clearly, Rawls's theory is not able to support this goal adequately.

Part of the problem with Rawls's theory is that it remains con-strained by the realist view of international society and its emphasis on 'power politics' in an adversarial system of autonomous, sovereign states. This narrow focus on states in the abstract is problematic since, as I mentioned above, the illegitimacy of particular states that are institutionally unjust may not be recognized. So long as realism remains the dominant tradition, attempts to recreate the international system in a manner consistent with the requirements of universal human rights will be doomed to failure. Thus, it seems to me that a law of peoples must assume a cosmopolitan rather than realist or narrowly internationalist point of view, if it is to be able to accom-modate the crucial interdependence of human rights, democracy and peace. Here the work of Kant again provides an attractive basis for thinking through this interdependence.

In many ways, Kant can be regarded as the foremost philosophical proponent of a peaceful international order based on freedom and equality. Kant was convinced of the necessity of establishing a cosmopolitan world order because violence and war undermine freedom and equality. 'We have to admit that the greatest evils which oppress civilised nations', he wrote, 'are the result of *war* – not so much of actual war in the past or present as of the unremitting, indeed ever-increasing *preparation* for war in the future.'[10] In order to achieve peace, states must recognize the principle of right not only externally but internally, as a principle of humanity. For Kant, only republican constitutional states that practise cosmopolitan hospitality can maintain an international federation. This is because republicanism relies on the consent of citizens, and citizens, if consulted by executives, are unlikely to consent to war given its many costs and risks. By contrast, in a non-republican regime, the ruler, who is not a fellow citizen obligated to contribute to or participate in war, is free and willing to declare war.

In Kant's view, then, the republican constitution is the most conducive to perpetual peace. Grounded upon public accountability, commerce and representative-democratic norms – including separation of the legislative, judicial and executive powers, the rule of law and respect for human rights – republicanism provides the conditions for a lasting peace when extended to a world order of confederated communities, each of which would reciprocally recognize the equal rights of their members as world citizens. As Kant recognized, 'peace can be neither inaugurated nor secured without a general agreement between the nations; thus a particular kind of league, which we might call a *pacific federation (foedus pacificum)* is required'.[11]

Kant discusses the mutually beneficial relationships between human rights, peace and democracy – or at least a republican constitutionalism compatible with the modern ideals of liberal democracy – at length.[12] Ultimately, unlike Rawls's account, a Kantian notion of cosmopolitan right appeals to a moral conception of all persons as free and equal. For Kant, a moral conception of the person is of a free and equal rational being, recognized as an autonomous member of the kingdom of ends. Moral persons are autonomous and free to choose, and are thus ends in themselves. The categorical imperative provides a rule of respect for human freedom, that is, respect for the right of all persons to determine their own ends, which is clearly expressed in the formulation known as the principle of humanity: 'So act as to treat humanity, both in your own person and in the person of every other, always at the same time as an end, never simply as a means.'[13] As ends in themselves, all persons possess absolute and equal worth. A Kantian notion of cosmopolitan right is committed as well to creating the basic social conditions, institutions and practices through which all human beings can actually realize themselves as free and equal in non-violent and peaceful polities. Kant observes that a cosmopolitan law of peoples ought to be governed by considerations of universal principles of right if we are realistically to expect peace among states, and thus a cosmopolitan realm of ends:

> The peoples of the earth have thus entered in varying degrees into a universal community, and it has developed to the point where a violation of rights in one part of the world is felt everywhere. The idea of a cosmopolitan right is therefore . . . a necessary complement to the unwritten code of political and international right, transforming it into a universal right of humanity. Only under this condition can we flatter ourselves that we are continually advancing towards a perpetual peace.[14]

Kant also provides a strong case for the necessity of republican forms of governance in *all* states which are grounded on the constitutional protection of equal human rights and liberties, in order to secure peace both *within* and *among* states. A republican constitution is 'the only constitution which can be derived from the idea of an original contract' as well as the 'pure concept of right'.[15] As a representative form of government, republicanism grounds the legitimacy of state sovereignty upon the existence of popular sovereignty. As a result, Kant's conception of global justice indicates that non-liberal hierarchical states must be transformed into states that uphold democratic, egalitarian and secular principles of justice for all persons. This conception of global or cosmopolitan justice includes incorporating much stronger claims to civil and political rights than those acknowledged by Rawls, so as to eliminate discrimination based on race, ethnicity, sex, language, religion and political opinion. Ironically, the reformation of hierarchical states into states embodying the principles of equal rights and liberties was mentioned approvingly by the early Rawls in *A Theory of Justice*:

> We have to concede that as established beliefs change, it is possible that the principles of justice which it seems rational to acknowledge may likewise change. Thus when the belief in a fixed natural order sanctioning a

hierarchical society is abandoned, assuming here that this belief is not true, a tendency is set up in the direction of the two principles of justice in serial order. The effective protection of the equal liberties becomes increasingly of first importance in support of self-respect. (1971: 548)

Through the expanding democratization of illiberal states, the international system can then be modified into a universal community of cooperatively interacting states constrained by the institutionalized rights of all persons as world citizens, that is, by a *cosmopolitan* law of peoples. Because of the normative demands of human rights and democratic accountability, internal sovereignty will no longer be regarded as inviolable and the state considered immune from public criticism as long as it falls short of a republican form of government based on principles of right. In other words, to establish a global culture of peace, sovereignty should depend upon the moral and political legitimacy of states, a standard that hierarchical and otherwise tyrannical states cannot meet.

From the perspective of Kantian cosmopolitanism, we are better able to pursue the possibility that the transformation of non-liberal societies into republican, democratic ones can result in an international system that promotes enduring peace rather than war and violence. This possibility agrees nicely with the conclusions of the theory of democratic or liberal peace, based upon Kant's hypothesis that, as states with a republican form of government become more numerous, international conflicts will decrease. The theory of democratic peace in essence refers to either of two separate contentions. One is that democracies can be expected to keep the peace between themselves, but not necessarily with other non-democratic states, and the other is that democracies are also more likely than other states to be more pacific in their relations overall, including with non-democracies. These theories draw upon research which suggests that democracies possess normative and institutional or structural features making them much less likely than other forms of government to commit the state to war.[16] While there is substantial debate about the strength of the empirical evidence used to support the theory, I endorse the claim that there are structural features inherent to liberal democracies which make them peaceful with one another, but not necessarily with non-democratic or hierarchical systems.

Perhaps the most important of these features is the liberal democratic commitment to taking civil, political and socio-economic rights seriously (if still imperfectly) and to maintaining the universality of the full range of individual human rights. Contrary to Rawls's claims, liberal democracies do not in principle undermine this universality by trading off some rights for others; civil and political rights, and social, cultural and economic rights are indivisible and interdependent. Democratic governments rest upon popular sovereignty, account-ability and the impartial rule of law, reinforced by the principle of tolerance and protection of minority rights. Thus, a series of checks have been incorporated into the structure of democratic states, which non-democratic states lack. The division of administrative, legislative and military power within the formal institutions of the state and the need to build broad-based consensus restrict and slow the process of decision-making and mobilization for war.

Another relevant feature highlighted in the literature on democratic peace is that liberal democracies accept the norms of compromise and conflict resolution, and have developed internal mechanisms for con-flict resolution which do not rely on a resort to violence.[17] Democratic states will then attempt to apply the same mechanisms to the resolu-tion of external conflicts, and will expect other democratic states to do the same. These normative and institutional attributes are viewed as responsible for creating and maintaining the pacific union between democratic states.[18] In this way we can regard democracy as a vehicle for peacekeeping as well as for peacemaking.

Liberal democratic societies, Rawls states, must tolerate non-liberal societies, organized by comprehensive doctrines but meeting certain conditions of well-orderedness, in the same way that liberal citizens must respect citizens with other comprehensive views, provided they are pursued in accordance with domestic justice. The constructivist account which holds that the original position procedure is to represent peoples symmetrically and equally situated, so that the liberal conception does not impose on other societies, is thought by Rawls to be the best manner of showing such toleration since it asks of other societies only what they can reasonably grant (1999: 59–60). But liberal societies, or rather the citizens of liberal societies, must also be responsive to the fundamental needs and interests of all other persons qua persons, and this equally. This is simply a feature of liberal persons that cannot be waived, and it is necessary if the dignity of all persons is to be respected. Typically, the idea of human dignity is taken to entail an idea of equal worth, an idea that is absent from hierarchical societies.

It is commonly accepted that the liberal political tradition requires us to tolerate others out of respect, if not for the views of any particular individuals at least for the rights those individuals are thought to possess. Yet this way of thinking runs up against a certain difficulty, namely, the claim that liberal democracy has the authority to curtail norms that disrespect, cause harm and violate the rights of some persons. We have, then, a dilemma posed by the coexistence of neutrality or tolerance on the one hand, and the limits of pluralism on the other. In Chapters 1 and 2 it was noted that rights-based theories are in some sense neutral with respect to competing conceptions of the good. By 'conception of the good' is meant a conception that encompasses both personal values and societal circumstances. It consists of a more or less determinate scheme of ends that the agent aspires to carry out for his or own sake, as well as for the sake of attachments to other individuals and loyalties to various groups and associations. Under this scheme, which Rawls embraces, liberal democracies should allow freedom to citizens to develop their own conceptions of the good (1971: 327–8). One question that arises from this assertion is whether – in the name of liberty, tolerance and pluralism – *all* conceptions of the good should be open as options to be pursued not only in a liberal democratic society but also in an international society of peoples committed to honouring human rights. Should neutrality prescribe governments to remain silent in the face of phenomena that discriminate against certain members of society, for example, on the basis of race, ethnicity, gender and sexual orientation? The basic problem here is whether or not a place exists for every norm which may be valued by some individuals or groups to endure within the framework of a cosmopolitan society of peoples.

Reflecting on the dilemma of whether or not all conceptions of the good may have a place in liberal democracies, Rawls concedes that no society can include within itself all forms of life. He argues that, in a democratic culture, a workable conception of political justice must allow for a diversity of doctrines and a plurality of conflicting, indeed incommensurable, conceptions of the value and purpose of human life by the members of existing democratic societies.[19] But, given the profound differences in beliefs and conceptions of the good, we must recognize that, just as on questions of religious and moral doctrine, public agreement on the basic questions of philosophy cannot be obtained without the state's infringement of basic liberties. Rawls explains that conceptions of the good which directly conflict with the principles of justice, or wish to control the machinery of state and practices so as to coerce the citizenry by employing effective intolerance, should be excluded. The assumption is that these principles of justice underlie any conception of the good. Rawls further asserts that, if a conception of the good is unable to persist and gain adherents under institutions of equal freedom and mutual toleration – such as we might find in a hierarchical society – we must question whether it is a viable conception of the good, and whether its passing is to be regretted.[20]

In *Political Liberalism*, Rawls reiterates that some conceptions of the good will die out in a just constitutional (republican) regime. He further clarifies his position by distinguishing between comprehensive doctrines and *reasonable* comprehensive doctrines. Rawls explains that comprehensive doctrines include conceptions of what is of value in human life, as well as ideals of personal virtue and character, of friendship and of familial and social relationships.[21] While reasonable comprehensive doctrines cover the major religious, philosophical and moral aspects of human life in a more or less consistent and coherent manner, they organize and characterize recognized values so that they are compatible with one another and express an intelligible view of the world.[22]

Rawls maintains that a modern democratic society is characterized not simply by a pluralism of comprehensive religious, philosophical and moral doctrines but by pluralism of incompatible yet reasonable comprehensive doctrines. Political liberalism assumes that, for political purposes, this plurality is the normal result of the exercise of human reason within the framework of the free institutions of a constitutional democratic regime. Political liberalism also assumes that reasonable comprehensive doctrines do not reject the essentials of a democratic regime.

To argue that some conceptions of the good may have no place requires a recognition that there are some values that underlie a liberal society which bring members of society to view some other conceptions as incompatible. Rawls implies that some norms and moral codes must be shared by members of the community, despite their cultural diferences. This is not to say that one dominant culture or one dominant conception of the good exists; but that some basic norms should be safeguarded in order to make the working of a liberal-democratic system possible and to ensure its survival. These accepted norms, by virtue of their existence, enable each individual and group to pursue their conceptions of the good, as long as convictions are not contradictory to them. These norms set limitations on the range of values that society can respect. The most basic norms democracy has to secure are, first, respecting others as human beings and, second, not intentionally causing harm to others. These norms are also fundamental to the human rights culture characteristic of contemporary liberal democracies.

The norm of respect for others is founded on the assertion that we ought to respect others as autonomous human beings who exercise self-determination to live according to their own life plans; that is, we respect people as self-developing beings who are able to develop their capacities as they choose. At the same time we insist on the require-ment of mutuality, in that we ought to show respect for those who respect others. This prescription to respect those who respect others is then qualified by the boundaries of toleration, insofar as restrictions on liberty are justified when there are clear threats of immediate violence against some individuals or groups, that is, actions which would violate the obligation to respect the rights of that individual or group. Together, these two norms safeguard the rights of those who might find themselves in a disadvantageous position in society.

Now Rawls believes that the public culture of democracy is obligated to pursue forms of social cooperation which can be achieved on a basis of mutual respect. This cooperation involves the acceptance of common procedures to regulate political conduct. Citizens should be accorded equal respect in their pursuit of their idea of the good. Rawls's concept of justice is independent from and prior to the concept of goodness in that its principles limit the conceptions of the good that are permissible. He explains that the principles of any reasonable political conception must impose restrictions on per-missible comprehensive views, and the basic institutions those prin-ciples require inevitably encourage some ways of life and discourage others, or even exclude them altogether.[23] Rawls's ideal polity would not be congenial towards those who believe that their personal con-ception of the good involves enforcing others to abide by it. It would exclude some beliefs, such as those that entail coercion of others, causing harm to others, or depriving others of the equal exercise of their basic rights.

The justification for excluding controversial beliefs from the original position lies in the social role of justice, which is to enable individuals to make mutually acceptable to one another their shared institutions and basic arrangements. This justification is accompanied by an agreement on ways of reasoning and rules for weighing evidence that govern the applications of the claims of justice. Mutual respect would enable social cooperation between individuals who affirm fundamentally different yet reasonable conceptions of the good. Thus, for instance, Rawls does not exclude religious groups with strong beliefs who may demand strict conformity and allegiance from their members, but he could not endorse the formation of a theocracy, for such a hierarchical society can exist only through coercion and the denial of equal rights.

Rawls mentions a case where one group wants to make the entire community accept its own conception of the good.[24] He supports opposition and state intervention to prevent this scenario in order to protect the rights of individuals who disassociate themselves from the intensive and all-embracing conception of the given cultural group. A minority culture could not force its ideas upon the entire community. This form of minority coercion is repudiated by Rawls just as we reject majority coercion. Democracy is a form of government that secures the rights of all, majority and minority alike. We oppose majority rule when it does not protect the rights of minorities, and likewise we object to minority coercion that does not respect the rights of the majority.

Rawls's theory of justice as fairness is a moral conception that provides us with an account of the cooperative virtues suitable for a political doctrine in view of the conditions and requirements of a constitutional regime. It is a theory, in his view, of an 'overlapping consensus' between different groups and individuals with divergent and even conflicting doctrines as to the fair procedures for making political demands in a democratic society, where mutual respect, toleration and fairness must be the norm. Such a consensus, Rawls argues, is moral both in its object and grounds, and so is distinct from a consensus founded solely on self- or group-interest. He acknowledges that such a consensus is not always possible. Nevertheless, I think that a convergence on a conception of global justice may be achieved such that the principles of toleration, respect and human rights are sustained through an ever-widening circle of democratization.

Consequently, an acceptance of a concept of justice can be achieved in spite of differences, but some conceptions will have no place within a well-ordered society of peoples. Rawls notes that a society is well-ordered by justice as fairness so long as, first, citizens who affirm reasonable comprehensive doctrines generally endorse justice as fairness as giving the content of their political judgements; and, second, unreasonable comprehensive doctrines do not gain enough currency to compromise the essential justice of basic institutions, including primary goods such as rights and liberties, opportunities and powers, income and wealth, and a sense of one's own worth. Rawls's reasoning, then, is designed to protect the fundamental rights and liberties of all, majority and minorities alike, based on respect for others, while at the same time permitting restriction on toleration at the point where respect ceases.

From the perspective of Rawls's theory it is possible to conceptualize the fundamental norms of political liberalism in terms of the institutionalization of universal human rights. This is because human rights claims are not made on behalf of any particular social group but for all instances of humanity in general, and such claims are referenced against coercive social groups or political bodies; in short, human rights are both universal and political in character. When such claims and entitlements are effectively institutionalized as laws, rules and regulations, they function as norms that a political community recognizes as fundamental to the humanity of its members, irrespective of their differing reasonable comprehensive doctrines of the good. Ronald Dworkin offers a similar reading of Rawls's two principles, suggesting that they imply the 'right of all men and women to equality of concern and respect, a right they possess not by virtue of birth or characteristic or merit or excellence but simply as human beings with the capacity to make plans and give justice'.[25] The establishment of individual civil and political rights in a constitutional democracy protects the fundamental right of all citizens to equal respect and concern, providing a convergence or overlapping consensus on core human rights norms within the context of a political society representing a diversity of interests.

What this suggests is that, on the basis of institutionalizing human rights norms, liberal democracies can interfere to curtail some state practices that undermine the basic principle of granting equal respect and concern to all. Political liberalism cannot endure conceptions and practices that deny respect to individuals, such as those which discriminate based on sex, race, ethnicity and religion. Liberal democracies have to play the role of umpires both in the sense of applying just considerations when reviewing different conceptions of the good and also in trying to reconcile conflicting interests. This is a delicate task that requires integrity as well as impartiality. Yet liberal democratic governments should not cling to neutrality when this policy is thought to contradict basic human rights norms and rules. In other words, the political liberal cannot be tolerant when it comes to conduct that fails to respect others to the extent that their fundamental rights and interests are violated and harm is caused. Political liberalism must always promote the view that each person has a claim to equal concern and respect which all of us are obligated to honour.

A final critical point to be raised here is that, even though democracies hardly, if ever, go to war with each other, they are generally hostile to non-democracies. As a result, democracies are hardly immune from engaging in war, at least with non-democracies. This is an important point, yet in the end it is one which I think underscores the argument I have made throughout this section, namely, that liberal democracies must actively – yet peacefully and justly – encourage and support transitions from non-liberal to liberal democratic societies. Such transitions require *enhancing* the democratic commitment to norms of peaceful conflict resolution and *extending* these norms from domestic to international politics. In Kant's view, for instance, the peaceful resolution of conflicts is a characteristic of 'mature', stable democracies that repudiate the incessant preparation for war and embrace the ideals of social justice and non-violence. The possibility for attaining a just and lasting peace for all peoples is one reason why I think it would be permissible, indeed obligatory, for mature democracies (or those democracies striving for maturity) to exert greater diplomatic and legal pressure for democratic reform and the protection of equal human rights. In other words, actively promoting global democracy and human rights is essential to the pursuit of perpetual peace.

The possibility of a human right to peace

How might we further integrate the elements of global justice, democracy and peace? An answer to this question leads me to suggest a new role for human rights within the society of peoples. In the past several decades, discussion of the protection of human rights has been at the forefront of the agenda of peace scholars, activists and organizations. As a result, human rights have gained greater visibility and recognition through their increased assertion in situations of conflict that threaten such rights. However, less attention has been paid to the claim that peace itself is a genuine human right. The task of articulating this claim, persuading critics that peace is a right which merits national and international recognition and translating this recognition into meaningful implementation, is one of the primary human rights challenges of the twenty-first century. This section presents a small contribution to that task, as it articulates a normative defence of the human right to peace (HRP). Overall, I argue that a right to peace is a genuine human right because it satisfies appropriate justificatory tests.

Some controversy exists at present about how extensively rights discourse should be used in expressing values and norms favourable to peace. Enthusiasts among theorists and activists argue that rights discourse ought to be the primary and fundamental approach to most if not all issues of peace, including warfare, disarmament and political oppression.[26] By contrast, others hold that discussion of peace issues should make very limited appeal to the discourse of rights and the formal legalisms that allegedly accompany it, or that rights talk ought to occupy a place of secondary importance to discussions of positive peace. Still others deny that there can even be such a thing as a right to peace.[27]

However, speaking of rights within a broader discourse of social justice is both necessary and useful for dealing with some of the most serious consequences of human violence and conflict. In particular, the right to peace can play a useful role in protecting human interests and in providing a link between the peace and human rights movements. This is not to say, however, that HRP is justified solely on the instrumental grounds that it will be useful to peace activists. Yet it is important to note that HRP will prove useful to peace activists only if people find plausible the claim that it is a genuine human right satisfying appropriate justificatory tests.[28] Thus, if employed wisely, HRP can prove to be a valuable normative asset in trying to resolve violence and security crises. For this reason, HRP can play a central role in justifying and guiding a wide range of peace principles and programmes, but it should do this together with other norms of social justice such as the fair distribution of social goods and obligations to future generations.

The idea that peace is a condition conducive to the realization of basic human rights has been formally recognized since the adoption

of the United Nations Charter in 1945. To 'save succeeding generations from the scourge of war', to 'live together in peace' and 'to
maintain international peace and security' are phrases concerning the
purpose of the United Nations that appear in the Preamble to the UN
Charter. In subsequent international instruments, we find similar expressions on the contribution of human rights to peace. For example,
the UDHR provides in the Preamble that recognition of 'the equal and
inalienable rights of all members of the human family is the foundation of freedom, justice and peace in the world'. The International
Covenants repeat this claim.

Further references to the relationship between the maintenance of
peace and human rights are to be found in various other resolutions
and declarations. However, all of these documents share the view that
the recognition and implementation of human rights will aid in
creating conditions conducive to the emergence of peace. They do not
speak of the right to peace *per se*. We do not find an explicit reference
to peace as a human right until the 1981 African Charter on Human
and Peoples' Rights (Article 23.1), which asserts that 'All peoples shall
have the right to national and international peace and security'. In
1984 the UN General Assembly approved the succinct Declaration on
the Right of Peoples to Peace. In four points, the Declaration provides
(1) that the peoples of our planet have a sacred right to peace; (2) that
the preservation of the right of peoples to peace and the promotion of
its implementation constitute a fundamental obligation of each state;
(3) that ensuring the exercise of the right of peoples to peace demands
that the policies of states be directed towards the elimination of the
threat of war and the renunciation of the use of force in international
relations; and (4) that all states adopt appropriate measures at both
the national and international level to implement the right of peoples
to peace.

Clearly, the actual commitments and policies of states as yet
contain no recognition of such a right. The existence of prudential
relations, but not of peace exactly, between states is generally
regarded as pragmatically helpful for the continuance of basic human
rights within the conventional scope of international law and relations. Yet to say, as the Declaration on the Right of Peoples to Peace
does, that all peoples, both individual and collective, have a right to
domestic and international peace is to make the more powerful claim
that all persons are entitled to the existence of peace whether or not
the state in which they live recognizes this fact. Such an entitlement, I

suggest, must have a place among people's other basic entitlements affirmed in the international human rights documents.

Human rights are often delineated according to three stages. Under this scheme civil and political rights are defined as first-generation human rights, and economic, social and cultural rights are defined as second-generation rights. More recently a third generation of human rights has been articulated. These third-generation or 'solidarity' rights are thought to include development, a healthy environment and peace.[29] The concept of generations of human rights serves some analytical and pragmatic purposes in helping to identify the character and content of different types of rights, yet it is important to recognize the indivisibility and interdependence of all human rights.[30] Civil and political rights are sometimes characterized as 'negative' rights insofar as they entail the freedom of individuals from governmental interference. Economic, social and cultural rights are generally characterized as 'positive' rights insofar as they require the promotion of governmental policies designed to create the social conditions that enable individuals to flourish. It is clear, though, that the realization of civil and political rights often requires state intervention in order to guarantee the participatory rights of individuals, while the progressive realization of economic, social and cultural rights requires safeguards to protect against the possible abuse of individual rights by the actions of government.

Third-generation rights are typically characterized as rights that inhere in groups and not merely individuals. The concern for solidarity rights stems from the recognition of the broad common interests of humanity, especially to certain basic conditions of life that are indispensable to the promotion of human dignity and well-being and to the effective fulfilment of other human rights. There is much disagreement as to whether group rights are in fact human rights, but the details of that particular debate need not occupy us here.[31] Instead, we can understand third-generation rights as referring to the rights of individuals existing as members of social groups. The right to peace, then, means broadly the right of individuals, acting collectively, to conditions of peace indispensable to living a fully human life. To this point very little indication has been given as to what is meant by conditions of peace and the range of issues this concept raises, such as the content of such a right and the correlative duties needed to secure the right in question.

Although one might propose a broad formulation of HRP that claims a right to a non-violent, secure, pleasant, cooperative, friendly, harmonious and even loving world, a narrow formulation focusing exclusively on human security and non-violence has the best chance of gaining acceptance as a genuine human right. Consequently, I will argue for a right to a secure and non-violent world, meaning a world that is not destructive of the central capabilities characteristic of flourishing human existence.

The meaning of a 'peaceful' or safe and non-violent world is ambiguous, since the term 'peace' may be defined in both a positive and a negative sense. In its negative sense, peace is defined as the formal absence of war. Negative peace refers to the state that exists during the period between wars, such as between the First and Second World Wars. In its positive sense, peace is defined as the presence of such 'life-affirming and life-enhancing values' as cooperation, harmony, friendship and love.[32] Positive peace refers to a condition that is greater than the mere absence of war, although the precise characteristics of this condition are difficult to identify.

None the less, proponents of the concept of positive peace point out that mere negative peace falls short of the fundamental goal of absolute non-violence. The absence of the overt violence of war does not preclude the presence of various forms of indirect or 'structural' violence within a given society.[33] For example, one state may not be literally at war with another state, but its social, cultural and legal institutions may be structured according to discriminatory beliefs and policies that deny rights and access to education, employment or healthcare to certain individuals. In cases where social practices deny education, housing, the opportunity to work or to participate in governance because of race, religion, sex and so forth, great psychological, social and economic harm is being done to human beings, even if tanks and bombs are not being used. Such 'unjust social arrangements', Rawls has noted, 'are themselves a kind of extortion, even violence, and consent to them does not bind' (1971: 343). In addition, as Kant pointed out, it is common for 'peacetime' to be viewed as little more than a temporary suspension of hostilities that allows the various parties the luxury of preparing for war.[34]

However, proponents of the concept of positive peace also claim that genuine peace cannot be had unless, in addition to the absence of war and structural violence, a radical transformation of human consciousness also occurs. In their view, every individual should alter his or her beliefs and modes of thought so as to prefer 'affirmative' values such as cooperation, harmony, brotherhood, compassion and love (as well as others like faith, hope, humility, courage and trust). Both Martin Luther King, Jr. and Mohandas Gandhi exemplify this perspective. King believed, for example, that 'only love' can 'drive out hate' from the human heart. Gandhi's and King's claim is that we must reject all forms of violence *and* reshape human consciousness if we are to create a world that is free of violence. Thus proponents of positive peace share not only the supposition that all violence is morally impermissible, but also the assumption that violent beliefs and structures of consciousness can be, and must be, eliminated from human thought by challenging the ideological bases of such beliefs and structures.

My argument for HRP does not address the psychological issue of the transformation of human consciousness. Rather HRP is concerned only with a particular set of threats to human security and safety, namely those *large-scale threats which stem from war and the brutalities of despotic regimes*. Broadly speaking, HRP is concerned with security from armed conflict, whether domestic or international, and the structural violence associated with political oppression. Given this, peace can be equated with the absence of direct and structural collective violence. My argument for HRP is further distinguished from the ideal of positive peace insofar as there are, under some strict conditions, limited and justifiable uses of force and violence.[35] Specifically, these are for purposes of protecting the human rights of individuals against harm caused by wars of aggression and widespread violence perpetrated by despotic regimes against their own citizens.

The complete and permanent elimination of conflict is, I believe, highly unlikely. Therefore, the argument offered in support of HRP is grounded in a conception of 'just peace' rather than positive peace. Just peace moves beyond mere negative peace but does not require the highly utopian features of positive peace. Just peace is a realistic yet stringently normative position, which requires the presence of basic social and political institutions committed to principles of fairness, equality, respect, opportunity, democratization and the protection of human rights. While just peace maintains a preference for non-violent mediation and resolution of conflict, it also recognizes the legitimate use of force in certain limited cases where violence must be used to resist and abolish greater instances of injustice, such as genocide and other gross violations of human rights.[36] Rawls also asks whether forceful intervention is ever called for, and responds that if 'the offenses against human rights are egregious and the society does not respond to the imposition of sanctions, such intervention in the defense of human rights would be acceptable and would be called for' (1999: 93–4 n.).

Following the recommendations of the Carnegie Commission for the Prevention of Deadly Conflict I support the use of force for preventing the outbreak or recurrence of violent conflict in circumstances of post-conflict peacekeeping and preventive deployments of humanitarian intervention, under the following conditions:

1. Any threat or use of force must be governed by universally accepted principles, as the UN Charter requires. Decisions to use force must not be arbitrary, or operate as the coercive and selectively used weapon of the strong against the weak.

2. The threat or use of force should not be regarded only as a last resort in desperate circumstances. Opportunities may arise when clear demonstrations of resolve and determination can establish clear limits to unacceptable behaviour.

3. States – particularly the major powers – must accept that the threat or use of force must be part of an integrated, usually multilateral strategy (such as with a UN Security Council resolution specifying a clear mandate and detailing the arrangements under which force will be used), and used in conjunction with political and economic instruments.

Under these conditions, the circumstances in which military action is justified and the goals that can be accomplished are extremely limited, and must be measured against the international norms against conflict embodied in the UN Charter and human rights instruments. In this way, the argument for HRP does not force us to choose between either peace or justice in such difficult cases.

We might think of the position advocated here as being 'realistically utopian' in the sense proposed by Rawls for his law of peoples. Rawls writes that political philosophy 'is realistically utopian when it extends what are ordinarily thought of as the limits of practical political possibility' insofar as 'it depicts an achievable social world that combines political right and justice for all liberal and decent peoples'. A 'realistic utopia' would 'set limits to the reasonable exercise of power' by employing 'political (moral) ideals, principles, and concepts to specify a reasonable and just society' (1999: 6, 12–14).

Threats to human well-being are the primary focus of HRP because the most severe effects of military conflict and political violence are death, dislocation and harm to physical and mental health. Violent threats to human well-being – such as the use of bombs, guns and torture – not only kill, but maim, disfigure, shorten a person's life, cause permanent physical and emotional disabilities and lead to temporary or recurring illness. Threats to human well-being also extend beyond the traditional limits of physical health and affect aspects of what Amartya Sen and Martha Nussbaum call the 'central human capabilities'. These capabilities are functions characteristically performed by human beings and 'are so central that they seem definitive of a life that is truly human'.[37] Without the availability of these capabilities, Nussbaum writes, 'we would regard a life as not, or not fully, human'.[38] The central capabilities Nussbaum identifies[39] are:

1. *Life.* Being able to live to the end of a human life of normal length; not dying prematurely or before one's life is so reduced as to be not worth living.

2. *Bodily health.* Being able to have good health, including reproductive health; being adequately nourished; being able to have adequate shelter.

3. *Bodily integrity.* Being able to move freely from place to place; being able to be secure against violent assault, including sexual assault, marital rape, and domestic violence; having opportunities for sexual satisfaction and for choice in matters of reproduction.

4. *Senses, imagination, and thought.* Being able to use the senses; being able to imagine, to think, and to reason – and to do these things in a 'truly human' way, a way informed and cultivated by an adequate education, including, but by no means limited to, literacy and basic mathematical and scientific training; being able to use imagination and thought in connection with experiencing and producing express-ive works and events of one's choice (religious, literary, musical, etc.); being able to use one's mind in ways protected by guarantees of freedom of expression with respect to both political and artistic speech and freedom of religious exercise; being able to have pleasur-able experiences, and to avoid nonbeneficial pain.

5. *Emotions.* Being able to have attachments to things and persons outside ourselves; being able to love those who love and care for us; being able to grieve in their absence; in general, being able to love, to

grieve, to experience longing, gratitude, and justified anger; not
having one's emotional development blighted by overwhelming fear
and anxiety. (Supporting this capability means supporting forms of
human association that can be shown to be crucial in their development.)

6. *Practical reason*. Being able to form a conception of the good and
to engage in critical reflection about the planning of one's own life.
(This entails protection for the liberty of conscience.)

7. *Affiliation*. (a) Being able to live for and in relation to others, to
recognize and show concern for other human beings, to engage in
various forms of social interaction; being able to imagine the situation
of another and to have compassion for that situation; having the
capability for both justice and friendship. (Protecting this capability
means, once again, protecting institutions that constitute such forms
of affiliation, and also protecting the freedom of assembly and
political speech.) (b) Having the social bases of self-respect and
nonhumiliation; being able to be treated as a dignified being whose
worth is equal to that of others. (This entails provisions of
nondiscrimination.)

8. *Other species*. Being able to live with concern for and in relation
to animals, plants, and the world of nature.

9. *Play*. Being able to laugh, to play, to enjoy recreational activities.

10. *Control over one's Environment*. (a) *Political*: being able to
participate effectively in political choices that govern one's life; having
the rights of political participation, free speech, and freedom of
association. (b) *Material*: being able to hold property (both land and
movable goods); having the right to seek employment on an equal
basis with others; having the freedom from unwarranted search and
seizure. In work, being able to work as a human being, exercising
practical reason and entering into meaningful relationships of mutual
recognition with other workers.

These capabilities point to some basic aspects of well-being in HRP,
namely, those that pertain to avoiding unnecessary misery and to
securing the possibility of a minimally good human life for all
persons.[40] For example, having to live without access to adequate
educational facilities, without the opportunity freely to express one's
opinions, or without the possibility of participating in political
governance might not destroy one's physical health, but each deprivation would seriously harm human functioning, cause humiliation and

assault one's dignity. In sum, HRP should address forms of military and political violence that create significant risks of killing people or depriving them of the possibility of a minimally good life defined in terms of the central human capabilities. This is a general criterion that sets the level of the elimination of violence at an attainable standard, and describes the level of protections against violence that states should guarantee. Because the quality of life and threats to human functioning vary from one country to the next, assessment of conditions and implementation of relevant public policy must remain open to plural specification. International human rights typically set broad normative standards that can be interpreted and applied by appropriate legislative, judicial or administrative bodies at the national level, even as the standards offer reasonable guidance to policy-makers. Standards for non-violence should be specified further at the national level through democratic legislative and regulatory processes open to all citizens.[41]

In order further to define the scope of HRP it is necessary to describe the duties that individuals, governments, corporations and international organizations must bear in relation to this right. We must do so because a right is not merely a claim to some freedom or benefit; it is also a claim against certain parties to act so as to make that freedom or benefit available. With respect to the duties of individuals and corporations, then, it should first be recognized that persons, organizations and corporations have a duty to refrain from activities that generate unacceptable levels of direct or structural violence. For example, individuals have a duty to refrain from dis- criminating against others on the basis of race, gender, religion or sexual orientation, and to refrain from the deliberate or predictable harming, injuring, mutilating or killing of others. Hospitals have a duty to provide access to basic medical care to all persons in need of such care regardless of their race, gender, religion or sexual orienta- tion. Companies that manufacture advanced technological goods have a duty to take strong precautions against the illicit acquisition and use of such technology for purposes of illegitimate violence against individuals or states. Corporations that produce such goods also have a duty to compensate victims should harm occur.

Similar to individuals and corporations, governments have negative duties to refrain from actions that give rise to serious threats of violence to human life and well-being. For example, governments have a duty not to produce, stockpile and use nuclear weapons since these weapons indiscriminately maim and kill thousands of innocent human beings.[42] In addition to these negative duties, governments also have a duty to protect the citizens of their states against violence generated by other governmental or private agencies. An effective system of human rights protection requires a governmentally enacted system of regulation to ensure that police, intelligence and security agencies comply with its standards, and impose significant penalties on those who fail to comply. An adequate system of human rights regulation also requires that citizens, non-governmental human rights organizations and governmental organizations have the power to prosecute violators, whether public or private, and seek compensatory damages. Furthermore, all citizens should be allowed to exercise rights to political participation, enabling democratic participation in decisions about significant risks of violence. As Kant recognized, a constitutional democratic (or republican) form of government offers the best prospect of attaining peace. This is because 'the consent of the citizens is required to decide whether or not war is to be declared' and 'it is very natural that they will have great hesitation in embarking on so dangerous an enterprise'.[43]

Finally, international organizations have negative duties to refrain from generating significant risks of violence. For example, the United Nations has a duty to ensure the safety of non-combatants when using military force to conduct peacekeeping operations and in cases of humanitarian intervention. The World Bank has a negative duty to refrain from loaning money to countries and projects that will produce major risks of violence to human well-being, such as facilities that can produce weapons-grade nuclear materials. These international organizations also have positive duties to promote and protect HRP through declarations, regulations and enforcement measures providing for the reporting of violations, the mediation of disputes, the use of diplomatic, political and economic pressure to coerce violators to comply, and the use of international military force to rescue endangered peoples, stop ethnic cleansing or genocide and restore territorial integrity.

Human rights are fundamental international moral and legal norms that aim to protect people from severe social, political and legal abuses, simply because one is a human being. Human rights are justified in general for broad normative reasons. They secure claims to life, liberty, equality and fairness and in so doing protect our fundamental interests and central human capabilities. The argument of this section is that they should also secure a claim to non-violence and security. To qualify as a human right, however, HRP must satisfy at least four criteria. First, proponents must demonstrate that the proposed right-holders have a strong claim to the object of the right by showing that this object is of great value to individuals and society, and by showing that these values are frequently threatened by military and political abuses. Second, they must show that this claim cannot be adequately satisfied unless people are granted rights rather than weaker forms of protection which might prove inadequate. Third, proponents must demonstrate that the parties that bear duties under the right can legitimately be subjected to the negative and positive duties required for compliance with and implementation of the right. Finally, the proposed right must be practicable, given current economic and institutional resources.

The rights specified in various documents ranging from the Magna Carta to the UDHR were enumerated in response to perceived abuses by governments. Legal rights, such as the rights to habeas corpus and protection against arbitrary arrest and detention (UDHR, Articles 9–11) reflect the fact that repressive governments often use the legal system to harass, torture and kill political opponents. There is good reason, then, to view the articulation of the specific right of HRP against the background of those threats and forms of violence that frequently lead to the abuse of human dignity and destruction of the central human capabilities.

Technological developments underlying the proliferation of relatively inexpensive, mass-produced weapons have contributed to the creation of major, direct violent threats to human security and well-being. Globally, military expenditures amounted to approximately US$780 billion in 1999, an increase of roughly 2 per cent over 1998 expenditures. The largest spender in 1999 was the United States, whose $260 billion expenditure accounted for 36 per cent of the world total, followed by Japan, France, Germany and the UK, whose combined expenditures account for another 23 per cent of the world total.[44] Although military expenditure and arms production have declined since the end of the cold war, in 1998 the combined sales of the top 100 companies in the world arms industry amounted to $155 billion. Conventional weapons, particularly small arms and light weapons, are the major items exchanged in the global arms market, which is subject to minimal control and provides for massive illicit weapons trafficking. In the past decade alone, more than four million people have been killed in violent conflicts and, in 1997, there were more than thirty-five million refugees and internally displaced persons around the world as a result of war or mass violence.[45]

When violent threats reach this level of severity the security and well-being of many people are significantly degraded. Few human rights violations, other than genocidal programmes of mass extermination, cause such extensive and large-scale damage to the welfare of so many individuals and communities. Yet the very existence and use of these weapons is typically accepted as a common feature of modern society, and is rarely viewed as the violation of a specific human right.

Even in an apparently less severe case, such as when a government denies its citizens the opportunity to organize peacefully and to express themselves freely, substantial harm to people's well-being is caused. This is not to say that every person living in these states is physically harmed in a direct sense. Nevertheless, the indirect effects of state repression on the central human capabilities are extensive and far-reaching. The long-term emotional, mental and physical traumas caused by political oppression and social marginalization, in hierarchical societies for instance, are well documented and constitute a persisting legacy of violent conflict which undermines the quality of life for many survivors.[46] The effects of structural violence are not trivial. State repression kills some people, injures and shortens the lives of others, and causes emotional and material suffering. While the basic interests in life, health and a minimal level of welfare are identified for protection by a number of existing human rights, such as rights against murder, torture or physical injury, war and structural violence are significant and frequent threats to collective interests that are not yet protected by a human right to peace. The human right to peace aims to protect people against war and structural violence and their consequences, *in their entirety as systemic problems* and not merely as isolated instances of otherwise acceptable domestic and international activities.

Because a rights claim is a demand for some sort of social action, it is also important to show that the right-holder's enjoyment of the object of the right cannot be secured by any norms weaker than a right. For example, one might contend that severe conflict and repression could be eliminated by expressions of diplomatic disapproval, or by mass non-violent movements. If the vast majority of people could be drawn into a Gandhian movement of non-violence and love, this might make it unnecessary to declare and implement HRP. Alternatively, one might criticize the very notion of human rights for being an inappropriate source of social and political change. Karl Marx, for example, argued against basing social and political change on rights because such rights supposedly are predicated on the egoistic separation of humans from one another and weaken the bonds of community relations.[47] In similar fashion, some pacifists might instead advocate developing a non-violent consciousness of positive peace rather than supposedly perpetuating the status quo in the guise of legalistic reform.

While the spread of non-violent consciousness would certainly be a welcome development, it is nevertheless imperative to retain the language of rights when the enjoyment of the object of a rights claim is threatened or denied. Present circumstances around the globe attest, I think, to the prevalence of threats to peace and to the widespread denial of peace. The claim to a human right to peace is in effect a final appeal because weaker norms and the absence of such a right have proven to be ineffective in protecting collective human interests to non-violence and security. The hope that non-violent consciousness can make HRP unnecessary is an example of what James Nickel has called the 'threat-elimination strategy'. According to Nickel, the 'threat-elimination strategy has sometimes been advocated by those who see the possibility of a transformation of human motivation and consciousness through religion or other forms of enlightenment. They hope that such a transformation will eliminate selfishness, greed, conflict, and corruption.'[48] In the case of HRP, this strategy suggests that, if people had the right sort of non-violent consciousness, they would not willingly pursue violent ends through violent means, thus eliminating the need for HRP. The approach represented by those who prefer consciousness-raising strategies overemphasizes the importance of good motivation and underestimates the need to institutionalize human rights, thereby giving effective legal force to these rights. If the time should come when all people voluntarily eschew violence, then the claim to HRP will no longer be necessary.

Effective rights empower right-holders by imposing moral or legal burdens on duty-bearers. Proponents of HRP must show not only that the right-holders have a strong case for the object of the right, but also that the burden of providing for the enjoyment of this right can be legitimately imposed on the duty-bearers. As discussed above, individuals, organizations and corporations have negative duties to refrain from activities that create unacceptable levels of violence. Governments and international organizations also have positive duties to protect citizens from violence and promote their security and well-being. Those who engage in activities which harm citizens' security and well-being should bear the burden of regulations which require compensation.

One complex aspect of violent risks and harms is that they often result from activities engaged in by many people, as is the case with armed conflict and state repression. These activities produce risks or harms as the result of the cumulative effect of individual decisions and actions made by hundreds or thousands of people. Such collective action can bring about a variety of human deprivations, such as population displacement, illness and starvation, which may not be attributed to a single actor. This raises the issue of collective responsibility for actions leading to the widespread violation of HRP.

An extensive discussion of this issue is beyond the scope and aim of this section. Nevertheless, some basic points can be addressed. Collective responsibility has long been a problematic topic for philosophers. The paradigm of moral responsibility is the individual actor who has intentionally harmed some other person or persons. In this case the actor's causal relation to the harm is a necessary but not sufficient condition for assigning moral blame or obligation. Authentic responsibility also requires some element of intentionality on the actor's part. In the case of groups, the roles of agency and intentionality are less clear than with individuals. A group may collectively produce a certain result without each individual agent's knowledge or awareness that he is contributing to that result, such as when a traffic jam occurs when many drivers just happen to be on the road at the same time.

Despite this difficulty, it can be said that responsibility for some result is assignable to particular individuals, including the members of groups, for their contributory acts. Individuals may be held responsible for choosing to become and remain members of groups pursuing goals that involve harming others, as well as for their degree of active contribution to a harmful result.[49] An individual may argue of course that his particular contribution to a result is insignificant and thus avoids responsibility, but if every member of a group makes this claim the possibility is raised that no one can be held responsible for the result (or at most that a few 'bad apples' were responsible). Derek

Parfit has countered that, although an individual contribution may seem insignificant, even a seemingly minor act contributes directly to the harmful effects of the 'set of acts' that results from its combination with the actions of others. Therefore, an individual who performs an act knowing that it will contribute, even in some small way, to the overall result of harming others can be held morally responsible.[50]

Responsibility also may be assignable to the group itself, provided that intentionality as well as causality is present. Certain activities, especially those of waging war and harming large numbers of people through government oppression, can succeed only by means of organized group effort. Such coordination and unification of individual actions into collective actions introduces the element of overt purposiveness to the group as a whole. Group responsibility thus follows from the existence of collaborative coordination – evidenced by consensus, representative endorsement or delegative authorization – that establishes collective and not merely individual intentionality.[51] Given the possibility of normative responsibility for the kinds of collective actions violative of HRP, negative and positive duties can be imposed on organizations, corporations and governments, as well as individuals, for the protection of right-holders. Doing so then makes it possible to hold accountable those who commit abuses of HRP and other human rights.

The final matter that must be addressed is the possibility that HRP could fail to be a justified human right if its costs were unduly onerous. Many financial resources and significant institutional endeavours are needed to implement rights, and if these resources are limited or unavailable it may be impossible for duty-bearers to satisfy the obligations flowing from the rights. Because human rights impose correlative duties, and 'ought' implies 'can', one might contend that it would be incoherent to hold that HRP is to be implemented if it were economically impossible.

It is often argued that war is 'good' for the economy of a state insofar as a state's military spending is a contributor to its overall economic health. High military spending, it is thought, supports both the expansion of military forces and the growth of domestic economies; if that is the case, reducing military spending will have unfavourable economic consequences. Consequently, a reduction in military spending and in military forces for the purpose of eliminating sources of deadly conflict will incur a prohibitive economic cost that threatens the feasibility of HRP. Yet the connection between military spending and economic health is less favourable than this argument would have us think. Consider, for example, that during the cold war the state with the highest military spending – the Soviet Union at approximately 20 per cent of GDP – had the worst economic performance among leading powers, while the leading power with the lowest military spending – Japan at approximately 1 per cent GDP – had the highest economic performance.[52] Over time military spending tends to compete with other economic needs, such as investment in other government projects or civilian industry, and reduces economic growth by depriving the rest of the economy of valuable resources, technology and talent. Fewer jobs are created, per dollar of US government funds, in the military than in education, housing, construction, healthcare and similar areas that are of great social need.[53] It can be argued, then, that reducing military spending and transforming military development towards civilian sector development within a process of economic conversion will allow for the more productive use of economic resources and strengthen economic growth in the long term. Moreover, the resources saved by preventing losses due to the destruction of property, land, farms, factories, health and life can help to finance the implementation of HRP. Indeed it is quite likely that, in eliminating the drain on resources caused by constant expenditures for the preparation and executing of war, economic development will become more successful in both developed and developing nations. Overall, the economic feasibility of HRP would appear to be no less than, and quite likely greater than, military development.[54] Given this, the standard of protection prescribed by HRP would prove affordable with the refocusing of resources towards the production of goods and services that enhance rather than threaten human security and well-being.[55]

One of the greatest challenges facing the post-cold-war world is establishing a global order that creates the conditions for the peaceful coexistence of all peoples. One way to meet this challenge is to recognize and implement a human right to peace. I have argued in this section that a strong case exists for HRP. Defined in terms of the absence of large-scale collective violence rather than the harmonization of all interests and the transformation of human consciousness, HRP has a coherent scope. The possibility of reducing collective violence and maintaining peace requires, first and foremost, implementing a juridical system of rights within international law. If a strong and enforceable human right to peace with the scope articulated here were effectively implemented at the national and international levels, it would protect human beings against the substantial and recurrent harms associated with collective violence, protection which cannot be afforded by weaker norms. In addition, HRP has identifiable duty-bearers that can legitimately satisfy the normative and economic obligations flowing from such a right. As a norm that satisfies the tests appropriate to human rights, HRP should be recognized both as a general human right and as an important basis for claims to peace. Implementing HRP would obviously require substantial efforts, but as we begin the new millennium the goal of peace requires nothing less than our sustained commitment and perseverance.

Rawls and cosmopolitan justice

I have argued in this and the previous chapter that a more robust conception of global justice can accommodate both the civil and political and the economic and social rights of the Universal Declaration of Human Rights, and provide the impetus for the claim of a human right to peace. In doing so, my arguments have sought to preserve, against Rawls, the universality of human rights as a justified principle of global justice.

I have also suggested that one of the problems with Rawls's argument in *The Law of Peoples* is that it tends to obscure the ideal dimension that the notion of social cooperation has in his early theory of social justice. For instance, Rawls neglects the ideal of cooperation among free and equal persons within a global context. I showed in Chapter 2 that in *A Theory of Justice*, all rights – civil and political as well as economic and social (what Rawls refers to as means contributing to the worth of freedom) – are justified by appeal not only to their necessity and efficacy given societal cooperation under the circumstances of justice, but also by appeal to the normative ideal of cooperation among free and equal persons. This led me to the question I raised in the previous chapter of whether Rawls's principles of international justice are able to vindicate this ideal. In overlooking this normative ideal Rawls unnecessarily fragments the justificatory bases of human rights.

If human rights are rights that all individuals have simply because they are human, what ought to be argued is that there is one single normative ideal of the human being – as equally free – and that ideal is to be realized, logically, in society. The idea conveyed by the international human rights documents is that all rights are instrumental in society in helping to secure equally free humanity. Jack Donnelly has argued that the 'humanity' which grounds human rights is both historically embedded and utopian, in other words, it is a moral ideal.[56] To say that human rights derive from the inherent dignity of the human person is to say that human rights are needed for a life of dignity, a life worthy of a human person, a life of freedom and equality. Humanity's moral status, as free and equal and possessing dignity, not only appeals to the 'nature' of persons and their societies, given contemporary psychological, sociological and moral facts. It is also a moral vision of humanity resting on an account of some of the requirements needed to realize that vision. Human rights include, then, the demand that basic legal, political and economic institutions and practices help realize that moral vision precisely through the implementation of those rights.

The Rawlsian version of global justice discussed in Chapter 3 is in agreement on this last point. That discussion, it will be recalled, sought to answer the question, what sort of international order makes possible the full realization of the human rights of the Universal Declaration, given the fact of societal interdependence? I have suggested in the present chapter that the answer is more closely related to Kant's notion of cosmopolitan right than it is to Rawls's notion of a law of peoples.

The Kantian response to the ideal of equal freedom for all persons is to create an order of global justice that recognizes and protects the same and equal human rights for all, and the measures that guarantee the maximum worth or value of those rights. In other words, the response is the creation of or the working towards a global scheme that satisfies and harmonizes with Rawls's principles of justice if they are globalized, chosen by individuals as free and equal and chosen for basic institutions in general. Such Rawlsian principles of global justice are the principles that free and equal moral persons would agree upon when confronting a world in the circumstances of heavy interdependence and pluralism. The ideal of the human person as free and equal – or its equivalent, the ideal of well-ordered cooperation among citizens regarded as such persons – is a normative conception that must be realized. The task is then to attempt to create, not to presuppose the basic institutions (a liberal basic structure) and to implement the principles that will bring about, as far as possible, such an ideal person and such ideal cooperation. A cosmopolitan law of peoples would validate the universal public rights of all human beings, because of the recognition of cosmopolitan right or justice (international rule of law) nationally and internationally by peoples who are all to some extent connected.

This discussion on the importance of normativity allows us to draw together the analysis of Rawls's theory with the argument in favour of the cosmopolitan account of social justice. While I have attempted to show that Rawls's theory should move in a global direction, and that such a move can only help the universalization of human rights, the larger issue examined throughout Part II is that of whether Rawls's later conception of justice and rights is the best available fully to realize human rights. This is an important question because a cosmopolitan law of peoples aspires to more than universality of rights standards. It aspires also to the universal realization of the free and equal human being, an ideal underlying economic and social as much as civil and political rights. If the same ideal of equal freedom underlies Rawls's rights, opportunities and means in *A Theory of Justice*, one needs to extend Rawls's criterion so that it coheres with the ideal of human rights on the global level. The question then is: does Rawls provide a theory of social justice that is capable of grounding universal human rights? I believe that in his early theory of justice as fairness he does, and in my estimation there is much to be gained by thinking of human rights in a Rawlsian framework, that is, as universal requirements of domestic and international social justice and as standards specifying the legitimacy of institutional patterns across the globe. However, a properly Rawlsian conception of justice and human rights must eliminate the separation between the creation of a domestic democratic climate in which equal freedom can flourish and the creation of a global scheme in which such a domestic democratic climate becomes possible. A just world order would require the institutionalization of human rights, the democratization of all states and the implementation of a cosmopolitan law of peoples. Doing so would improve the chances for living together in conditions of cooperation, peace and security.

As far as international justice is concerned in *A Theory of Justice*, Rawls assumes a conception of social cooperation which is tied directly to the realist perspective of conventional international relations and the law of nations. Given this assumption, I have argued that Rawls's account of international justice is severely hampered by its dependence on a background *modus vivendi* framework. The inequality and instability resulting from this framework are hardly conducive to the principles of justice endorsed by Rawls at the domestic level. Consequently, I believe that the choice situations of the original position ought to reflect an alternative conception of social cooperation in order to generate a much stronger conception of global justice. This would be achieved, in part, by eliminating Rawls's stipulation that the original position may be extended into the international domain only *after* principles have been chosen for domestic purposes. Instead, the parties to the original position would immediately address the principles for the basic structure of *global* society, which includes at the same time domestic social systems and individuals as the bearers of rights.

Under this interpretation, the majority of the elements found in Rawls's description of the original position still remain in place, such as the formal constraints of the concept of right (universality, generality, publicity, finality and reciprocity), the condition of mutual disinterestedness and the conception of the parties as rational. However, what is most significantly different is that the parties to the original position are to be considered persons from different societies and not representatives of states. The parties can still be regarded as the citizens (not merely subjects) of states, but they would not possess knowledge of the particular features of the states in which they happen to reside. In other words the parties retain, from Rawls's original domestic conception, their identities as free and equal moral persons in the world at large but a veil of ignorance precludes them from assuming the identity of states' representatives.[57]

Adopting this position allows for a cosmopolitan characterization of the international original position. For instance, the parties do not know the particular circumstances of any society, nor do they know any society's political structure or economic situation. Moreover, the parties do not know the particular circumstances of the international community. Because Rawls would allow the international original position only after the principles have been chosen for the domestic original position, in his model the parties must know that they are representatives of states whose interests are necessarily determined by an existing national context. This would seem to me to defeat the purpose of keeping a veil of ignorance and an original position before choosing appropriate principles of global justice.

As Rawls maintains, justice is the object of the basic structure of society; yet I suggest that the basic structure is that of an interdependent global society rather than that of a single more-or-less self-contained state. This claim is significant because the basic structure is conceived by Rawls as the system of institutions that distributes rights and liberties and determines the division of advantages of domestic cooperation. It is my argument that the basic structure is now to be understood as the system which distributes *universal* rights and liberties and determines the advantages of *international* social cooperation. It should also be noted that, if the parties are persons, rather than representatives of states in a *modus vivendi* framework, then they would be more liable to adopt a moral rather than merely prudential understanding of their existence in the circumstances of justice. This recognition is a factor absent from Rawls's model. In the revised model of global justice, the interests, equality and autonomy of individual persons are now given priority over the interests of states.

The cosmopolitan conception of justice defended here suggests that, although the parties recognize that a basic structure of some sort exists, it remains open as to what its final form will be, although I do assume it would match up with a Rawlsian liberal, democratic society. It does not assume that the selected principles of global justice will be the rules of the conventional law of nations, which necessarily differ from the principles of domestic justice described by Rawls. Thus, the parties understand that extended principles of justice are required to order these social institutions for the mutual advantage of all, precluding the immediate imposition of a *modus vivendi* framework from a position external to that of the parties in the original position. The principles of domestic justice would coincide with the principles of global justice, meaning that the basic rights and liberties of people as national citizens would coincide with the basic rights and liberties of people as global citizens. Employing a global original position from the outset conforms with the universal status of human rights. As the rights of all human beings everywhere, the institutionalization of human rights proceeds from the international level to the domestic and local levels, rather than from the local or domestic to the international. Starting from a global rather than domestic choice situation therefore entails the following modifications of Rawls's principles of justice that can be derived and used to appraise the basic structure of international society:

1. The first principle of equal liberty requires the distribution of the most extensive total system of universal rights and liberties from the start to all human beings in the global community.

2. The second principle concerning equality of opportunity and social and economic inequalities applies from the start to the global, not just the domestic, community.

Rawls observes in his theory of domestic justice that, from the participant's point of view, it would not be reasonable to expect agreement on a principle of justice granting a greater than equal share in any division of the social primary goods; nor would it be reasonable to expect agreement on a principle distributing less than an equal share. The same can be said if one takes the original position, and thus the background ideal of social cooperation, to be immediately global rather than only domestic. The basic result of the modifications given above is, then, a view of cosmopolitan justice in which all social primary goods – equal rights and liberties, fair equality of opportunities, the bases of self-respect and respect for others – are to be distributed *equally and universally*.

This Rawlsian framework of principles of global justice would appear to embody the ideals that are essential to the achievement of universally substantive human rights. This is because such universal principles are justified by appeal not only to their necessity and efficacy given international interdependence, but also by appeal to the normative ideal of social cooperation among free and equal persons. As I argued in Chapter 2, if we understand Rawls's basic or fundamental rights to mean human rights, such rights depend both on the normative ideal of social cooperation among free and equal persons and on their realization in the socio-political institutions of the basic structure of global society. It is only if the ideals of free and equal persons and of social cooperation are as prescriptive at the international level as Rawls holds them to be at the domestic level that a specifically Rawlsian conception of global justice can be obtained.

Conclusion

In working against the evil propensity in human nature . . . our will is in general good, but the accomplishment of what we will is made more difficult by the fact that the attainment of the end can be expected . . . only through the progressive organization of citizens of the earth into and toward the species as a system that is cosmopolitically combined. (Immanuel Kant, *Anthropology from a Pragmatic Point of View*, 251)

Rawls's work on social justice has been widely, and rightly, acclaimed as one of the most important contributions to political theory in the twentieth century. Whether one agrees or disagrees with Rawls's ideas, they cannot be ignored by anyone seriously interested in theories of justice, either domestic or international. My analysis in this book has illustrated the fundamental aspects of Rawls's theory, but also has been sharply critical of it. Rawls's early focus on achieving justice within a single society left unanswered the question of how justice may be achieved across societies. As I have attempted to show, Rawls's initial response to the issue of international justice was severely limited. Moreover, the issue of human rights remains inadequately addressed even in the more robust theory of international justice developed in his recent account of the law of peoples.

Overall, I have been concerned to show that the most fundamental problem contained in Rawls's theory of international justice and human rights is that it fails to carry forward the normative significance of the domestic account into the international arena, even while being based on his domestic account of justice as fairness. As it now stands, his theory cannot adequately support a genuinely universal human rights project. Although Rawls's theory of justice can, I think, be utilized to contribute to a theory of universal human rights, this contribution must depend on a greater commitment to extending the priority and principles of justice to all persons and not only to those already living in established liberal democracies. Let us review the arguments made throughout the book to support this conclusion.

Chapter 1 presented an introduction to the moral and political concerns of social contract theory and served to state the focus of this study. First, the essential contours of contractarianism were set out. Then the important elements of rights and freedom were shown as central to contractarianism, establishing the further connection between social justice and the existence of basic rights and freedoms. Next, the emergence of the modern discourse of universal human rights was discussed along with various aspects of that discourse in relation to the social contract tradition. With this basic groundwork thus set out, the book moved to consider Rawls's role in the social contract tradition and the intersection of his work with the issues of international justice and human rights.

Chapter 2 continued the discussion from Chapter 1 on the fundamental theses and ideas that form the core of Rawls's moral and political theory of justice as fairness. This included accounts of the original position, the veil of ignorance, the thin theory of the good, the formal constraints, the principles of justice and the sense of justice. In the course of investigating the place of rights within Rawls's theory, it was shown that Rawls places a priority on the social primary goods of basic rights and liberties. It was argued that Rawls's views on the rights and liberties in *A Theory of Justice* can be understood in terms of basic human rights which are to be recognized for all persons. I then explored the influence of social pluralism on Rawls's later political conception of justice as fairness and addressed some communitarian criticisms of Rawls's theory.

In Chapter 3, the arguments Rawls provides for his description of international justice were examined. Essentially, Rawls contends that an extension of justice as fairness from the domestic to the international level results in a picture of international justice that is identical to the traditional law of nations framework. I argued that Rawls's description contains two fundamental problems that lead to an unnecessarily weak account of international justice, namely, the priority he assigns to the domestic original position over the international original position, and the analogy he draws between individuals and states. I also discussed the doctrine of self-determination and how certain difficulties with this doctrine problematize the law of nations scheme endorsed by Rawls. Finally, I examined the possibility of extending Rawls's two principles of justice to a global scale by eliminating the priority Rawls gives to the domestic original position.

Chapter 4 built on the analysis of the previous chapters through a discussion of Rawls's most recent, and most comprehensive, attempt to account for human rights through the extension of justice as fairness into an international law of peoples. In the case of the law of peoples, it was shown that Rawls's distinction between liberal and hierarchical societies leads him to propose a concept of human rights that provides for different sets of rights with respect to each type of society. I then argued that the more limited set of rights ascribed to persons in hierarchical societies undermines the universality of human rights and allows for the possibility of unfair inequality between persons in the same societies as well as between different societies. From there I discussed the intersection of democracy and human rights, and offered a justification for a human right to peace. The chapter concluded with an appeal to a more cosmopolitan ideal of social justice informed by Rawlsian ideal theory, according to which all persons are regarded as free and equal in worth and dignity, and are considered to possess equally certain fundamental human rights. Consequently, I believe that this latter approach better represents a conception of global justice committed to universally promoting and protecting human equality and dignity than does the approach taken in Rawls's law of peoples. A cosmopolitan scheme of global justice is needed if the rights of all peoples are to be respected, and international peace and security ensured.

The traditional law of nations approach, which supports the rights of states over and above the rights of individuals, remains an integral part of existing international law. Because of this, a tension persists between the domestic and international spheres of law and politics when it comes to the issue of human rights, insofar as human rights principles and law represent a challenge to the strong sovereignty claimed by states with respect to their internal domestic affairs. Furthermore, this same tension is to be found within political liberalism itself since liberalism affirms both the doctrine of state sovereignty and the principle of universal rights that belong to all people equally. As a way of resolving this tension, and thus of securing human rights on a truly universal basis, I have argued that the law of nations approach must be superseded by a system of cosmopolitan law and justice committed first and foremost to the ideals of human freedom and equality.

Cosmopolitan justice gives expression to the ideals of human freedom and equality, and denounces the abuses of state power

protected by the exclusiveness of state sovereignty. It affirms unconditionally the rights to freedom under law and to equality possessed by
all peoples, and condemns the obstruction to the full realization of
those rights by oppressive regimes. The realization of the full spectrum of human rights becomes all the more important as the con-
solidation of greater economic and political interdependence of states
reveals the extent of the disparities that exist within the global basic
structure. If economic and political inequalities are to be eradicated
rather than perpetuated, a commitment to the ultimate ends of global
justice, supported by the principles of universal human rights, must
obtain. As I suggested in Chapter 4, this commitment to global justice
and human rights can also contribute to the realization of lasting
peace between all the nations and peoples of the world.

I discussed also how a cosmopolitan theory of global justice based
on Rawlsian principles appeals not only to a particular conception of
moral persons but also seeks to create the basic social conditions,
institutions and practices through which human beings can actually
realize themselves as free and equal. In other words, Rawlsian principles of global justice are those upon which free and equal moral
persons would agree given the circumstances of a global original
position. However, while such principles are ideals of well-ordered
cooperation among persons, they are clearly also more than that: they
are ideals that must be realized to the greatest degree possible if real
justice is to be had. The further task, then, is to construct the social
institutions and implement the principles that will bring about the
type of global social cooperation of moral persons that cosmopolitan
justice requires.

According to Article 1 of the UDHR, the normative premiss
justifying universal rights is the principle that each human being as a
moral person is entitled to freedom and to equal dignity. Persons are
so entitled because human beings are due freedom and equal dignity
as a matter of reciprocal moral recognition. Human rights are 'part of
what is involved in being a member of the moral community' and
include 'forms of inviolability in the status of every member of the
moral community'.[1] According to the Preamble of the UDHR and the
discussions of the Third Committee of the General Assembly in 1948,
the atrocities of war and genocide are additional justifications for
prescribing the international system of human rights and generating a
global consensus on human rights norms. Thus, the justificatory
theory of the UDHR is an exercise in situated moral-political

rationality that makes a commitment to freedom and equality on the basis of political, sociological and historical analyses of the circumstances confronting all societies of the world. This position fits well with the one I outlined in Chapter 2 concerning Rawls's theory of basic or human rights. As I stated there, while the moral interests and obligations representative of those protected by human rights do not suddenly come into existence only within a formal political unit, they are only *fully* realized when implemented and protected within a legitimate legal and political system.

A central question facing a theory of global justice incorporating universal human rights is that of how cooperation between sovereign states can be possible while they are competing against each other for power and influence. In order to enable the protection of human rights, the realist tradition and its reliance on prudential rationality must be supplanted by a robust scheme of implementation at the local, national, regional and international levels, motivated by a moral commitment to the view that every human being has certain basic rights. Global implementation of human rights should not be dependent upon the continuance and convenience of national power and interests; it requires a firm commitment to cosmopolitan norms and rules by the actors involved, including individual citizens, civil society associations, NGOs, states and regional and international organizations such as the European Union and the United Nations. Through the strengthening of cosmopolitan norms, the elaboration of stronger international legal principles and the setting aside of national self-interest through recognition of the advantages received from the expansion of a pacific union, cooperation can be greatly enhanced.[2] For global principles, rules and norms to be politically significant, they cannot be merely a reflection of self-interest; rather, there must be a sense of being bound despite countervailing self-interest. This sense of being bound arises out of concern for the rights of all persons, and encompasses a corresponding sense of obligation to which those rights give rise. For this reason, the implementation and protection of human rights should provide a constraint on national self-interest, for the benefit of *all* human beings.

The codification of human rights into the UDHR affirms that only an international community based on and ensuring the same and equal human rights for all, and the measures guaranteeing the maximum worth or value of those rights, can adequately respond to the circumstances of social justice in the contemporary world. The conception of cosmopolitan justice presented here suggests that, in accepting the basis of human rights to be the freedom and equal dignity of all persons, hierarchical states must be transformed to some extent into states which uphold more democratic, egalitarian and secular principles of justice. This is because the goal of cosmopolitan justice is to transform the political sphere of global society from a sphere of mere subjects to one of world citizens. The normative content of cosmopolitan justice thus entails a concept of democracy that cannot be restricted to isolated national contexts, but must point beyond such restrictions towards a global democratic community that would ensure human rights worldwide. Because Rawls declines to extend the principles of justice to such an extent, however, his law of peoples falls short of providing the type of cosmopolitan justice needed for the realization of truly universal human rights. While it may be very difficult to bring about a scheme of global justice that fully supports the universality of human rights in world society, this book has been written to promote that effort.

Notes

Introduction

1 John Rawls, *A Theory of Justice* (Cambridge, MA: Harvard University Press, 1971). A revised edition of *A Theory of Justice* was published in 1999; all references throughout this book will be to the 1st edition.

2 In 1950, Peter Laslett stated that 'for the moment, anyway, political philosophy is dead'. In Peter Laslett (ed.), *Philosophy, Politics and Society* (Oxford: Blackwell, 1950), vii.

3 John Rawls, *The Law of Peoples, with 'The Idea of Public Reason Revisited'* (Cambridge, MA: Harvard University Press, 1999); John Rawls, 'The Law of Peoples', in Stephen Shute and Susan Hurley (eds), *On Human Rights: The Oxford Amnesty Lectures, 1993* (New York: Basic Books, 1993), 41–82.

1 Contractarian Theory and the Principles of Justice

1 Useful discussions of the different representatives of the social contract tradition can be found in Michael Lessnoff (ed.), *Social Contract Theory* (New York: New York University Press, 1991); David Boucher and Paul Kelly (eds), *The Social Contract from Hobbes to Rawls* (London and New York: Routledge, 1994); Christopher W. Morris (ed.), *The Social Contract Theorists: Critical Essays on Hobbes, Locke, and Rousseau* (Lanham, MD: Rowman & Littlefield, 1999).

2 A classic statement of this position is W. D. Ross, *The Right and the Good* (Oxford: Clarendon Press, 1930).

3 For discussions of the role of right-based theories see Ronald Dworkin, *Taking Rights Seriously* (Cambridge, MA: Harvard University Press, 1977); Alan Gewirth, *Reason and Morality* (Chicago: University of Chicago Press, 1978); J. L. Mackie, 'Can There be a Right-Based Moral Theory?', in Jeremy Waldron (ed.), *Theories of Rights* (Oxford: Oxford University Press, 1984).

4 Nozick employs the concept of side constraints in his conception of rights. Robert Nozick, *Anarchy, State, and Utopia* (New York: Basic Books, 1974), 30–42.

5   Peter Vallentyne, 'Contractarianism and the Assumption of Mutual Unconcern', *Philosophical Studies*, 56 (1989), 187.

6   For a clear discussion of the idea of natural rights see Michael Freeden, *Rights* (Minneapolis: University of Minnesota, 1991), especially chs. 2 and 3.

7   For analyses of gender issues in relationship to social contract theory see, for example, Susan Moller Okin, *Women in Western Political Thought* (Princeton, NJ: Princeton University Press, 1979); Carole Pateman, *The Problem of Political Obligation* (Berkeley, CA: University of California Press, 1986); and Anne Phillips, *Engendering Democracy* (University Park, PA: Pennsylvania State University Press, 1991).

8   Plato, *The Republic*, trans. by Benjamin Jowett (New York: Vintage Books, 1991), 46.

9   Thomas Hobbes, *Leviathan* (New York and London: Collier Macmillan, 1962), 103.

10 Ibid.

11 Ibid., 105.

12 John Locke, *The Second Treatise on Civil Government* (Buffalo, NY: Prometheus Books, 1986), 9–10.

13 Ibid., 70.

14 Ibid., 49.

15 Ibid., 94–5.

16 Jean-Jacques Rousseau, *The Social Contract*, in Roger D. Masters and Christopher Kelly (eds), *The Collected Writings of Rousseau* (Hanover and London: University Press of New England, 1994), 138.

17 The following discussion is based on Immanuel Kant, *Foundations of the Metaphysics of Morals*, trans. Lewis White Beck (Indianapolis: Bobbs-Merrill Co., 1959).

18 For an extensive examination of this Kantian ideal see Christine M. Korsgaard, *Creating the Kingdom of Ends* (Cambridge: Cambridge University Press, 1996).

19 Immanuel Kant, 'On the Common Saying "This may be true in theory, but it does not apply in practice"', in *Kant's Political Writings*, ed. Hans Reiss, trans. H. B. Nisbet (Cambridge: Cambridge University Press, 1970), 79.

20 Ibid., 80.

21 Immanuel Kant, *Lectures on Ethics*, trans. Louis Infield (Indianapolis, Hackett Co., 1981), 193–4.

22 The reasoning Rawls offers for his claim that the maximin rule is the most rational decision strategy in the context of the original position has been extensively criticized, and a variety of alternative decision strategies have been suggested for how persons in the original position would specify the minimum for their society. See, for example, Brian Barry, *The Liberal Theory of Justice* (Oxford: Clarendon Press, 1973), 87–127.

23 Brian Barry, *Justice as Impartiality* (Oxford: Clarendon Press, 1995), 58.
24 Ibid.
25 Ibid., 11–15.
26 Ibid., 57–60.
27 This characterization of Rawls's theory illustrates his concern for the priority of the right over the good. As I shall discuss below, Rawls continues to stress in *Political Liberalism* the need for a conception of justice to be concerned with the right, and not the good in any strong sense, in order to accommodate different reasonable conceptions of the good within a just and stable political sphere.
28 Barry writes, 'Rawls's incorporation of this notion of a social structure into his theory represents the coming of age of liberal political philosophy'. Ibid., 214.
29 Ibid.
30 See Nozick, *Anarchy, State, and Utopia*, 198–204, 235–8.
31 Barry, *Liberal Theory of Justice*, 29–30.
32 The most well-known intuitionists are associated with the British tradition of moral sense theory, such as Shaftesbury, Francis Hutcheson, Samuel Clarke and Thomas Reid. A classic twentieth-century account of utilitarianism based on intuitionism is G. E. Moore's *Principia Ethica* (Cambridge: Cambridge University Press, 1903).
33 Rawls makes this connection very clear when he writes that his 'principles of justice are also categorical imperatives in Kant's sense'. *A Theory of Justice*, 253.

2 The Basic Rights and Liberties

1   Onora O'Neill, *Towards Justice and Virtue: A Constructive Account of Practical Reasoning* (Cambridge: Cambridge University Press, 1996), 47.
2   Ibid., 41.
3   Another reason why Rawls employs an abstract conception of the persons in the original position is that not all features of real individuals are morally relevant. Moral choices and decisions depend upon criteria of what is and is not morally relevant with respect to persons, and thus an abstraction is performed in moral deliberation. Yet abstraction does not necessarily result in a free-floating, transparent self completely divorced from historical and social context. Therefore I think Rawls rightfully engages in abstraction, and not in idealization. This last point will return in the discussion of Michael Sandel's critique of Rawls in the last section of Chapter 2.
4   Ronald Dworkin, *Taking Rights Seriously* (Cambridge, MA: Harvard University Press, 1977), 114.

5   For a useful analysis of Kant's idea of autonomy see Allen W. Wood, *Kant's Ethical Thought* (Cambridge: Cambridge University Press, 1999), especially chapter 5. Onora O'Neill discusses both Kantian and non-Kantian accounts of autonomy in chapter 2 ('Agency and Autonomy') of her *Bounds of Justice* (Cambridge: Cambridge University Press, 2000), 29–49.

6   John Rawls, 'Social Unity and Primary Goods', in Amartya Sen and Bernard Williams (eds), *Utilitarianism and Beyond* (Cambridge: Cambridge University Press, 1982), 165–6.

7   John Rawls, 'Some Reasons for the Maximin Criterion', *American Economic Review*, 64 (1974), 143.

8   John Rawls, 'Fairness to Goodness', *Philosophical Review*, 84 (1975), 548.

9   Norman Daniels, 'Equal Liberty and Unequal Worth of Liberty', in Norman Daniels (ed.), *Reading Rawls: Critical Studies on Rawls' 'A Theory of Justice'* (Oxford: Basil Blackwell, 1975), 278.

10 John Rawls, *Justice as Fairness: A Restatement*, ed. Erin Kelly (Cambridge, MA, and London: Harvard University Press, 2001), 148–51.

11 John Rawls, *Political Liberalism* (New York: Columbia University Press, 1996). All citations of *Political Liberalism* will be from the 1996 paperback edition.

12 It might well be replied that the ideas and institutions found in the public political culture of contemporary democratic societies are there to be drawn upon only because of the influence of classical liberalism in helping to create that very culture over time. Thus Rawls might be accused of developing his 'political not metaphysical' conception of justice based on the very source from which he is seeking to distance himself. At any rate, it seems to me that Rawls's political conception of justice maintains a strong continuity with his earlier conception of justice as fairness as to its essential features.

13 Thomas Nagel, 'Moral Conflict and Political Legitimacy', *Philosophy and Public Affairs* (Summer 1987), 229.

14 Ibid., 229–30.

15 Nagel has more recently dropped the argument of epistemological restraint, while still holding to its conclusion. See Thomas Nagel, *Equality and Partiality* (Oxford: Oxford University Press, 1991), 163, n. 9.

16 Rawls also includes a version of the first principle in *Political Liberalism* which reads: 'Each person has an equal claim to a fully adequate scheme of equal basic rights and liberties, which scheme is compatible with the same scheme for all; and in this scheme the equal political liberties, and only those liberties, are to be guaranteed their fair value' (p. 5).

17 These correspond to the 'highest-order interests' of *A Theory of Justice* discussed earlier in the chapter.

[18] Ronald Dworkin, *Taking Rights Seriously* (Cambridge, MA: Harvard University Press, 1977).

[19] This question is raised in L. W. Sumner, *The Moral Foundation of Rights* (Oxford: Clarendon Press, 1987), 159.

[20] Incidentally, Rawls rejects Dworkin's characterization of justice as fairness as right-based for being a too narrow definition of his theory. Rawls explains that he prefers to regard his theory as 'working up into idealized conceptions certain fundamental intuitive ideas such as those of the person as free and equal' rather than, apparently, building upon the notion of natural rights. Again, however, I am not certain how a fundamental intuitive idea such as that of a person as free and equal differs from the idea of the natural right of equal concern and respect, which might also be regarded as a fundamental intuitive idea for those in a liberal-democratic society. See John Rawls, 'Justice as Fairness: Political Not Metaphysical', *Philosophy and Public Affairs*, 14 (1985), 236, n. 19.

[21] John Rawls, 'Kantian Constructivism in Moral Theory', *Journal of Philosophy*, 77 (1980), 517.

[22] Rex Martin, *Rawls and Rights* (Lawrence, KS: University of Kansas Press, 1985), 41.

[23] For a concise discussion of the influence of natural rights theory on contemporary human rights doctrines see Jack Donnelly, 'Human Rights as Natural Rights', *Human Rights Quarterly*, 4 (1982), 391–405.

[24] The range of rights that are to be recognized is, of course, one of the more contentious issues in human rights debates, particularly concerning the relationship between civil and political rights and economic, social and cultural rights.

[25] The UDHR and other human rights documents can be consulted in Henry J. Steiner and Philip Alston, *International Human Rights in Context: Law, Politics, and Morals* (Oxford: Clarendon Press, 1996).

[26] Recent years have seen claims made for a 'third generation' of human rights, namely, those of peace, solidarity and development, as well as rights to a clean and healthy environment. I discuss the possibility of justifying a human right to peace in Chapter 4. See the useful discussion of how the ideas of positive and negative freedoms intersect with the contract tradition in Jürgen Habermas, 'Human Rights and Popular Sovereignty: The Liberal and Republican Versions', *Ratio Juris*, 7 (March 1994), 1–13.

[27] The Vienna Declaration and Programme of Action, adopted by the 1993 UN World Conference on Human Rights, emphasized that human rights are treated as 'indivisible and interdependent and interrelated' (Paragraph 5).

[28] See Louis Henkin, *The International Bill of Rights: The Covenant on Civil and Political Rights* (New York: Columbia University Press, 1981), 24–5 and 259.

29 Jack Donnelly, 'Human Rights as Natural Rights', 400.

30 Fernando Tesón provides an excellent analysis of cultural relativism in all of its varieties, against the background of human rights standards, in his 'International Human Rights and Cultural Relativism', *Virginia Journal of International Law*, 25 (1985), 869–98.

31 See John O. Nelson, 'Are there Inalienable Rights?', *Philosophy*, 64 (1989) and 'Against Human Rights', *Philosophy* 65 (1990). In the latter essay, Nelson unabashedly asserts that human rights are nothing more than a 'wicked' and 'genocidal' imposition of foreign values (pp. 347–8).

32 Jack Donnelly, 'Human Rights as Natural Rights', 400–1.

33 Ibid., 404–5.

34 Rhoda E. Howard, 'Cultural Absolutism and the Nostalgia for Community', *Human Rights Quarterly*, 15 (1993), 329 ff.

35 Thomas Nagel, 'Personal Rights and Public Space', *Philosophy and Public Affairs*, 24 (1995), 84.

36 Kymlicka is addressing the special case of minority cultures, on the verge of extinction as cultures, within liberal-democratic multinational states. See Will Kymlicka, *Liberalism, Community, and Culture* (Oxford: Clarendon Press, 1989) and *Multicultural Citizenship* (Oxford: Clarendon Press, 1995).

37 James W. Nickel, *Making Sense of Human Rights: Philosophical Reflections on the Universal Declaration of Human Rights* (Berkeley and Los Angeles: University of California Press, 1987), 38.

38 Carl Wellman, 'A New Conception of Human Rights', in Eugene Kamenka and Alice Erh-Soon Tay (eds), *Ideas and Ideologies: Human Rights* (London: Edward Arnold, 1978), 53–6.

39 Thomas Nagel, *Equality and Partiality* (Oxford: Oxford University Press, 1991), 57.

40 See, for instance, Shlomo Avineri and Avner de-Shalit (eds), *Communitarianism and Individualism* (Oxford: Oxford University Press, 1992).

41 Michael Sandel, *Liberalism and the Limits of Justice* (Cambridge: Cambridge University Press, 1982), 20.

42 Ibid., 19.

43 John Rawls, 'Justice as Fairness: Political Not Metaphysical', 226.

44 Ibid., 225.

45 Ibid., 230.

46 Ibid., 235–6.

47 Ibid., 229.

48 Sandel, *Liberalism*, 28.

49 John Rawls, 'The Priority of Right and Ideas of the Good', *Philosophy and Public Affairs*, 17 (1988), 251.

50 John Stuart Mill, *On Liberty and Other Essays* (Oxford: Oxford University Press, 1991), 63.

51   John Rawls, 'The Domain of the Political and Overlapping Consensus',
     New York University Law Review, 64 (1989), 262.

52   Ibid., 246.

53   John Rawls, 'Justice as Fairness: Political Not Metaphysical', 232.

54   John Rawls, 'The Priority of Right and Ideas of the Good', 255.

55   Ibid., 256.

56   Ibid., 257.

57   Sandel, *Liberalism*, 20–4.

58   Norberto Bobbio correctly observes: 'The evident plurality of religious
     and moral perceptions is a historical fact . . . It is precisely this pluralism
     which constitutes the most powerful argument in favour of some of the
     most significant human rights, such as religious freedom and freedom of
     thought in general.' See Norberto Bobbio, *The Age of Rights* (Cam-
     bridge: Polity Press, 1996), 6.

59   Thomas Nagel, 'Personal Rights and Public Space', 106.

60   John Rawls, 'The Domain of the Political and Overlapping Consensus',
     249.

61   Gerald Gaus provides a nice description of the role of individual rights
     that meshes well with the account I have offered: 'A system of [publicly]
     justified rights thus allows people to live together in peace and coordinate
     their activities while honoring their commitment to publicly justify
     themselves, despite the fact that they regularly, if not typically, disagree
     on the merits or justice of particular actions . . . A liberal regime, in which
     individuals live together honoring their commitment to public
     justification in the face of pervasive moral disagreement, must be a
     regime of rights. A regime of justified rights copes with the fact of moral
     disagreement by decentralizing and dispersing moral authority.' Gerald
     Gaus, *Justificatory Liberalism: An Essay on Epistemology and Political
     Theory* (Oxford: Oxford University Press, 1996), 201. A publicly justified
     scheme of basic rights thus allows us to negotiate through conflicting
     comprehensive doctrines, without succumbing to the tyranny of the
     moral dogmatism that would result if a single comprehensive doctrine
     were elevated above all others.

3   From Domestic to International Justice

1   The 'law of nations' referred to by Rawls is the traditional name for
    international law, and is defined as the body of legal rules commonly
    considered binding on states in their relations with one another.
    Contemporary international law is defined more broadly to encompass
    the relations not only between states but also between states and persons
    and between persons and persons. On this difference, see Ray August,

Public International Law (Englewood Cliffs, NJ: Prentice Hall, 1995), 2. James Brierly, *The Law of Nations*, 6th edn (Oxford: Clarendon Press, 1963) is Rawls's one and only cited authority for international law and relations. Rawls claims that Brierly's book 'is all that we need' for the discussion of international justice.

2 On this point see Mark R Wicclair, 'Rawls and the Principle of Nonintervention', in H. Gene Blocker and Elizabeth H. Smith (eds), *John Rawls' Theory of Social Justice* (Athens, OH: Ohio University Press, 1980), 289–308.

3 Rawls does concede that the 'conditions for the law of nations may require different principles arrived at in a somewhat different way' than those put forward in his own discussion (*A Theory of Justice*, 8).

4 Thomas W. Pogge, *Realizing Rawls* (Ithaca, NY: Cornell University Press, 1989), 242 ff.

5 John Rawls, *Justice as Fairness: A Restatement*, ed. Erin Kelly (Cambridge, MA, and London: Harvard University Press, 2001), 16.

6 Thucydides, one of the earliest realists, developed several basic premisses of realism in his treatise on the Peloponnesian War. First, he asserted that states are the primary actors in the world's political system. Second, he argued that states seek power as a means and as an end to ensure their survival in an anarchical world. Power is defined in terms of the possession of resources, such that the more resources an actor possesses the more power it has. Third, he suggested that states are rational actors insofar as they pursue what is in their best interests, through appeal to prudential rather than moral reasons. State interests are driven primarily by the necessity of national survival. See Thucydides, *The Peloponnesian War*, trans. Rex Warner (New York: Penguin Books, 1972).

7 Kurt Baier, 'Justice and the Aims of Political Philosophy', *Ethics*, 99 (1989), 774.

8 Consider, for example, the following claim made by Nicholas Spykman: 'In international society all forms of coercion are permissible, including wars of destruction. This means that the struggle for power is identical with the struggle for survival, and the improvement of their relative power position becomes the primary objective of the internal and external policy of states. All else is secondary.' *America's Strategy in World Politics: The United States and the Balance of Power* (New York: Harcourt, Brace, 1942), 18.

9 Hans J. Morgenthau, *Politics Among Nations: The Struggle for Power and Peace*, 2nd edn (New York: Alfred A. Knopf, 1954), 5.

10 Pogge, *Realizing Rawls*, 224–7.

11 Hedley Bull contends that international relations occurs in an 'anarchical society', that is, a society of states ordered by the distribution of power with no effective government beyond the nation-state. The lack of an

effective supranational body with the capabilities to develop and enforce codes of conduct on individual states renders nonprudential cooperation unlikely. The dictates of power politics ordinarily makes such cooperation undesirable, and take precedence over justice. See Hedley Bull, *The Anarchical Society: A Study of Order in World Politics* (New York: Columbia University Press, 1977).

[12] Pogge, *Realizing Rawls*, 256.

[13] Pogge reiterates this point in 'An Egalitarian Law of Peoples', *Philosophy and Public Affairs*, 23 (1994).

[14] Onora O'Neill, 'Political Liberalism and Public Reason: A Critical Notice of John Rawls' Political Liberalism', *Philosophical Review* 106 (1997), 417.

[15] Charles Beitz, *Political Theory and International Relations* (Princeton, NJ: Princeton University Press, 1979), 145.

[16] See Barry Eichengreen, 'The Global Gamble on Financial Liberalization: Reflections on Capital Mobility, National Autonomy, and Social Justice', *Ethics and International Affairs*, 13 (1999), 205–26.

[17] Charles Beitz, *Political Theory and International Relations*, 137–43. Cf. Terry Nardin, *Law, Morality, and the Relations of States* (Princeton, NJ: Princeton University Press, 1983), 268: 'International justice has come to be identified with reforms aimed at securing a more equal distribution of wealth rather than with conduct according to the common rules of international society.'

[18] I use 'intervene' here somewhat loosely and in a strong sense, since people clearly cannot live together in society without interfering to some degree with each other's lives. The classic argument for a concept of negative freedom from constraint or interference is, of course, provided by John Stuart Mill in *On Liberty*.

[19] See C. W. Previté-Orton, *The Defensor Pacis of Marcilius of Padua* (Cambridge: Cambridge University Press, 1928).

[20] On the contributions of early-modern theorists see David P. Calleo, 'Reflections on the Idea of the Nation-State', in Charles A. Kupchan (ed.), *Nationalism and Nationalities in the New Europe* (Ithaca, NY: Cornell University Press, 1995), esp. p. 19.

[21] Avishai Margalit and Joseph Raz, 'National Self-Determination', *Journal of Philosophy*, 87 (1990), 444.

[22] I shall offer a more extensive discussion of the connection between human rights and peace in Chapter 4.

[23] See Hurst Hannum, 'Rethinking Self-Determination', *Virginia Journal of International Law*, 34 (1993).

[24] Janice E. Thomson, 'State Sovereignty in International Relations: Bridging the Gap between Theory and Empirical Research', *International Studies Quarterly*, 39 (1995), 219.

25   Rupert Emerson, *Self-Determination Revisited in the Era of Decoloniza-tion* (Cambridge, MA: Harvard University Press, 1964), 61.

26   See also the Declaration on Principles of International Law Concerning Friendly Relations and Cooperation Among States in Accordance with the Charter of the United Nations (1970): 'Nothing in the foregoing paragraphs [asserting the principle of equal rights and self-determination of peoples] shall be construed as authorizing or encouraging any action which would dismember or impair, totally or in part, the territorial integrity or political unity of sovereign and independent States . . .'

27   F. H. Hinsley, *Power and the Pursuit of Peace: Theory and Practice in Relations Between States* (London: Cambridge University Press, 1963), 26.

28   On the conventional dichotomy that divides international relations and domestic politics, that is, on how the international and the national are viewed as oppositions in international relations theory and practice, see R. B. J. Walker, 'Security, Sovereignty, and the Challenge of World Politics', *Alternatives*, 15 (1990), 3–28.

29   Nicholas Greenwood points out that another interesting development is the increasing role of non-state actors, such as NGOs, in devising new methods of intervention and promoting the view that it is no longer the state which can claim sole responsibility for 'the common good'. Nicholas Greenwood, 'Intervention for the Common Good', in Michael Mastanduno and Gene Lyons (eds), *Beyond Westphalia? National Sovereignty and International Intervention* (Baltimore: Johns Hopkins University Press, 1994). Based on his work with the United Nations International Criminal Tribunals for the former Yugoslavia and Rwanda, Justice Richard Goldstone convincingly asserts that 'sovereignty, which was previously a state's best shield against any international intervention, is no longer absolute'. *For Humanity: Reflections of a War Crimes Investigator* (New Haven and London: Yale University Press, 2000), 126.

30   Hurst Hannum, *Autonomy, Sovereignty, and Self-Determination: The Accommodation of Conflicting Rights* (Philadelphia: University of Pennsylvania Press, 1990), 27.

31   Hugh Seton-Watson, *Nations and States* (London: Methuen, 1977), 1.

32   James Crawford, 'The Rights of Peoples: "Peoples" or "Governments"?', in James Crawford (ed.), *The Rights of Peoples* (Oxford: Oxford University Press, 1988), 55.

33   Hans Kelsen, *The Law of the United Nations: A Critical Analysis of its Fundamental Problems* (New York: Praeger, 1951), 51–3.

34   Charles A. Kupchan, 'Introduction: Nationalism Resurgent', in Charles A. Kupchan (ed.), *Nationalism and Nationalities in the New Europe* (Ithaca, NY: Cornell University Press, 1995), 4.

35   On this point see Donald L. Horowitz, 'Self-Determination: Politics,

Philosophy, and Law', in Ian Shapiro and Will Kymlicka (eds), *Ethnicity and Group Rights* (New York: New York University Press, 1997). Consider the difficulties presented by the events in Eastern Europe and especially the former Yugoslavia since 1989. As the Soviet Bloc disintegrated, the principle of self-determination appeared as an effective mechanism to justify the autonomy and freedom of the states recognized by the established international system. Yet this same system was thrown into turmoil as the principle of self-determination was invoked by ever-smaller groups of peoples existing across, within, or beyond recognized territorial borders. As the drive towards self-determination became more local, the doctrine became always more exclusive. A nice discussion of these matters is presented in Mervyn Frost, *Ethics in International Affairs* (Cambridge: Cambridge University Press, 1996), ch. 7. For an argument that international justice, contra Rawls, requires intervention (given certain legitimate criteria) see Barbara Harff, 'Rescuing Endangered Peoples: Missed Opportunities', *Social Research*, 62 (1995).

36 An extensive discussion of these and related issues is found in Will Kymlicka, *Multicultural Citizenship* (Oxford: Clarendon Press, 1995).

37 Pogge, *Realizing Rawls*, 227.

38 Sissela Bok has suggested that we can identify the following categories of values that are broadly shared across national, ethnic, religious and other boundaries: (1) some form of positive duties regarding mutual support, loyalty and reciprocity; (2) negative duties to refrain from harmful action; (3) norms for at least rudimentary fairness and procedural justice in cases of conflict regarding both positive and negative injunctions. Such common values, she argues, can provide the basis for international dialogue and negotiations that build more robust global norms concerning how to treat all human beings justly. Sissela Bok, *Common Values* (Columbia and London: University of Missouri Press, 1995), esp. ch. 1.

39 Pogge, *Realizing Rawls*, 228.

40 Ibid.

41 Charles Beitz, *Political Theory and International Relations* (Princeton, NJ: Princeton University Press, 1979); Brian Barry, *The Liberal Theory of Justice* (Oxford: Clarendon Press, 1973); T. M. Scanlon, 'Rawls' Theory of Justice', *University of Pennsylvania Law Review*, 121 (1973).

42 Beitz, *Political Theory*, 151.

43 For Pogge's discussion of these features, see 'Cosmopolitanism and Sovereignty', in Chris Brown (ed.), *Political Restructuring in Europe: Ethical Perspectives* (London: Routledge, 1994), 89–122.

44 Pogge, *Realizing Rawls*, 272.

45 R. J. Vincent, *Human Rights and International Relations* (Cambridge: Cambridge University Press, 1986), 38.

46 John Rawls, 'Reply to Alexander and Musgrave', *Quarterly Journal of Economics*, 88 (1974), 634.
47 Bok, *Common Values*, ch. 2.
48 Pogge, *Realizing Rawls*, 270.
49 Ibid., 272–3.
50 Ibid., 138.
51 Ibid., 147.

4 The Problem of Human Rights

1 Note that the list of principles making up the law of peoples is expanded by Rawls from seven in 1993 to eight in 1999. The new principle he has added is number eight in the 1999 list.
2 See Immanual Kant, *Metaphysics of Morals*, trans. Mary Gregor (Cambridge: Cambridge University Press, 1996), 89–124.
3 These ideas are reiterated by Rawls in *The Law of Peoples*, 71–2. Rawls maintains in both the 1993 and 1999 versions that non-liberal persons are not to be considered as free and equal individuals, as in liberal societies. Rather, at the level of the second original position, only non-liberal peoples *as a whole* are considered as free and equal parties in the choice procedure. In other words, individual persons are not recognized as such within Rawls's conception of non-liberal hierarchical societies.
4 Recall that in *A Theory of Justice* Rawls secures in the original position a deep separation between choice and the contingent features of the agent's society, with the result that choice depends primarily upon the nature of the agent as a moral and rational being and very little upon contingent social circumstances. From this position, the claims of human rights that follow from the principles of justice as fairness are based upon the possession of moral personality and not upon social convention, custom or tradition.
5 Eugene Kamenka, 'Human Rights: Peoples' Rights', in James Crawford (ed.), *The Rights of Peoples* (Oxford: Clarendon Press, 1988), 133.
6 As Henkin explains, because international law is made by states assuming legal obligations, states party to international human rights agreements can be seen in two different roles: as legislators, making law, and as obligors, having obligations to ensure the human rights of their inhabitants. International law focuses on the state's obligations; but under that law, once it is in effect, the rights are rights of the individual. It is true that there are controversies in the literature as to whether the individual has human rights in international law – whether rights (and obligations) in this case work only among states, or also between an individual and his or her state. But there are no disagreements that the

individual has human rights, under international law, against his or her domestic society. Louis Henkin, *The International Bill of Rights: The Covenant on Civil and Political Rights* (New York: Columbia University Press, 1981).

7   Martha Nussbaum, *Sex and Social Justice* (New York and Oxford: Oxford University Press, 1999), 97.

8   See Ken Booth, 'Three Tyrannies', in Tim Dunne and Nicholas Wheeler (eds), *Human Rights in Global Politics* (Cambridge: Cambridge University Press, 1999), 36–46.

9   For an alternative perspective, see Jürgen Habermas, 'Remarks on Legitimation Through Human Rights', *Philosophy and Social Criticism*, 24 (1998), 157–71.

10 Immanuel Kant, 'Conjectures on the Beginning of Human History', in *Political Writings*, ed. Hans Reiss (Cambridge: Cambridge University Press, 1970), 231–2.

11 Immanuel Kant, 'Perpetual Peace', in *Political Writings*, ed. Reiss (Cambridge: Cambridge University Press, 1970), 104.

12 The reader should bear in mind that the discussion here represents a modernized and liberal Kantian interpretation, setting aside some of Kant's more specific and conservative views. For example, even though Kant defines citizens as free, equal and independent, he suggests that women, servants, minors and other 'passive' citizens are not to be enfranchised. Such a view reveals the historically limited nature of some of Kant's thinking on social issues. To be fair, though, it should also be noted that Kant contends that, in a just state, 'passive' citizens ought to be enabled to work up to the full status of 'active' citizens, who satisfy special property qualifications. Even on this matter, then, Kant opens the way for some kind of liberal reform. See Kant, 'On the Common Saying "This may be true in theory, but it does not apply in practice"', in *Kant's Political Writings*, ed. Reiss, 75–9, and Kant, *Metaphysics of Morals*, trans. Mary Gregor (Cambridge: Cambridge University Press, 1996), 89–113. Allen D. Rosen usefully discusses many of these issues in his *Kant's Theory of Justice* (Ithaca, NY, and London: Cornell University Press, 1993).

13 Immanuel Kant, *Foundations of the Metaphysics of Morals*, trans. Lewis White Beck (Indianapolis: Bobbs-Merrill Co., 1959), 46.

14 Ibid., 107–8.

15 Ibid., 99–100.

16 See, for example, Michael Doyle, 'Kant, Liberal Legacies, and Foreign Affairs, Part I', *Philosophy and Public Affairs*, 12 (1983), 205–35 and 'Kant, Liberal Legacies, and Foreign Affairs, Part II', *Philosophy and Public Affairs*, 12 (1983), 323–53; David P. Forsythe, *Human Rights and Peace: International and National Dimensions* (Lincoln, NE, and London:

University of Nebraska Press, 1993); Nils Peter Gleditsch, 'Democracy and Peace: Good News for Human Rights Advocates', in Donna Gomien (ed.), *Broadening the Frontiers of Human Rights* (Oxford: Oxford University Press, 1993); James Lee Ray, *Democracy and International Conflict* (Columbia, SC: University of South Carolina Press, 1995); and Bruce Russett, *Grasping the Democratic Peace: Principles for a Post-Cold War World* (Princeton, NJ: Princeton University Press, 1993).

[17] Russett, *Grasping the Democratic Peace*, 30–8.

[18] See Zeev Maoz and Bruce Russett, 'Normative and Structural Causes of Democratic Peace, 1946–1986', *American Political Science Review*, 87 (1993), 624–38. On the importance of economic interdependence to the reduction of interstate conflict, see John R. O'Neal and Bruce Russett, 'The Kantian Peace', *World Politics*, 51 (1999), 1–36.

[19] Rawls, 'The Idea of an Overlapping Consensus', 4.

[20] Rawls, 'The Priority of Right and Ideas of the Good', 266.

[21] Rawls, *Political Liberalism*, 13, 175.

[22] Ibid., 59.

[23] Ibid., 195.

[24] Ibid., 197–8.

[25] Ronald Dworkin, *Taking Rights Seriously*, 182.

[26] See Philip Alston, 'Peace as a Human Right', *Bulletin of Peace Proposals*, 11 (1980), 319–30; Marek Thee, 'Towards a Culture of Peace Based on Human Rights', *The International Journal of Human Rights*, 1 (1997), 18–34; and Katrina Tomasevski, 'The Right to Peace', *Current Research on Peace and Violence*, 5 (1982), 42–69.

[27] See, for example, David P. Forsythe, *Human Rights and Peace: International and National Dimensions* (Lincoln, NE: University of Nebraska Press, 1993), 3–7, who dismisses the notion of a right to peace as 'diplomatic rhetoric' that leaves the claimed right without 'independent and specific meaning', such that we cannot 'know what we are obligated to do under' such a right. In what follows I attempt to clarify the meaning of, and specify the obligations that follow from, the right to peace. For an approach that emphasizes the secondary role of rights in the creation of a peace culture, see Rajni Kothari, 'Peace, Development and Life', *Bulletin of Peace Proposals*, 18 (1987), 261–7.

[28] For discussions about the appropriate justificatory tests for human rights, see Maurice Cranston, 'Human Rights, Real and Supposed', in D. D. Raphael (ed.), *Political Theory and the Rights of Man* (Bloomington: Indiana University Press, 1967), 43–54; Jack Donnelly, *Universal Human Rights in Theory and Practice* (Ithaca, NY: Cornell University Press, 1989), 9–45; Henry Shue, *Basic Rights: Subsistence, Affluence, and U.S. Foreign Policy*, 2nd edn (Princeton, NJ: Princeton University Press, 1996), 13–20.

29 On third-generation rights see UNESCO, *Symposium on the Study of New Human Rights: The Rights of Solidarity* (Paris: UNESCO, 1980); Stephen Marks, 'Emerging Human Rights: A New Generation for the 1980s?', *Rutgers Law Review*, 33 (1981), 435–52.

30 On the dangers of employing the metaphor of successive generations of human rights, see Carl Wellman, 'Solidarity, the Individual and Human Rights', *Human Rights Quarterly*, 22 (2000), 639–57, at 640–1.

31 See, for example, Stephen Marks, 'Emerging Human Rights: A New Generation for the 1980s?', *passim*; Philip Alston, 'Conjuring up New Human Rights: A Proposal for Quality Control', *American Journal of International Law*, 78 (1984), 607–21; and Donnelly, *Universal Human Rights*, 143–54.

32 David P. Barash (ed.), *Approaches to Peace: A Reader in Peace Studies* (Oxford: Oxford University Press, 2000), 2.

33 Johan Galtung has pioneered the idea of structural violence. See his 'Violence, Peace and Peace Research', in Johan Galtung (ed.), *Essays in Peace Research* (Copenhagen: Ejlers, 1975).

34 Immanuel Kant, 'Perpetual Peace', 94–5. See also 'Conjectures on the Beginning of Human History', 231–2.

35 Gandhi rejects the use of violence as a way of eradicating violence, stating that 'it would be absurd to say that violence has ever brought peace to mankind'. Mahatma Gandhi, *Collected Works*, vol. 84 (New Delhi: Ministry of Information and Broadcasting, 1946), 127. He reasoned that, while resorting to violence in order to eradicate violence 'appears to do good, the good is only temporary; the evil it does is permanent'. Gandhi, *Collected Works*, vol. 27 (New Delhi: Ministry of Information and Broadcasting, 1925), 134.

36 See Carnegie Commission, *Preventing Deadly Conflict: Final Report* (Washington, DC: Carnegie Commission on Preventing Deadly Conflict, 1997), pp. xxv–xxvi. For a justification of humanitarian intervention on the basis of a human rights liberalism see Michael J. Smith, 'Humanitarian Intervention: An Overview of the Ethical Issues', in Joel H. Rosenthal (ed.), *Ethics and International Affairs: A Reader* (Washington, DC: Georgetown University Press, 1999). On this point see also Fernando Tesón, 'Kantian International Liberalism', in David R. Mapel and Terry Nardin (eds), *International Society: Diverse Ethical Perspectives* (Princeton, NJ: Princeton University Press, 1998). Tesón argues for a modified Kantian view recognizing a limited right of humanitarian intervention, according to which 'force may only be used in defense of persons, not of states as such'. Under this scheme force will 'sometimes have to be used against nonliberal regimes as a last resort in self-defense or in defense of human rights' (pp. 111–12).

37 Martha C. Nussbaum, *Sex and Social Justice* (Oxford: Oxford University

Press, 1999), 39. Amartya Sen discusses various aspects of the capabilities approach to human rights in his *Development as Freedom* (New York: Anchor Books, 2000).

[38] Nussbaum, *Sex and Social Justice*, 39.

[39] Ibid., 41–2.

[40] A minimally good human life means that all people should have at least their basic capabilities protected from violent harm, whatever else they have and pursue. For an alternative discussion of the possibility of generating a list of goods valuable to all agents, see Thomas Pogge, 'Human Flourishing and Universal Justice', *Social Philosophy and Policy*, 16 (1999), 333–61.

[41] For more on the argument that human rights norms require democratic governance, and on the linkage between democratic norms, human rights and the peaceful resolution of conflict, see David Beetham, 'Linking Democracy and Human Rights', *Peace Review*, 9 (1997), 351–6; David Held, *Democracy and the Global Order* (Cambridge: Polity Press, 1995); James Lee Ray, *Democracy and International Conflict* (Columbia, SC: University of South Carolina Press, 1995); Bruce Russett, *Grasping the Democratic Peace*.

[42] One response to the claim that governments have a duty not to have and use nuclear weapons is that it conflicts with the duty to protect one's citizens, or human beings more widely, as a corollary to the right to self-defence. However, the principle of self-defence is not unlimited and is constrained, for example, by humanitarian laws of war derived from the just war principle of non-combatant immunity. Under the *jus in bello* tradition, discrimination between combatants and non-combatants is intended to prevent intentional harm to innocent persons not involved in attempting to harm others. While even conventional warfare presents a very real threat of harm to non-combatants, conventional weapons at least offer the possibility of a discriminate response to aggression. On the other hand, nuclear weapons, due to their awesome destructive power, produce huge numbers of indiscriminate casualties. Because of their very design and purpose, the use of nuclear weapons evidences intentional harm directed at non-combatants. The presence of intent also leads the use of nuclear weapons to violate the other *jus in bello* principle, of proportionality, insofar as evil (or injustice) may not be used as a means to achieve good (or justice), in this case indiscriminately sacrificing the lives of numerous innocents to stop aggression. I conclude, then, that the use of nuclear weapons can never be just. For more on the just war tradition, see Richard Regan, *Just War: Principles and Cases* (Washington, DC: Catholic University of America Press, 1996), and Michael Walzer, *Just and Unjust Wars: A Moral Argument with Historical Illustrations*, 2nd edn (New York: Basic Books, 1992).

[43] Kant, 'Perpetual Peace', 100.

[44] The source for all information in this section is the *SIPRI Yearbook 2000: Armaments, Disarmament and International Security* (Oxford: Oxford University Press, 2000). Additional information can be found in Carnegie Commission, *Preventing Deadly Conflict*.

[45] See Berto Jongman, 'War and Political Violence', *Jaarboek Vrede en Veilegheid* (1996), 148 and the US Committee for Refugees, *World Refugee Survey 1997*, 84.

[46] These issues are surveyed in Carnegie Commission, *Preventing Deadly Conflict*. A significant effort to document the traumatic effects of state oppression and violent conflict is *The Truth and Reconciliation Commission of South Africa Report* (New York: Grove's/St Martin's, 1999), which includes extensive testimony by both victims and perpetrators of political violence.

[47] See Karl Marx, 'On the Jewish Question', in Robert Tucker (ed.), *The Marx-Engels Reader*, 2nd edn (New York: W. W. Norton, 1978).

[48] James Nickel, *Making Sense of Human Rights* (Berkeley, CA: University of California Press, 1987), 117.

[49] Virginia Held, 'Can a Random Collection of Individuals Be Morally Responsible?', *Journal of Philosophy*, 67 (1971), 471–81. See also the essays collected in Peter French (ed.), *Individual and Collective Responsibility*, 2nd rev. edn (Rochester, VT: Schenkman Books, 1998).

[50] Derek Parfit, *Reasons and Persons* (Oxford: Oxford University Press, 1986), 67–86.

[51] See Nicholas Rescher, 'Collective Responsibility', *Journal of Social Philosophy*, 29 (1998), 49–50.

[52] Alex Mintz and Steve Chan, *Defense, Welfare and Growth: Perspectives and Evidence* (New York: Routledge, 1992).

[53] Ibid. See also Alex Mintz (ed.), *The Political Economy of Military Spending in the United States* (New York: Routledge, 1992).

[54] See Lawrence Klein, Fu-chen Lo and Warwick J. McKibben (eds), *Arms Reduction: Economic Implications in the Post Cold War Era* (New York: UN University Press, 1995). See also Lloyd J. Dumas and Marek Thee (eds), *Making Peace Possible: The Promise of Economic Conversion* (New York: Pergamon Press, 1989).

[55] For an early ethical argument in support of this type of economic conversion, see William James (1871), 'The Moral Equivalent of War', in *Essays on Faith and Morals* (Cleveland and New York: Meridian Books, 1962), 311–28.

[56] This argument is advanced by Donnelly in *Universal Human Rights*, 16–19. As he puts it, human rights say in effect 'treat human beings as free and equal and you'll get free and equal human beings'.

[57] Darrel Moellendorf, in 'Constructing the Law of Peoples', *Pacific*

Philosophical Quarterly 77 (1996), argues for a similar conception of the original position with respect to Rawls's later account of international justice. See also Scanlon, 'Rawls' Theory of Justice', 1066–7.

Conclusion

1   Thomas Nagel, 'Personal Rights and Public Space', *Philosophy and Public Affairs*, 24 (1995), 85.
2   An excellent and extensive discussion of developing the types of institutional mechanisms advocated by the present discussion can be found in David Held's account of a cosmopolitan democratic law, implemented within the context of a reformed United Nations system, in his *Democracy and the Global Order*, especially chs. 10, 11 and 12.

Bibliography

Alston, Philip, 'Peace as a Human Right', *Bulletin of Peace Proposals*, 11 (1980), 319–30.

——, 'Conjuring up New Human Rights: A Proposal for Quality Control', *American Journal of International Law*, 78 (1984), 607–21.

August, Ray, *Public International Law*. Englewood Cliffs, NJ: Prentice Hall, 1995.

Avineri, Shlomo and Avner de-Shalit (eds), *Communitarianism and Individualism*. Oxford: Oxford University Press, 1992.

Baier, Kurt, 'Justice and the Aims of Political Philosophy', *Ethics*, 99 (1989), 771–90.

Barash, David P. (ed.), *Approaches to Peace: A Reader in Peace Studies*. Oxford: Oxford University Press, 2000.

Barry, Brian, *The Liberal Theory of Justice*. Oxford: Clarendon Press, 1973.

——, *Justice as Impartiality*. Oxford: Clarendon Press, 1995.

Beitz, Charles, 'Human Rights and Social Justice', in Peter G. Brown and Douglas MacLean (eds), *Human Rights and U.S. Foreign Policy*. Lexington, MA: Lexington Books, 1979.

——, *Political Theory and International Relations*. Princeton, NJ: Princeton University Press, 1979.

——, 'Rawls's Law of Peoples', *Ethics*, 110 (2000), 669–96.

Beetham, David, 'Linking Democracy and Human Rights', *Peace Review*, 9 (1997), 351–6.

Blocker, H. Gene and Elizabeth H. Smith (eds), *John Rawls' Theory of Social Justice*. Athens, OH: Ohio University Press, 1980.

Bobbio, Norberto, *The Age of Rights*. Cambridge: Polity Press, 1996.

Bok, Sissela, *Common Values*. Columbia, MO, and London: University of Missouri Press, 1995.

Booth, Ken, 'Three Tyrannies', in Tim Dunne and Nicholas Wheeler (eds), *Human Rights in Global Politics*. Cambridge: Cambridge University Press, 1999, 31–70.

Boucher, David and Paul Kelly (eds), *The Social Contract from Hobbes to Rawls*. London and New York: Routledge, 1994.

Brownlie, Ian, *Basic Documents on Human Rights*. Oxford: Oxford University Press, 1981.

Buchanan, Allen, 'Rawls's Law of Peoples: Rules for a Vanished Westphalian World', *Ethics*, 110 (2000), 697–721.

Buergenthal, Thomas, *International Human Rights*. Minneapolis: West Publishing Co., 1988.

Bull, Hedley, *The Anarchical Society: A Study of Order in World Politics*. New York: Columbia University Press, 1977.

Calleo, David P., 'Reflections on the Idea of the Nation-State', in Charles A. Kupchan (ed.), *Nationalism and Nationalities in the New Europe*. Ithaca, NY: Cornell University Press, 1995, 15–36.

Carnegie Commission, *Preventing Deadly Conflict: Final Report*. Washington, DC: Carnegie Commission on Preventing Deadly Conflict, 1997.

Cassese, Antonio, *International Law in a Divided World*. Oxford: Clarendon Press, 1986.

Cohen, G. A., 'Freedom, Justice, and Capitalism', in *History, Labour, and Freedom*. Oxford: Clarendon Press, 1988, 286–304.

Cranston, Maurice, 'Human Rights, Real and Supposed', in D. D. Raphael (ed.), *Political Theory and the Rights of Man*. Bloomington: Indiana University Press, 1967, 43–54.

Crawford, James, 'The Rights of Peoples: "Peoples" or "Governments"?', in James Crawford (ed.), *The Rights of Peoples*. Oxford: Oxford University Press, 1988, 55–67.

Daniels, Norman, 'Equal Liberty and Unequal Worth of Liberty', in Norman Daniels (ed.), *Reading Rawls: Critical Studies on Rawls' 'A Theory of Justice'*. Oxford: Basil Blackwell, 1975, 253–81.

Donnelly, Jack, 'Human Rights as Natural Rights', *Human Rights Quarterly*, 4 (1982), 391–405.

——, *Universal Human Rights in Theory and Practice*. Ithaca, NY: Cornell University Press, 1989.

Doyle, Michael, 'Kant, Liberal Legacies, and Foreign Affairs, Part I', *Philosophy and Public Affairs*, 12 (1983), 205–35.

——, 'Kant, Liberal Legacies, and Foreign Affairs, Part II', *Philosophy and Public Affairs*, 12 (1983), 323–53.

Dumas, Lloyd J. and Marek Thee (eds), *Making Peace Possible: The Promise of Economic Conversion*. New York: Pergamon Press, 1989.

Duncan, Graeme, *Democratic Theory and Practice*. Cambridge: Cambridge University Press, 1983.

Dunne, Tim and Nicholas Wheeler (eds), *Human Rights in Global Politics*. Cambridge: Cambridge University Press, 1999.

Dworkin, Ronald, *Taking Rights Seriously*. Cambridge, MA: Harvard University Press, 1977.

Eichengreen, Barry, 'The Global Gamble on Financial Liberalization: Reflections on Capital Mobility, National Autonomy, and Social Justice', *Ethics and International Affairs*, 13 (1999), 205–26.

Emerson, Rupert, *Self-Determination Revisited in the Era of Decolonization*. Cambridge, MA: Harvard University Press, 1964.

Finnis, John, *Natural Law and Natural Rights*. Oxford: Clarendon Press, 1980.

Forsythe, David P., *Human Rights and Peace: International and National Dimensions*. Lincoln, NE, and London: University of Nebraska Press, 1993.

Freeden, Michael, *Rights*. Minneapolis: University of Minnesota Press, 1991.

French, Peter (ed.), *Individual and Collective Responsibility*, 2nd rev. edn. Rochester, VT: Schenkman Books, 1998.

Frost, Mervyn, *Ethics in International Affairs*. Cambridge: Cambridge University Press, 1996.

Galston, William A., 'Pluralism and Social Unity', *Ethics*, 99 (1989), 711–26.

Galtung, Johan (ed.), *Essays in Peace Research*. Copenhagen: Ejlers, 1975.

Gandhi, Mahatma, *Collected Works*, vol. 27. New Delhi: Ministry of Information and Broadcasting, 1925.

——, *Collected Works*, vol. 84. New Delhi: Ministry of Information and Broadcasting, 1946.

Gaus, Gerald, *Justificatory Liberalism: An Essay on Epistemology and Political Theory*. Oxford: Oxford University Press, 1996.

Gauthier, David, 'The Social Contract as Ideology', *Philosophy and Public Affairs* 6 (1977), 130–64.

——, *Morals by Agreement*. Oxford: Clarendon Press, 1986.

Gewirth, Alan, *Reason and Morality*. Chicago: University of Chicago Press, 1978.

Gleditsch, Nils Peter, 'Democracy and Peace: Good News for Human Rights Advocates', in Donna Gomien (ed.), *Broadening the Frontiers of Human Rights*. Oxford: Oxford University Press, 1993, 287–306.

Goldstone, Richard J., *For Humanity: Reflections of a War Crimes Investigator*. New Haven, CT, and London: Yale University Press, 2000.

Greenwood, Nicholas, 'Intervention for the Common Good', in Michael Mastanduno and Gene Lyons (eds), *Beyond Westphalia? National Sovereignty and International Intervention*. Baltimore: Johns Hopkins University Press, 1994, 43–58.

Gurr, Ted Robert, *Minorities at Risk: A Global View of Ethnopolitical Conflict*. Washington, DC: United States Institute of Peace Press, 1993.

Habermas, Jürgen, *Legitimation Crisis*. Boston: Beacon Press, 1975.

——, 'Human Rights and Popular Sovereignty: The Liberal and Republican Versions', *Ratio Juris*, 7 (1994), 1–13.

——, 'Remarks on Legitimation Through Human Rights', *Philosophy and Social Criticism*, 24 (1998), 157–71.

Hannum, Hurst, *Autonomy, Sovereignty, and Self-Determination: The Accommodation of Conflicting Rights*. Philadelphia: University of Pennsylvania Press, 1990.

——, 'Rethinking Self-Determination', *Virginia Journal of International Law*, 34 (1993), 1–69.

Harff, Barbara, 'Rescuing Endangered Peoples: Missed Opportunities', *Social Research*, 62 (1995), 25–40.

Hart, H. L. A., 'Are there Any Natural Rights?', in Jeremy Waldron (ed.), *Theories of Rights*. Oxford: Oxford University Press, 1984, 77–90.

Held, David, *Democracy and the Global Order: From the Modern State to Cosmopolitan Governance*. Cambridge: Polity Press, 1995.

Held, Virginia, 'Can a Random Collection of Individuals be Morally Responsible?', *Journal of Philosophy*, 67 (1971), 471–81.

Henkin, Louis, 'International Human Rights as "Rights"', in J. Roland Pennock and John Chapman (eds), *Human Rights: Nomos XXIII*. New York: New York University Press, 1981, 257–80.

——, *The International Bill of Rights: The Covenant on Civil and Political Rights*. New York: Columbia University Press, 1981.

Hinsley, F. H., *Power and the Pursuit of Peace: Theory and Practice in Relations between States*. London: Cambridge University Press, 1963.

Hobbes, Thomas, *Leviathan*. New York and London: Collier Macmillan, 1962.

Hooker, Richard, *Of the Laws of Ecclesiastical Polity*. New York: E. P. Dutton, 1925.

Horowitz, Donald L., 'Self-Determination: Politics, Philosophy, and Law', in Ian Shapiro and Will Kymlicka (eds), *Ethnicity and Group Rights*. New York: New York University Press, 1997, 421–63.

Howard, Rhoda E., 'Cultural Absolutism and the Nostalgia for Community', *Human Rights Quarterly*, 15 (1993), 315–38.

Hume, David, *Enquiries Concerning Human Understanding and Concerning the Principles of Morals*. Oxford: Clarendon Press, 1961.

James, William, 'The Moral Equivalent of War', in *Essays on Faith and Morals*. Cleveland and New York: Meridian Books, 1962, 311–28.

Jongman, Berto, 'War and Political Violence', *Jaarboek Vrede en Veilegheid 1996* (1996), 142–60.

Kamenka, Eugene, 'Human Rights: Peoples' Rights', in James Crawford (ed.), *The Rights of Peoples*. Oxford: Clarendon Press, 1988, 127–40.

—— and Alice Erh-Soon Tay, *Ideas and Ideologies: Human Rights*. London: Edward Arnold, 1978.

Kant, Immanuel, *Foundations of the Metaphysics of Morals*, trans. Lewis White Beck. Indianapolis: Bobbs-Merrill Co., 1959.

——, *Kant's Political Writings*, ed. Hans Reiss, trans. H. B. Nisbet. Cambridge: Cambridge University Press, 1970.

——, *Anthropology from a Pragmatic Point of View*, trans. Victor Lyle Dowdell. Carbondale and Edwardsville, IL: Southern Illinois University Press, 1978.

——, *Lectures on Ethics*, trans. Louis Infield. Indianapolis: Hackett Publishing Co., 1981.

——, *Metaphysics of Morals*, trans. Mary Gregor. Cambridge: Cambridge University Press, 1996.

Kelsen, Hans, *The Law of the United Nations: A Critical Analysis of its Fundamental Problems*. New York: Praeger, 1951.

Klein, Lawrence, Fu-chen Lo, and Warwick J. McKibben (eds), *Arms Reduction: Economic Implications in the Post Cold War Era*. New York: UN University Press, 1995.

Korsgaard, Christine M., *Creating the Kingdom of Ends*. Cambridge: Cambridge University Press, 1996.

Kupchan, Charles A., 'Introduction: Nationalism Resurgent', in Charles A. Kupchan (ed.), *Nationalism and Nationalities in the New Europe*. Ithaca, NY: Cornell University Press, 1995.

Kymlicka, Will, *Liberalism, Community, and Culture*. Oxford: Clarendon Press, 1989.

——, *Multicultural Citizenship*. Oxford: Clarendon Press, 1995.

Laslett, Peter (ed.), *Philosophy, Politics and Society*. Oxford: Blackwell, 1950.

Lessnoff, Michael (ed.), *Social Contract Theory*. New York: New York University Press, 1991.

——, *Political Philosophers of the Twentieth Century*. Oxford: Blackwell, 1999.

Locke, John, *The Second Treatise on Civil Government*. Buffalo, NY: Prometheus Books, 1986.

MacIntyre, Alisdair, *After Virtue*, 2nd edn. Notre Dame, IN: University of Notre Dame Press, 1984.

Mackie, John L., 'Can there be a Right-Based Moral Theory?', in Jeremy Waldron (ed.), *Theories of Rights*. Oxford: Oxford University Press, 1984, 168–81.

Maoz, Zeev and Bruce Russett, 'Normative and Structural Causes of Democratic Peace, 1946–1986', *American Political Science Review*, 87 (1993), 624–38.

Margalit, Avishai and Joseph Raz, 'National Self-Determination', *The Journal of Philosophy*, 88 (1990), 439–61.

Marks, Stephen, 'Emerging Human Rights: A New Generation for the 1980s?', *Rutgers Law Review*, 33 (1981), 435–52.

Martin, Rex, *Rawls and Rights*. Lawrence, KS: University of Kansas Press, 1985.

Marx, Karl, 'On the Jewish Question', in Robert Tucker (ed.), *The Marx-Engels Reader*, 2nd edn. New York: W. W. Norton, 1978, 26–52.

Mastanduno, Michael, and Gene Lyons (eds), *Beyond Westphalia? National Sovereignty and International Intervention*. Baltimore: Johns Hopkins University Press, 1994.

Mill, John Stuart, *On Liberty and Other Essays*. Oxford: Oxford University Press, 1991.

Mintz, Alex (ed.), *The Political Economy of Military Spending in the United States*. New York: Routledge, 1992.

—— and Steve Chan (eds), *Defense, Welfare and Growth: Perspectives and Evidence*. New York: Routledge, 1992.

Moellendorf, Darrel, 'Constructing the Law of Peoples', *Pacific Philosophical Quarterly*, 77 (1996), 132–54.

Moore, G. E., *Principia Ethica*. Cambridge: Cambridge University Press, 1903.

Morgenthau, Hans J., *Politics Among Nations: The Struggle for Power and Peace*, 2nd edn. New York: Alfred A. Knopf, 1954.

Morris, Christopher W. (ed.), *The Social Contract Theorists: Critical Essays on Hobbes, Locke, and Rousseau*. Lanham, MD: Rowman & Littlefield, 1999.

Nagel, Thomas, 'Moral Conflict and Political Legitimacy', *Philosophy and Public Affairs*, 16 (1987), 215–40.

——, *Equality and Partiality*. Oxford: Oxford University Press, 1991.

——, 'Personal Rights and Public Space', *Philosophy and Public Affairs*, 24 (1995), 83–107.

Nardin, Terry, *Law, Morality, and the Relations of States*. Princeton, NJ: Princeton University Press, 1983.

Nelson, John O., 'Are there Inalienable Rights?', *Philosophy*, 64 (1989), 519–24.

——, 'Against Human Rights', *Philosophy*, 65 (1990), 341–8.

Nickel, James W., *Making Sense of Human Rights: Philosophical Reflections on the Universal Declaration of Human Rights*. Berkeley and Los Angeles: University of California Press, 1987.

Nielsen, Kai, 'Relativism and Wide Reflective Equilibrium', *The Monist*, 76 (1993), 316–32.

—— and Roger Shiner (eds), *New Essays on Contract Theory*. Guelph, Ontario: Canadian Association for Publishing in Philosophy, 1977.

Nozick, Robert, *Anarchy, State, and Utopia*. New York: Basic Books, 1974.

Nussbaum, Martha, *Sex and Social Justice*. New York and Oxford: Oxford University Press, 1999.

—— and Jonathan Glover (eds), *Women, Culture, and Development*. Oxford: Clarendon Press, 1993.

—— et al., *For Love of Country: Debating the Limits of Patriotism*. Boston: Beacon Press, 1996.

O'Neal, John R. and Bruce Russett, 'The Kantian Peace', *World Politics*, 51 (1999), 1–36.

O'Neill, Onora, *Towards Justice and Virtue: A Constructive Account of Practical Reasoning*. Cambridge: Cambridge University Press, 1996.

——, 'Political Liberalism and Public Reason: A Critical Notice of John Rawls' Political Liberalism', *Philosophical Review*, 106 (1997), 411–28.

——, *Bounds of Justice*. Cambridge: Cambridge University Press, 2000.

Parfit, Derek, *Reasons and Persons*. Oxford: Oxford University Press, 1986.

Pennock, J. Roland and John Chapman (eds), *Human Rights: Nomos XXIII*. New York: New York University Press, 1981.

Plato, *The Collected Dialogues*, ed. Edith Hamilton and Huntington Cairns. Princeton, NJ: Princeton University Press, 1961.

——, *The Republic*, trans. Benjamin Jowett. New York: Vintage Books, 1991.

Pogge, Thomas W., *Realizing Rawls*. Ithaca, NY: Cornell University Press, 1989.

——, 'An Egalitarian Law of Peoples', *Philosophy and Public Affairs*, 23 (1994), 195–224.

——, 'Cosmopolitanism and Sovereignty', in Chris Brown (ed.), *Political Restructuring in Europe: Ethical Perspectives*. London: Routledge, 1994, 89–122.

——, 'Human Flourishing and Universal Justice', *Social Philosophy and Policy*, 16 (1999), 333–61.

Previté-Orton, C. W., *The Defensor Pacis of Marcilius of Padua*. Cambridge: Cambridge University Press, 1928.

Rawls, John, *A Theory of Justice*. Cambridge, MA: Harvard University Press, 1971.

——, 'Reply to Alexander and Musgrave', *Quarterly Journal of Economics*, 88 (1974), 633–55.

——, 'Some Reasons for the Maximin Criterion', *American Economic Review*, 64 (1974), 141–6.

——, 'Fairness to Goodness', *The Philosophical Review*, 84 (1975), 536–55.

——, 'Kantian Constructivism in Moral Theory', *Journal of Philosophy*, 77 (1980), 515–72.

——, 'Social Unity and Primary Goods', in Amartya Sen and Bernard Williams (eds), *Utilitarianism and Beyond*. Cambridge: Cambridge University Press, 1982, 159–86.

——, 'Justice as Fairness: Political not Metaphysical', *Philosophy and Public Affairs*, 14 (1985), 223–52.

——, 'The Idea of an Overlapping Consensus', *Oxford Journal of Legal Studies*, 7 (1987), 1–25.

——, 'The Priority of Right and Ideas of the Good', *Philosophy and Public Affairs*, 17 (1988), 251–76.

——, 'The Domain of the Political and Overlapping Consensus', *New York University Law Review*, 64 (1989), 233–55.

——, 'The Law of Peoples', in Stephen Shute and Susan Hurley (eds), *On Human Rights: The Oxford Amnesty Lectures*. New York: Basic Books, 1993, 41–82.

——, *Political Liberalism*, paperback edn. New York: Columbia University Press, 1996.

——, *The Law of Peoples*. Cambridge, MA: Harvard University Press, 1999.

——, *Justice as Fairness: A Restatement*, ed. Erin Kelly. Cambridge, MA, and London: Harvard University Press, 2001.

Ray, James Lee, *Democracy and International Conflict*. Columbia, SC: University of South Carolina Press, 1995.

Regan, Richard, *Just War: Principles and Cases*. Washington, DC: Catholic University of America Press, 1996.

Rescher, Nicholas, 'Collective Responsibility', *Journal of Social Philosophy*, 29 (1998), 49–58.

Rosen, Allen D., *Kant's Theory of Justice*. Ithaca, NY, and London: Cornell University Press, 1993.

Ross, W. D., *The Right and the Good*. Oxford: Clarendon Press, 1930.

Rousseau, Jean Jacques, *Social Contract*, in Roger D. Masters and Christopher Kelly (eds), *The Collected Writings of Rousseau*. Hanover and London: University Press of New England, 1994.

Russett, Bruce, *Grasping the Democratic Peace: Principles for a Post-Cold War World*. Princeton, NJ: Princeton University Press, 1993.

Sandel, Michael, *Liberalism and the Limits of Justice*. Cambridge: Cambridge University Press, 1982.

——, 'The Procedural Republic and the Unencumbered Self', *Political Theory*, 12 (1984), 81–96.

Scanlon, T. M., 'Rawls' Theory of Justice', *University of Pennsylvania Law Review*, 121 (1973), 1020–69.

Scanlon, T. M., *What we Owe to Each Other*. Cambridge, MA: Harvard University Press, 1998.

Sen, Amartya, 'Freedoms and Needs', *The New Republic*, 31 (1994), 31–8.

——, *Development as Freedom*. New York: Anchor Books, 2000.

—— and Bernard Williams (eds), *Utilitarianism and Beyond*: Cambridge: Cambridge University Press, 1982.

Seton-Watson, Hugh, *Nations and States*. London: Methuen, 1977.

Shapiro, Ian and Will Kymlicka (eds), *Ethnicity and Group Rights*. New York: New York University Press, 1997.

Shue, Henry, *Basic Rights: Subsistence, Affluence, and U.S. Foreign Policy*, 2nd edn. Princeton, NJ: Princeton University Press, 1996.

Shute, Stephen and Susan Hurley (eds), *On Human Rights: The Oxford Amnesty Lectures*. New York: Basic Books, 1993.

Smith, Michael J., 'Humanitarian Intervention: An Overview of the Ethical Issues', in Joel H. Rosenthal (ed.), *Ethics and International Affairs: A Reader*. Washington, DC: Georgetown University Press, 1999, 271–95.

Spykman, Nicholas, *America's Strategy in World Politics: The United States and the Balance of Power*. New York: Harcourt, Brace, 1942.

Steiner, Henry J. and Philip Alston, *International Human Rights in Context: Law, Politics, and Morals*. Oxford: Clarendon Press, 1996.

Sumner, L. W., *The Moral Foundation of Rights*. Oxford: Clarendon Press, 1987.

Tesón, Fernando, 'International Human Rights and Cultural Relativism', *Virginia Journal of International Law*, 25 (1985), 869–98.

——, 'Kantian International Liberalism', in David R. Mapel and Terry Nardin (eds), *International Society: Diverse Ethical Perspectives.* Princeton, NJ: Princeton University Press, 1998, 103–13.

Thee, Marek, 'Towards a Culture of Peace Based on Human Rights', *International Journal of Human Rights*, 1 (1997), 18–34.

Thomson, Janice E., 'State Sovereignty in International Relations: Bridging the Gap between Theory and Empirical Research', *International Studies Quarterly*, 39 (1995), 213–34.

Thucydides, *The Peloponnesian War*, trans. Rex Warner. New York: Penguin Books, 1972.

Tocqueville, Alexis de, *Democracy in America.* New York: Vintage Books, 1990.

Tomasevski, Katrina, 'The Right to Peace', *Current Research on Peace and Violence*, 5 (1982), 42–69.

UNESCO, *Symposium on the Study of New Human Rights: The Rights of Solidarity.* Paris: UNESCO, 1980.

Vallentyne, Peter, 'Contractarianism and the Assumption of Mutual Unconcern', *Philosophical Studies*, 56 (1989), 187–92.

Vincent, R. J., *Human Rights and International Relations.* Cambridge: Cambridge University Press, 1986.

Waldron, Jeremy (ed.), *Theories of Rights.* Oxford: Oxford University Press, 1984.

Walker, R. B. J., 'Security, Sovereignty, and the Challenge of World Politics', *Alternatives*, 15 (1990), 3–28.

Walzer, Michael, *Just and Unjust Wars: A Moral Argument with Historical Illustrations*, 2nd ed. New York: Basic Books, 1992.

Wellman, Carl, 'A New Conception of Human Rights', in Eugene Kamenka and Alice Erh-Soon Tay (eds), *Ideas and Ideologies: Human Rights.* London: Edward Arnold, 1978, 48–58.

——, 'Solidarity, the Individual and Human Rights', *Human Rights Quarterly*, 22 (2000), 639–57.

Wicclair, Mark R., 'Rawls and the Principle of Nonintervention', in H. Gene Blocker and Elizabeth H. Smith (eds), *John Rawls' Theory of Social Justice.* Athens, OH: Ohio University Press, 1980, 289–308.

Wood, Allen W., *Kant's Ethical Thought.* Cambridge: Cambridge University Press, 1999.

Index